The Myth
of Religious Superiority

FAITH MEETS FAITH

An Orbis Series in Interreligious Dialogue
Paul F. Knitter & William R. Burrows, General Editors
Editorial Advisors
John Berthrong
Diana Eck
Karl-Josef Kuschel
Lamin Sanneh
George E. Tinker
Felix Wilfred

In the contemporary world, the many religions and spiritualities stand in need of greater communication and cooperation. More than ever before, they must speak to, learn from, and work with each other in order to maintain their vital identities and to contribute to fashioning a better world.

The FAITH MEETS FAITH Series seeks to promote interreligious dialogue by providing an open forum for exchange among followers of different religious paths. While the Series wants to encourage creative and bold responses to questions arising from contemporary appreciations of religious plurality, it also recognizes the multiplicity of basic perspectives concerning the methods and content of interreligious dialogue.

Although rooted in a Christian theological perspective, the Series does not limit itself to endorsing any single school of thought or approach. By making available to both the scholarly community and the general public works that represent a variety of religious and methodological viewpoints, FAITH MEETS FAITH seeks to foster an encounter among followers of the religions of the world on matters of common concern.

Faith Meets Faith Series

The Myth of Religious Superiority

Multifaith Explorations of Religious Pluralism

Edited by

Paul F. Knitter

ORBIS BOOKS

Maryknoll, New York 10545

Founded in 1970, Orbis Books endeavors to publish works that enlighten the mind, nourish the spirit, and challenge the conscience. The publishing arm of the Maryknoll Fathers and Brothers, Orbis seeks to explore the global dimensions of the Christian faith and mission, to invite dialogue with diverse cultures and religious traditions, and to serve the cause of reconciliation and peace. The books published reflect the opinions of their authors and are not meant to represent the official position of the Maryknoll Society. To obtain more information about Maryknoll and Orbis Books, please visit our website at www.maryknoll.org.

Library of Congress Cataloging-in-Publication Data

The myth of religious superiority : multifaith explorations of religious pluralism / Paul F. Knitter, editor.
        p. cm. — (Faith meets faith)
Proceedings of a conference held Sept. 6-9, 2003 in Birmingham, England.
Includes bibliographical references and index.
ISBN-13: 978-1-57075-627-6 (pbk.)
1. Religions—Relations. 2. Religious pluralism. I. Knitter, Paul F. II. Series.
BL410.M97 2005
201'.5—dc22
                                                              2005009192

Contents

Introduction

PAUL F. KNITTER

As the title indicates, *The Myth of Religious Superiority* is in some fashion a sequel to the 1987 book *The Myth of Christian Uniqueness*. At that time editors John Hick and I, together with the contributors to that volume, felt that we were standing before what had been likened to a "religious Rubicon." Like Caesar and Rome, Christians found themselves contemplating crossing a river that appeared to be as necessary as it was full of potential risk. Given their growing awareness of both the reality and the validity of other religions, followers of Christ found it increasingly difficult to stand before the entire world and claim that theirs was the only or the best religion.

Thus, in that book, we gatherered theologians from different denominations and cultures to explore how Christians could understand the uniqueness or distinctiveness of Christ and Christianity in such a way that they would no longer have to insist that they had the only, or the final, or the superior path to God and absolute Truth. Christianity would remain important and distinctive, but so would other religions.

Even though the animated and often controversial discussions that *The Myth of Christian Uniqueness* stirred up are still brewing,[1] many of the explorers under the flag of this so-called pluralistic model have felt that it would be helpful to broaden the discussion beyond its then *intra*-Christian confines. The religious Rubicon, we now know, runs not only through Christianity; it confronts all religions. Throughout their histories all religious traditions— some more than others, some more explicitly and aggressively than others— have made claims of superiority and of being the only or the most assured path for humans to reach their highest ends. Has humanity reached a point in its cultural and geo-political development where it is possible, even necessary, to move beyond such "better than thou" assertions? Are *all* religious traditions conscious and capable of such a move?

Of course, our pluralist proclivities urged a positive response to such questions. But to explore these proclivities as carefully and critically as we could,

---

[1] See Gavin D'Costa, ed., *Christian Uniqueness Reconsidered: The Myth of a Pluralistic Theology of Religions* (Maryknoll, NY: Orbis Books, 1990).

a group of us did in 2003 what we had done in 1987. John Hick, Perry Schmidt-Leukel, Leonard Swidler, and I put our heads and funding resources together and called an international conference (which some wags dubbed the Pluralist Summit). But this time it was not to be mono-religious but multi-religious. Our hopes were to explore, maybe facilitate, the possibility of an interreligious crossing of the Rubicon!

The letter of invitation to the conference stated these hopes as follows:

We want to gather together persons from various religious traditions who are committed to what has come to be called the "pluralist model" for understanding and responding to the reality of religious diversity. Put negatively, we mean by pluralists those who do not regard their own religion as the one and only "true" faith and way of "salvation," uniquely superior to all others. We hope to provide an opportunity for pluralists from different religious traditions to meet together to share their different understandings of pluralism, of its basis within their own tradition, of problems to be faced, and of prospects for the future.

The intricacy of our intent is captured in the title of this book. We did not wish to imperialistically throw out all past claims to religious superiority; rather, we hoped to deal with such claims for what we believed they are—*myths* of religious superiority—that is, religious people using religious language to express experiences or insights that are beyond language. So religious language bears the quality of the mythic, symbolic, metaphoric, poetic. Its truth, therefore, lies in its interpretation, which will be different in different times and cultures. Our hopes were to call upon specialists and practitioners in various religious traditions to reinterpret for our age whatever myths or claims of superiority or exclusivity they may have made in the past. How might assertions about "the only Savior" or "the highest Enlightenment" or "the final revelation" be understood and reformulated so that each religious community can make room for other communities in today's pluralistic community of religions?

Thanks to the financial support of the Identity Foundation (Düsseldorf), the Weisfeld Foundation (Glasgow), and the Allan & Nesta Ferguson Trust, and under the auspices of the Department of Theology of the University of Birmingham (which provided us with the indispensable administrative help of Ms. Carol Bebawi), some thirty-five religious scholars from Asia, Europe, and the United States gathered in Birmingham, England, September 6–9, 2003. Uncomfortably aware that the organizers were a quartet of white, Christian, Western men, we made sure that we had sufficient funds and contacts to make our gathering as religiously and gender diverse as possible (though we ended up, alas, with more Christians than any other religion, more men than women).

Papers had to be prepared in advance, were read by all, and then discussed in plenary sessions. And the discussions were indeed animated, revealing a pluralism of pluralistic viewpoints, both between and within religious traditions. Under the light and heat of criticism, papers were revised. And then came the difficult, often painful, editorial task of making a selection for our book, knowing that there was room for only about one-third of the papers. The primary guideline for that selection was to have strong, varied voices from all the traditions.

Both from the contents of the papers and of our conference discussions, it became clear that among the various motivations that had brought us all together, one was the most impelling: *the vital connection between the religions of the world and peace in the world.* Hans Küng's broadly known dictum rang true for us, especially in light of the events on and after 9/11: There will be no peace among nations without peace among religions; and there will be no peace among religions without greater dialogue among them.[2] But as is evident in many of this book's essays, we felt that a further piece needs to be added to Küng's statement: There will be no real and effective dialogue among the religions if each religion continues to make its claims of superiority.

For how can religious communities—or any diverse groups of people, for that matter—gather to cooperate and learn from one another if each of them is convinced that theirs is the only or the final word of truth, or if they believe that eventually God wills all peoples to become members of their religion? Claims of superiority, at the most, can ground competition; they cannot promote cooperation and mutual learning. They can allow tolerance but not mutuality. If religious people come together for peacemaking dialogue but retain their claims of religious superiority (even if only in their minds and hearts), they are no different, in their fundamental religious convictions, from the militant religious people who refuse such dialogue; both such peacemakers and the militants hold that theirs is the only or the best way. And this makes it difficult, if not impossible, for peacemakers to resist the militants.

In fact, as this collection of essays will also make clear, we agreed that there is a causal link between claims of religious superiority and calls to religious violence. If peace-filled religious people, therefore, proclaim defensively that the militants (either the "terrorists" or the "imperialists") are misusing and exploiting their religion, they must ask themselves *why* it is so easy for extremist leaders or politicians to exploit their religion. They must ask themselves whether claims of superiority—claims to have "the only Savior" or the "last revelation" or "the highest enlightenment"—are among the primarily reasons why their religion is so easily used as a divine seal of approval for violence.[3] John Hick, in his own reflections on our Birmingham conference, answers such questions with his usual clarity:

---

[2] Hans Küng, *Global Responsibility: In Search of a New World Ethic* (New York: Crossroad, 1991), xv.

[3] For a provocative answer to such questions, see Charles Kimball, *When Religion Becomes Evil* (HarperSanFrancisco, 2002).

We are acutely aware that throughout history almost all human conflicts have been validated and intensified by a religious sanction. God
has been claimed to be on both sides of every war. This has been possible because each of the great world faiths has either assumed or asserted its own unique superiority as the one and only true faith and path
to the highest good—in familiar Christian terms, to salvation. These
exclusive claims to absolute truth have exacerbated the division of the
human community into rival groups, and have repeatedly been invoked
in support of oppression, slavery, conquest, and exploitation.[4]

Claims of religious superiority all too easily, if not invariably, become calls
to religious violence. Thus, we felt, the urgency of our conference and of this
book.

But there were other points of agreement that emerged from our conference
and recur throughout this collection of essays. What follows are some of the
principal ingredients of what one might call the pluralist consensus that resulted from our multifaith exploration:

1. *All the religions possess the resources within their own traditions to
   adopt the pluralist model.* The pluralist turn, therefore, is not a foreign
   imposition; it is not a move toward heresy. While the renunciation of
   claims to be the "only" or the "definitive" religion may clash with past
   formulations of belief, there are resources within the religions themselves to justify and even require this move and to reformulate past
   claims of superiority. Pluralists, in other words, feel they are faithful to
   their religious identities.[5]
2. *Differences matter.* In asserting "ultimate reality" or "truth" as the basis for the real or potential commonalities among the religions, pluralists do not wish to deny, indeed they resolutely affirm, the real differences among the religions. Plurality requires diversity. The differences
   among the religions *matter;* such differences, as Raimon Panikkar reminds his fellow pluralists, can never be reduced to a neat "system."[6]

---

[4] John Hick, "Pluralism Conference," *Buddhist-Christian Studies* 24 (2004): 253.

[5] This statement is particularly relevant in view of declarations of some Christian
churches that the pluralist model, and the position of at least one Catholic pluralist,
represented in this book, "contains affirmations contrary to the truths of both divine
and catholic faith." Such declarations must be taken seriously, but they must also be
brought into conversation with the case that pluralists are making for the orthodoxy
of their positions. We hope our book will further such conversations. See the Vatican
Declaration *Dominus Iesus* (Congregation for the Doctrine of the Faith, August 6,
2000) and the CDF "Notification" on the work of Roger Haight published in
L'Osservatore Romano (February 8, 2005).

[6] Raimon Panikkar, "The Jordan, the Tiber, and the Ganges: Three Kairological
Moments of Christic Self-Consciousness," in *The Myth of Christian Uniqueness:
Toward a Pluralistic Theology of Religions,* ed. John Hick and Paul F. Knitter
(Maryknoll, NY: Orbis Books, 1987), 109–10.

And yet, the differences can connect; they offer the possibility of conversation and cooperation. "Greater unity amid abiding diversity"—this expresses the hope of the pluralists' perspective.

3. *All religious traditions, in varying ways, recognize that the ultimate reality or truth that is the object of their quest or discoveries is beyond the scope of complete human understanding.* Here, then, is one of the most evident and effective resources within each of the religions to counteract free-wielding claims of superiority. If there is "always more to learn" in the religious quest, if *Mystery* will never be mastered, then all claims to know It fully or finally can be nothing else but idolatrous.

4. *Pluralism does not imply relativism.* Contrary to current caricatures, pluralists do not assert that "all religions are essentially the same" or that "all religious beliefs or practices are equally valid." While pluralists do affirm the broad validity—or more practically, the equal rights— of the many religions, they also affirm the possibility, indeed the necessity, of distinguishing between specific "good and bad," or "helpful and harmful" religious affirmations or practices. Such evaluations are always dangerous and must be carried out carefully, open-mindedly, and (most important) *dialogically.*

5. *The most urgent (though not the only) form of interreligious encounter today is an ethical dialogue among the religions.* Such a dialogue must "engage the pressing problems of the world today, including war, violence, poverty, environmental devastation, gender injustice, and human rights violations."[7] The ethical issues and crises presently facing humankind provide the religions with both the *necessity* of an interreligious contribution to human and ecological well-being and at the same time an *opportunity* for the religions to understand each other and evaluate their differences.

6. *In all their encounters and dialogues, the religions must respect freedom of conscience.* To do this, they must distinguish between *witnessing* and *proselytizing.* Proselytization results from claims of superiority. Witnessing is based on the desire and need to share what one has found to be true and precious.

It is the resolute hope of the organizers and participants of our pluralist project that this book will stimulate and perhaps provide some direction for further conversations and efforts toward a more fruitful, peacemaking, life-giving dialogue and cooperation among the religious communities of the world. Whatever might be the future insights and developments regarding claims of superiority among the religions, what is most important is that such dialogue and cooperation take place.

---

[7] From the points of agreement affirmed at the Birmingham Conference.

PART I

Foundational Perspectives

1

The Next Step beyond Dialogue

JOHN HICK

Interfaith dialogue has been going on now on a growing scale and on many levels for more than a generation, and it must continue increasingly in the future. So to speak of the next step beyond dialogue is not intended to mean the end of dialogue and its replacement by something else. It is a way of enhancing dialogue, not replacing it. It is the step from dialogue between people who each believe, at the back of their minds and usually without saying it aloud, that theirs is really the one and only true or fully true faith, to dialogue between people who accept the genuine religious equality of the other, so that they can then benefit freely from one another's distinctive spiritual insights and be free to join together in facing the massive social and economic and political problems of the world.

So clearly this next step is not the different religions all becoming one, uniting to form some kind of new global religion. On the contrary, their plurality and diversity are positive and valuable. The variety around the world of our different ways of being human, which are the great cultures and religions of the earth, is something to celebrate and understand, not something to try to iron out.

In exploring the next step I use the word *salvation,* acknowledging, of course, that it is not a universally used term but one most at home in Christian discourse. Salvation, then, is the aim of each of the great world religions. Each has a keen awareness of the reality of human suffering and of the human neglect, cruelty, injustice, exploitation, sheer ignorance, or thoughtlessness that cause most of it. They all recognize that there is something deeply and tragically defective in our ordinary human situation, both individually and collectively. They conceptualize this in various ways. Some express it by saying that we are fallen and therefore sinful beings; others that we are frail, fallible creatures, made out of the dust of the earth; others that all life is, in the Buddhist phrase, *dukkha,* defective, involving all manner of suffering; others again that we are living in blindness to the reality of our own deeper nature and of the larger reality of which we are part. These are all ways of pointing to the same observable facts. But in the face of this dark side of life, which is all too evident, each of the great traditions nevertheless stands out as a form of what we can call cosmic optimism in that it proclaims the real possibility, which can even begin to be realized here and now, of a limitlessly better state. And in each case, the movement toward that state consists in a progressive transformation from natural self-centeredness to a new orientation centered in the Ultimate Reality on which the religions are focused from their different angles.

RELIGION: THE OUTER AND THE INNER

Let us distinguish between two different aspects of religion. One is the religions as socio-religious entities existing over against one another and interacting with all the other factors that go to make up human history. They have their own boundaries, even in principle their list of members, and they are related to each other as distinct and often rival institutions. It is religion in this sense that is studied by historians, sociologists, and anthropologists and is therefore the aspect of religion most studied in the universities. Whether a religion originated with an individual founder or holy book, or developed through a long line of sages or prophets, in each case it has become embodied in a continuing human institution or institutions. And in all human institutions, including religious ones, there has been a human-all-too-human influence on their development over time. Inevitably they reflect not only the best but also the worst in human nature.

And so we find that the religious institutions, as enormously powerful factors in human history, have not only done a great deal of good but also a great deal of harm. On the one hand they have been instruments for social cohesion, defining a tribe or a nation, and they have through the centuries provided a framework of meaning for the lives of hundreds of millions of people, challenging people morally and giving them comfort and support in time of trouble. They have played a central role in the formation of civilizations, in the development of language, education and science, the creation of hospitals and universities, and in inspiring literature, music, painting, sculpture, architecture. But on the other hand they have been instruments of social control by a dominant class; they have supported, and indeed embodied, the centuries-long patriarchal male dominance over women; and they have divided people into rival groups and have been used to validate and intensify almost all human conflicts, as we see so tragically in many parts of the world today. God has been claimed to be on both sides of every war, so that it has been said that the only industry that God seems to support is the arms industry! But if we ask, with all this in mind, whether institutional religion has done more good or more harm to humankind over the centuries, it seems to me that the goods and evils are of such different kinds as to be incommensurable, so that it is not really possible to reach any straightforward verdict.

But this institutional aspect of religion, with all its goods and evils, is only half the story. The other aspect is something for which we do not have an ideal word, but which can vaguely be called spirituality, meaning each individual's inner response to the Divine, the Transcendent, Ultimate Reality, the Ultimate, the Real. For all the world religions speak in their different ways of a limitlessly important reality that both transcends the material universe and is also present within it. There is no common term for this. Here in the West we most naturally speak of God. But in the global context we must do so as our way of referring to the Ultimate Reality, without prejudging whether that reality is an infinite person, or indeed three infinite persons in one, or is a trans-personal reality beyond the distinction between the personal and the impersonal. This is because with our knowledge of Buddhism, Taoism, Jainism, and some forms of Hinduism it is no longer possible to equate religion with belief in a personal God. And because it is so hard to speak of God without that implied connotation, I am going instead to speak of the Ultimate—not because this is better than the other terms but simply because one has to settle upon one of them.

And again, I wish we had a better word for the inner response to the Ultimate than *spirituality,* which is often used so loosely today—I have even heard in a TV commercial of the spiritual aspect of painting your toenails— but even so *spirituality* is probably a better word for my purpose than such alternatives as *piety, mysticism, religiosity,* or *faith*.[1]

The relationship between these two aspects, the outer reality of the historical religious institutions and the inner reality of spirituality, is twofold. On the one hand, the development of religious institutions was always inevitable because we are inherently social beings who need one another and who need to do things together, so that human response to the Ultimate was originally communal before becoming individual. And fortunately, within the great organized and institutionalized religions, despite all their faults, there has always been space for the spiritual life. But on the other hand, the spiritual life can also occur outside the institutions, though—it has to be added— when it does it is still parasitic upon them for the preservation of scriptures, for the accumulated wisdom of the past, for methods of prayer and meditation handed down within the institutions. So these two aspects of religion, spirituality and the institutions, need each other. But I also want to affirm strongly that the spiritual life, the transforming personal response to the Ultimate, is the living heart of religion and that the institutions, while necessary, are secondary; when they make themselves primary as absolute authorities they become potentially dangerous centers of power.

---

[1] *Faith* is the word used by Wilfred Cantwell Smith in his distinction between the "the cumulative traditions" and "faith." It was he who brought this very important distinction to the notice of us all in his classic book *The Meaning and End of Religion,* and in speaking of the religious institutions and spirituality I am repeating his distinction in different terms.

SPHERES OF INFLUENCE

Now when we stress the priority of the spiritual over the institutional, a conception of religion comes to light that is rather different from our usual Western way of thinking. We see this other understanding in China during the centuries when it was quite normal to be a Buddhist, a Confucian, and a Taoist. Again, in Japan today great numbers of people practice both Buddhism and Shinto. And in India the many different strands of religious thought and practice that are lumped together under the Western-invented name of Hinduism, such as the Vaishnavite and Shaivite streams of devotion, are not so much rivals as regional variations.

So on this other conception of religion, the different faiths are not seen as bounded entities set over against one another but more as spheres of spiritual influence—the influence emanating from the teachings of the Buddha, the influence emanating from the teachings of Confucius, and the Taoist influence emanating from the *Tao Te Ching*, and so on. Now while one cannot belong simultaneously to two different institutions with mutually exclusive memberships, one *can* live within two or more overlapping spheres of spiritual influence. One and the same person can respond to the influences that come from a variety of different sources, and indeed many of us and probably a growing number of us today are doing just that. In this model of religion the institutions still have their place. They are still necessary in preserving communal memories and providing communal symbols and rituals, but they are no longer closed entities whose established structures and professional priesthoods so easily become opposed to one another. For while religious institutions have almost always divided humanity, the inner openness to the Ultimate that I am calling spirituality has no tendency to divide people into opposing groups. Spirituality does indeed take characteristically different forms within the different traditions, but these differences are complementary rather than contradictory.

MY RELIGION SUPERIOR
TO YOURS?

However, here we are in the West with the prevailing understanding of the religions as bounded entities existing over against one another. Seen in this way, each is a unique totality of forms of spiritual practice, revered scriptures, treasured creeds, stories and myths, familiar symbols, systems of doctrine, moral codes, great paradigmatic figures, remembered histories, cultural ethos, authority figures. And in this situation the pluralist view is that it is a fundamental mistake to elevate any one of them—always of course one's own—as uniquely superior to all the others.

Why is that a mistake?

A great deal depends on whether we adopt a top-down method, starting with an established system of doctrines and making deductions from it, or a from-the-ground-up method, starting with the observable realities of human life and asking what they imply. Using this second method, I start from the obvious fact that the religion to which anyone adheres—and equally the religion against which anyone reacts and which they reject—depends in the vast majority of cases on where they were born. Someone born into a Christian family in Italy is much more likely to become a Christian than a Buddhist. If in Pakistan, much more likely to become a Muslim than a Jew. If in Thailand, much more likely to be a Buddhist than a Christian. And so on. The point is well made by a twelve-year-old boy I've been told of, born into a Christian family in Cairo, who remarked one day, "You know, if I'd been born next door I'd be a Muslim." Individual conversions from one faith to another do of course occur all the time in all directions, and whenever this happens I think we have to assume that it is a right move for that individual; but this remains statistically insignificant in comparison with the massive transmission of faith from one generation to another within the same tradition. The fact is that in the vast majority of cases we *inherit* our religion along with our nationality, our language, and our culture.

So what are the implications of this? Let me put them in Christian terms, though they can equally well be put in the terms of any other faith. Most Christians assume, or are certainly supposed to assume because of the claim that has traditionally been made, that there is a significant religious advantage in being a Christian rather than a Jew or a Muslim or a Buddhist, etc. The strongest form of this is the belief that only Christians go to heaven, all the rest to hell. But today the mainline Christian churches have moved a long way beyond that and have now mostly settled down in the belief that, on the one hand, salvation for anybody is brought about solely by Christ's atoning death on the cross, but nevertheless, on the other hand, that non-Christians can also benefit from Christ's saving work because of the universal presence of the Holy Spirit at work throughout the world. But they still believe that there is a significant religious advantage in being a member of the Christian church. To quote the 1997 statement of the Vatican's International Theological Commission, *Christianity and the World Religions*, "the universal presence of the Spirit can not be compared with his special presence in the Church of Christ. . . . Only the Church is the body of Christ, and only in it is given in its full intensity the presence of the Spirit" (p. 54). And the mainly Protestant World Council of Churches in its most recent Baar Statement on this subject in 1990 recognized truth and wisdom, love and holiness within the other religions, but added that this "is the gift of the Holy Spirit"—the second Person of the Christian Trinity.

This is at present, I would say, the majority view among both Catholic and Protestant theologians and church authorities. The prevailing view, in other words, is that non-Christians can be included within the sphere of Christian salvation—hence the term *inclusivism*. But Christianity nevertheless retains its unique centrality and normativeness and, to be frank, its superiority. If we take the analogy of the solar system, with God as the sun at the center and the religions as the planets circling around that center, inclusivism holds that the life-giving warmth and light of the sun falls directly only on our earth, the Christian church, and is then reflected off it in lesser degrees to the other planets, the other religions. Or if you prefer an economic analogy, the wealth of divine grace falls directly upon the church and then trickles down in diluted forms to the people of the other faiths below. And the very serious question that we have to ask is whether this is an honestly realistic account of the human situation as we observe it on the ground.

How can we judge? Only, surely, by the observable fruits of religion in human life. I think these are well described by the Christian writer Saint Paul as "love, joy, peace, patience, kindness, goodness, faithfulness, gentleness, self-control" (Gal 5:22–23), to which we have to add today the search for social and international justice and peace. These are values common to all the world religions. And what has made me, personally, come to doubt the assumption of the unique superiority of my own Christian faith is that these observable fruits do not seem to be specially concentrated in the Christian church but, on the contrary, seem to be spread more or less evenly around the world, with its different cultures and religions. Obviously this can be argued. I would only say that the onus of proof is upon anyone, of any religion, who claims that the members of his or her religion are in general better human beings, morally and spiritually, than the rest of the human race.

Let me put it again in Christian terms. If we take literally the traditional belief that in Christ we have an uniquely full revelation of God and an uniquely direct relationship with God, so that in the church we are members of the body of Christ, taking the divine life into our lives in the Eucharist, and living under the guidance of the Holy Spirit, then surely this ought to produce some noticeable difference in our lives. Christians *ought* to be better human beings than those who lack these inestimable spiritual benefits. Or does the new situation inaugurated by the life and death of Jesus make no practical difference? But in that case, what is its value? So we are stuck on the horns of a dilemma. We either have to claim, against the evidence of our experience, that as members of the body of Christ Christians in general are better human beings than non-Christians, or we are going to have to rethink those of our traditional doctrines that entail that.

But let me add at this point that there is a perfectly good sense in which for me—and "me" could be anyone—my religion is the truth and the true path of salvation. I was born into it, it has formed me and nourished me, it has so to speak made me in its own image, so that it fits me and I fit it as probably no other can. And this is true from within each of the world religions. The upshot is that normally we should each remain within our inherited faith and use its resources to the full. But what the pluralist insight is telling us is to recognize that exactly the same applies to the people of other faiths. They too have been formed by their own faith, and for them it is uniquely special; for them it is salvific.

A NEW FRAMEWORK OF UNDERSTANDING

So how do we go about forming a new framework of understanding? Two ways are in fact being actively explored—different but complementary.

One is to start from within one's own faith and work outward, so to speak, by exploring its resources for an acceptance of the salvific parity of the other world faiths, the acceptance of them, in other words, as equally authentic paths to—to use the term again—salvation. For each tradition does in fact have within it strands of thought that can be developed to authorize the pluralist point of view. This can only be done within each faith in its own terms and by its own adherents. But those who use scripture, whichever scripture it may be, to prove their point, in practice use it selectively, highlighting what supports their point of view and tacitly leaving aside what does not. We all do that, either consciously or unconsciously. My own hunch is that our basic point of view comes first and then selects its appropriate scriptural backing and theological interpretation. It is for this reason that I myself prefer to concentrate on advocating the basic pluralist point of view, confident that once this is accepted the theologians and exegetes, who operate when necessary as theological "spin doctors," will sooner or later find ways to give it the stamp of official approval.

So the way that I myself prefer is to set forth the intellectual grounding for religious pluralism. Some, I know, feel that philosophical thinking in this area is not necessary, or even not desirable. Others of us, however, feel that we have an obligation to try to make intelligible sense of the global religious situation, with all its complexities of similarity and difference. So let me very briefly outline my own suggestion.

I take my clue from something that is affirmed within all the great traditions. This is that the Ultimate is in itself beyond the scope of human description and understanding. As the great Christian theologian Thomas Aquinas said, God "surpasses every form that our intellect reaches."[2] God in God's ultimate eternal self-existent being is ineffable, or as I would rather say, transcategorial, beyond the scope of our human conceptual systems. And so we have a distinction between God in God's infinite self-existent being and God as humanly knowable. We find this in some of the great mystics, who distinguished between the Godhead, which is the ultimate ineffable reality, and the known God of the scriptures and of church doctrine and worship, imaged and understood in our limited human terms. We find parallel distinctions within the other great traditions. Within the mystical strands of Judaism and Islam the distinction is between, on the one hand, *Ein Sof*, the Infinite, or *al Haq*, the Real, and on the other hand, this infinite reality as revealed within our limited human thought forms and languages. The great Jewish thinker Maimonides expressed this as a distinction between the essence and

---

[2] Thomas Aquinas, *Summa contra Gentiles*, I, 14:3.

the manifestation of God. Within Hinduism it is the distinction between *nirguna* Brahman, Brahman without attributes and beyond human description, and *saguna* Brahman, which is that same reality as humanly known as the realm of the gods. And within Mahayana Buddhism it is the distinction between the *Dharmakaya*, the ultimate ineffable reality, and its embodiment in the realm of the compassionate *Buddhas*.

So we have a distinction between the Ultimate as it is in itself and that same ultimate reality as it impinges on us and is imaged by our little human minds. Our awareness of the Ultimate is thus a mediated awareness, receiving its form, and indeed its plurality of forms, from our human contribution to our awareness of it. The basic principle that in our awareness of anything the very activity of cognition itself affects the form in which we are conscious of it, is well established today in epistemology, in cognitive psychology, and in the sociology of knowledge. But it was brilliantly stated centuries ago by Thomas Aquinas in his dictum that "things known are in the knower according to the mode of the knower."[3] In ordinary sense perception the mode of the human knower is much the same throughout the world. But in religious awareness the mode of the knower differs significantly among the different religious traditions, which have been formed and developed within different historical and cultural situations. So my suggestion, my hypothesis, is that the world religions are oriented toward the same Ultimate Reality, which is, however, manifested within their different thought-worlds and modes of experience in different ways. There is a fascinating saying in the Hindu scriptures, "Thou art formless. Thine only form is our knowledge of Thee."[4]

To make in another way the point that we are related to the Ultimate through our varying concepts and images of it, consider the history of the Christian awareness of God. The concept of God within mainline Christianity today is above all that of a limitlessly loving God. But for several centuries in medieval Europe the Christian understanding of God was very different. God was thought of as the terrible judge, an object of fear and dread. The evils that befell society, the plagues and droughts and diseases, were assumed to be divine punishments. God must be very angry with his people, it was thought, because he visited so much suffering on them. When illness or calamity came to someone it was believed that this was a punishment for the person's sins. And Christ was likewise seen as the terrible judge whom they would face on the day of judgment. It was seriously and terrifyingly believed that the great majority of people were going to burn forever in hell. And for mercy people looked, not to Christ, but to their local saint or to the Virgin Mary. It was only in the thirteenth century that the image of God as love and of Christ as love incarnate began to be recovered, the image that we treasure today. Now is it God who has changed over the centuries, or our human images of God? Surely the latter. So in this historical perspective we

---

[3] Thomas Aquinas, *Summa Theologica*, II/II, Q. 1, art 2.

[4] *Yogava'sistha*, I, 28.

can see the divine presence being mediated to us in terms of our changing human images of God. We are related to the Ultimate through a screen of human concepts and images, and these concepts and images vary not only between the traditions but also even within them.

So the model that seems to me best to make sense of the total situation is that of one Ultimate Reality being humanly conceived and imaged or symbolized within the different major streams of religious life that we call Christianity, Islam, Hinduism, and so on. Or in the more poetic words of the great Muslim Sufi thinker Rumi, speaking of the religions of the world, "The lamps are different but the Light is the same; it comes from beyond."[5]

ALTERNATIVES?

If this seems a startling suggestion, what are the alternatives? One alternative is obviously the antireligious view that all the God figures and nonpersonal absolutes witnessed to by the religions are illusory, all products of the human imagination. But in this book we are not dealing with that prior question; we speak and write as people committed in each case to a positive faith and have come together to think through the problems that face us. So a second possibility is that the God or absolute of my own tradition, whichever it may be, is real and all the others illusory. But this is the traditional absolutism that we have left behind. A third possibility is to say that the Holy Trinity, Allah, Vishnu, and so on are different names for the same deity. One of my own earlier books has the unfortunate title *God Has Many Names*—which I blame on the publisher! But the Gods as described in the different scriptures are clearly not the same. They each have a different and unique personal profile and record of historical interventions in human life on earth. The strictly unitary Allah, for example, is manifestly not the same as the Holy Trinity. So different names is not the answer.

Yet another possibility is the ultra-pluralism that says that all the God figures and non-personal absolutes are alike real.[6] That is, the Holy Trinity is one reality, Allah is another reality, Adonai, the Lord blessed be he, of rabbinic Judaism is another reality, Vishu another, Shiva yet another, Brahman another again, and likewise the Tao, the Dharmakaya are all different realities. But consider the implications of this. Would it mean that the Holy Trinity

---

[5] R. A. Nicholson, trans., *Rumi: Poet and Mystic* (London and Boston: Unwin, 1978), 166.

[6] This is suggested by implication by Mark Heim (*The Depth of the Riches: A Trinitarian Theology of Religious Ends,* Grand Rapids, MI: Eerdmans, 2001) when he proposes that the different ends sought by the different religions—the Christian heaven, the Muslim paradise, the Buddhist nirvana, etc.—are all equally real. For in order for them to be real the universe must be organized by the Christian Trinity, the Qur'anic Allah, the eternal Dharma, etc., and it cannot be organized by more than one of them.

presides over and is worshiped in Christian countries, the Allah of Islam in Muslim countries, the God of the Sikh faith in the Punjab, while the transpersonal focus of Buddhist meditation is real in Burma, Thailand, Sri Lanka, Tibet, parts of China and Japan, and so on? This would be not only polytheism but also (to coin a phrase) polyabsolutism.

But is it a coherent possibility? I think not, for three reasons. One is that the monotheistic Gods are each defined as creator of everything other than God, and there can logically only be one such creator. A second is that a universe organized as the *non*-theistic traditions affirm is incompatible with there being even one such monotheistic God, let alone several. And third, several faiths are today mixed together in many countries and many cities, so that we would have to take the division of divine jurisdictions down to different cities and even to street level and indeed to individual houses. The picture becomes more and more incoherent the more it is spelled out. So, if we do not want to say any of these things, then what can we say? I suggest that the best religious account we can give of the global situation is that of a single ineffable Ultimate Reality whose universal presence is being differently conceived and experienced and responded to within the different human religious traditions.

WHY IT MATTERS

So that's my suggestion. But others among us have different suggestions, as is evident in the pages of this book. So let me end by asking, Why does all this matter? Indeed, does it matter? Well, yes, it does matter a very great deal. We live as part of a worldwide human community that is at war with itself. In many places men, women, and even children are killing and being killed in conflicts that are both validated and intensified by religion. And this is possible because each faith has traditionally made an absolute claim to be the one and only true faith. Today to insist on the unique superiority of your own faith is to be part of the problem. For how can there be stable peace between rival absolutes? In the words of the Catholic theologian Hans Küng: "There will be no peace among the peoples of this world without peace among the world religions."[7] And I would add that there will be no real peace among the world religions so long as each thinks of itself as uniquely superior to all the others. Dialogue between the faiths must continue on an ever-increasing scale. But the only stable and enduring basis for peace will come about when dialogue leads to a mutual acceptance of the religions as different but equally valid relationships to the Ultimate Reality.

---

[7] Küng, *Global Responsibility*, xv.

2

Exclusivism, Inclusivism, Pluralism

The Tripolar Typology— Clarified and Reaffirmed

PERRY SCHMIDT-LEUKEL

In 1983 and 1986 Alan Race and Gavin D'Costa introduced into the discussions on a Christian theology of religions the three options of *exclusivism,*
inclusivism, and *pluralism.*[1] Over the years, these terms have become pretty
much a standard part of the professional discourse. Recently, however, this
way of sorting out positions has become the object of some sharp criticisms,[2]
the strongest coming from one of its first users and former defenders,[3] that
is, from Gavin D'Costa himself, who now rejects the whole typology as an
"untenable" and "faulty typology."[4] Another critic, Wesley Ariarajah, holds

---

[1] Alan Race, *Christians and Religious Pluralism: Patterns in the Christian Theol-*
ogy of Religions (London: SCM, 1983); Gavin D'Costa, *Theology and Religious*
Pluralism: The Challenge of Other Religions (London: Blackwell, 1986).

[2] For example, J. A. DiNoia, *The Diversity of Religions: A Christian Perspective*
(Washington, DC: Catholic Univ. of America Press, 1992), 47–55; Schubert Ogden,
Is There Only One True Religion or Are There Many? (Dallas: Southern Methodist
Univ. Press, 1992), 79–104; Ian Markham, "Creating Options: Shattering the
Exclusivist, Inclusivist, and Pluralist Paradigm," *New Blackfriars* 74, no. 867 (1993),
33–41; Terrence W. Tilley, "Christianity and the World Religions: A Recent Vatican
Document," *Theological Studies* 60 (1999), 318–37.

[3] Gavin D'Costa, "Creating Confusion: A Response to Markham," *New*
Blackfriars 74, no. 867 (1993), 41–47.

[4] Gavin D'Costa, "The Impossibility of a Pluralist View of Religions," *Religious*
Studies 32 (1996), 233. See also the more elaborate version of his critique in Gavin
D'Costa, *The Meeting of Religions and the Trinity* (Maryknoll, NY: Orbis Books,
2000), 19–52.

that these terms have "increasingly become one of the stumbling blocks to progress in the discussions on how Christians should understand and relate to religious plurality."[5]

OBJECTIONS

Surveying the various criticisms, I can identify eight major objections:

1. *The typology has an inconsistent structure, "because the positions are not of the same genre and do not address the same questions."*[6]

2. *The typology is misleading, because it obscures or misses the real issues of a theology of religions.*[7]

3. *The typology is too narrow. There are more than three options.*[8] This criticism appears in a number of different forms, yet the critics offer no consistent alternative typology; rather, there are various individual proposals to expand the options to more than three. To mention a few examples: Schubert Ogden basically accepts the typology of exclusivism, inclusivism, and pluralism, but, in a criticism of all of them, he proposes a fourth option that holds "not that there *are* many true religions, but only that there *can be*."[9] We might call this a kind of potential pluralism. Andreas Grünschloß has argued

---

[5] Wesley Ariarajah, "The Need for a New Debate," in *The Uniqueness of Jesus: A Dialogue with Paul F. Knitter*, ed. L. Swidler and P. Mojzes, 29–34 (Maryknoll, NY: Orbis Books, 1997), 30. Similarly Tilley: "The continued utilization of this typology does not advance the discussion in the field" ("Christianity and World Religions," 326).

[6] Tilley, "Christianity and the World Religions," 324. Similarly Markham, "Creating Options," 34.

[7] DiNoia, *The Diversity of Religions*, 180: "Such typologizing obscures the more basic issue posed by current circumstances of religious interaction: how to affirm the universality of the Christian dispensation without sacrificing its particularity." DiNoia further claims that the typology gives a wrong priority to the question of salvation, which should rather be given to "questions about the varieties of aims proposed by religious communities" (ibid., 55). According to Terrence Tilley, "the typology . . . obscures another basic issue: the need to recognize the religious other as *other,* not as a mere outsider to, reflection of, extension of, or unwitting member of one's own tradition (e.g., 'non-Christian')" (Tilley, "Christianity and the World Religions," 323). D'Costa also holds that the typology is misleading because it does "not really focus on the important questions that are at stake when theologians and philosophers of religion argue about the status of other religions in regard to Christianity" (D'Costa, "The Impossibility of a Pluralist View of Religions," 225).

[8] This was also part of Markham's early criticism of the typology (cf. Markham, "Creating Options," 34).

[9] Ogden, *Is There Only One True Religion*, 83.

that, in order to be really comprehensive, the tripolar typology needs to be enlarged by a fourth option that he calls "inferiorism/exotism," that is, viewing other religions as superior to one's own.[10] Paul Knitter has recently also added a fourth model to the three options of the tripolar typology. He calls it the acceptance model and sees it instantiated in approaches like those of S. Mark Heim, Francis X. Clooney, and James Fredericks.[11]

Another proposal comes from Richard Plantinga, who also lists four options: exclusivism, inclusivism, pluralism, and universalism, which is more or less identical with the classical *apokatastasis* theory, the view that ultimately all will be saved. However, at the end of his deliberations Plantinga reckons with only two options, because "just as inclusivism is best understood as a variant of exclusivism, so universalism can best be understood as a variant of pluralism."[12] This leads us to the next objection:

4. *The typology is too broad. There are not really three options but only one.* According to Gavin D'Costa this one and only option is exclusivism because "both pluralism and inclusivism are subtypes of exclusivism." Each position follows "the logic of exclusivism" in so far as "there are certain claims to truth and those other claims that do not conform to these initial claims, explicitly or implicitly, are false."[13] D'Costa adds the remark that some people would perhaps be more inclined to see pluralism and exclusivism as being "only sub-types of inclusivism."[14] As far as I am aware, this is at least partly true for suggestions coming from Reinhold Bernhardt and Michael von Brück, who both hold that, hermeneutically, inclusivism is inevitable

---

[10] Andreas Grünschloß, *Der eigene und der fremde Glaube: Studien zur interreligiösen Fremdwahrnehmung in Islam, Hinduismus, Buddhismus und Christentum* (Tübingen: J.C.B. Mohr, 1999), 15–43.

[11] Knitter gives them new names, however, so that exclusivism becomes "the replacement model," inclusivism "the fulfillment model," and pluralism, "the mutuality model." Paul F. Knitter, *Introducing Theologies of Religions* (Maryknoll, NY: Orbis Books, 2002), 20, 173–215.

[12] Richard Plantinga, ed., *Christianity and Plurality: Classic and Contemporary Readings* (Oxford: Blackwell, 1999), 6. As a logical possibility he adds nihilism: "the claim that no one is saved" (ibid., 7n5), which is, of course, not a theological position and is equivalent to what I call atheism/naturalism.

[13] D'Costa, "The Impossibility of a Pluralist View of Religions," 225. In *The Meeting of Religions and the Trinity* D'Costa explains more fully why he thinks that inclusivism "logically collapses into exclusivism" (22). A similar argument has been made by Alvin Plantinga in order to defend exclusivism. In his defense he understands exclusivism in the broad epistemological sense that the truth of a particular view necessarily excludes the truth of any view that is incompatible with it. Alvin Plantinga, "Pluralism: A Defense of Religious Exclusivism," in *The Philosophical Challenge of Religious Diversity*, ed. P. Quinn and K. Meeker, 172–92 (New York: Oxford Univ. Press, 2000), esp. 174.

[14] D'Costa, "The Impossibility of a Pluralist View of Religions," 225.

and therefore propose reconstructing pluralism as a form of "mutual"[15] or "reciprocal"[16] inclusivism.

5. *The typology is too coarse or abstract. It does not do justice to the more complex and nuanced reality of real theologies.*[17] This objection has taken two different forms. First, there is the concern that the views of individual theologians are too complex to fit into one of the three categories.[18] Second, there is the view that within a differentiated evaluation of the non-Christian religions a theologian might assess various elements within them differently, that is, seeing some aspects of other religions as being entirely wrong, others as inferior, some as equal, and again others even as superior.[19]

6. *The typology is misleading, because it does not do justice to the radical diversity of the religions.* According to S. Mark Heim, who has forcefully advanced this objection, the entire typology is misleading, because it rests on the wrong "assumption that salvation is an unequivocal, single reality."[20] He holds that the religions' concepts and paths of salvation are so diverse that they constitute different roads to different destinations and

---

[15] Reinhold Bernhardt, "Prinzipieller Pluralismus oder mutualer Inklusivismus als hermeneutisches Paradigma einer Theologie der Religionen?" in *Die spekulative Philosophie der Weltreligionen*, ed. Peter Koslowski, 17–31 (Wien: Passagen Verlag, 1997). See also his essay in this volume for a more nuanced presentation of the same perspective.

[16] Michael von Brück, "Identifying Constructively Our Interreligious Moment," in Swidler and Mojzes, *The Uniqueness of Jesus*, 35–43. Also, Michael von Brück, "Heil und Heilswege im Hinduismus und Buddhismus—eine Herausforderung für christliches Erlösungsverständnis," in *Der einzige Weg zum Heil? Die Herausforderung des christlichen Absolutheitsanspruchs durch pluralistische Religionstheologien*, ed. M. von Brück and J. Werbick, 26–106 (Quaestiones Disputatae 143) (Freiburg: Herder, 1993), esp. 88–90.

[17] Ariarajah, "The Need for a New Debate," 30; Tilley, "Christianity and the World Religions," 326n19.

[18] This is the primary concern of Richard Skunks, "In universum mundum: Das Zeugnis des Evangeliums im Zeitalter pluralistischer Religionstheorien," in *Auf neue Art Kirche sein: Wirklichkeiten—Herausforderungen—Wandlungen* (Festschrift für Bischof Dr. Josef Homeyer), ed. Werner Schreer und Georg Steins, 514–30 (Munich: Bernward/Don Bosco, 1999).

[19] This objection is strongly put forth by Andreas Grünschloß, *Der eigene und der fremde Glaube*, 24–27. For an earlier and more moderate version of this objection see Reinhold Bernhardt: *Der Absolutheitsanspruch des Christentums: Von der Aufklärung bis zur Pluralistischen Religionstheologie* (Gütersloh: Gütersloher Verlagshaus Gerd Mohn, 1990), 234–35. For the same objection, see also M. M. Thomas, "A Christ-Centered Humanist Approach to Other Religions in the Indian Pluralistic Context," in *Christian Uniqueness Reconsidered: The Myth of a Pluralistic Theology of Religions*, ed. Gavin D'Costa, 49–62 (Maryknoll, NY: Orbis Books, 1990), 58.

[20] S. Mark Heim, *Salvations: Truth and Difference in Religion* (Maryknoll, NY: Orbis Books, 1995), 4. See also DiNoia, *The Diversity of Religions*, 47–55.

suggests the theological acknowledgment of a genuine plurality of salvations with different, but equally real, ultimate ends, so that each religion constitutes an exclusive path to its own specific fulfillment.

7. *The typology is offensive.*[21]

8. *The typology is pointless, because we are not in a position to choose any of these options and therefore have to refrain from all of them.*

This critique is primarily advanced by some of the defenders of a so-called comparative theology. The objection is presented in different degrees (some urge only a temporary moratorium,[22] while others apparently assume the fundamental impossibility of a theology of religions[23]), and for different reasons (that is, either for primarily epistemological reasons[24] or primarily for reasons of faithfulness to whatever is conceived as the unchangeable identity of one's own religious tradition[25]).

In addition to these criticisms, it should also be noted that despite (or perhaps because of) its widespread use, this threefold typology is not always employed in a uniform way. Therefore, one cannot assume that every author who speaks about exclusivism, inclusivism, and pluralism has precisely, or even broadly, the same understanding of these terms. A rather wide variety of different definitions is in the theological air—if definitions are given at all. Thus a classification that once seemed to provide a clear and helpful structure to the debate has turned into a reason for no little confusion and dissatisfaction.

Nevertheless, I firmly believe that the tripolar classification can be of great help in clarifying and profiling the available options for a theology of religions—whether Christian or other-than-Christian. In what follows I am *first*

---

[21] See Gerd Neuhaus, *Kein Weltfrieden ohne christlichen Absolutheitsanspruch: Eine religionstheologische Auseinandersetzung mit Hans Küngs "Project Weltethos"* (Quaestiones Disputatae 175) (Freiburg: HerderVerlag, 1999), 86–87. According to Neuhaus, the terms *inclusivism* and *exclusivism* in particular do not do justice to the self-understanding of those who hold these positions and serve only as polemical instruments in the hands of the pluralists.

[22] This seems to be the case with Francis Clooney. See particularly *Theology after Advaita Vedanta: An Experiment in Comparative Theology* (Albany: SUNY, 1993), 187–98. On the other hand, Clooney has on several occasions opted for an inclusivist position.

[23] This seems to be at least a strong tendency in James Fredericks, *Faith among Faiths: Christian Theology and Non-Christian Religions* (New York: Paulist Press, 1999).

[24] See James Fredericks, "A Universal Religious Experience? Comparative Theology as an Alternative to a Theology of Religions," in *Horizons* 22 (1995), 83–86. See also Francis Clooney, *Seeing through Texts* (Albany: SUNY, 1996), 298–99.

[25] This is a strong factor in Clooney's and Frederick's arguments and also in Klaus von Stosch, "Komparative Theologie—Ein Ausweg aus dem Grunddilemma einer Theologie der Religionen?" *Zeitschrift für Katholische Theologie* 124 (2002), 294–311.

proposing a logical reinterpretation of the typology, thereby transforming it from a descriptive, phenomenological typology into a logically precise and comprehensive classification.[26] *Second*, I give exact definitions for the three options within this reinterpretation. And *third*, I reaffirm this typology by showing how, in its clarified and reinterpreted form, it can respond to the various objections.[27] In doing all this, I hope to show why this typology can be used effectively and fruitfully in further theological discussions—as we are doing in this book.

REINTERPRETATION

It is not my intention to define *religion;* such a task, for a variety of good reasons, has proved impossible.[28] I do believe, however, that we can say that whatever else religions might be or do, they all affirm certain beliefs. Among these beliefs we find assertions about what exists or does not exist, value judgments, and also practical instructions. A central religious conviction is, as William Christian has framed it, that there is "something more important than anything else in the universe."[29] While this may also be true of the so-called secular religions (the great ideologies of the twentieth century), the traditional religions assume that this "something" that is more important than anything else in the world is a transcendent reality, that is, not one of the finite realities of this world.[30] In one way or another the religions claim to have some form of knowledge (or revelation) of this transcendent reality. And they do not only make the value judgment that this reality is the highest good, but they also instruct people to live their lives in such a way that they truly reflect this utmost importance of ultimate reality. Let us call such a proper orientation of life and the hopes connected with it salvation. Then we can say that religions, at least the traditional ones, claim—each in its own way—to mediate a salvific knowledge or revelation of a transcendent reality.

---

[26] I laid this out in greater detail in Perry Schmidt-Leukel, *Theologie der Religionen: Probleme, Optionen, Argumente* (Ars Una: Neuried, 1997), 65–97.

[27] A different attempt to reaffirm the tripolar typology, based on very similar motives, can be found in Alan Race, *Interfaith Encounter: The Twin Tracks of Theology and Dialogue* (London: SCM, 2001), 21–42. A very careful, cautious, and differentiated discussion of the typology is given in Michael Hüttenhoff, *Der religiöse Pluralismus als Orientierungsproblem* (Leipzig: Evangelische Verlagsanstalt, 2001), 29–77.

[28] See Walter Kerber, ed., *Der Begriff der Religion* (Munich: Peter Kindt Verlag, 1993).

[29] W. A. Christian, *Meaning and Truth in Religion* (Princeton, NJ: Princeton Univ. Press, 1964), 60.

[30] This is, of course, also true for Theravada Buddhism, which affirms the existence of an "unborn, unbecome, unmade, unconditioned" reality as the condition of ultimate liberation (see Udana VIII, 3; Ittivutaka 43).

We can call this property *P* (*P*=mediation of a salvific knowledge of ultimate/transcendent reality). Consequently, *P* is a property of a religious community or tradition if this community or tradition not only claims *P*, but correctly so claims—that is, if its claim is true.

If we ask whether *P* is a property of religions, that is, if *P* is given among the religions, we arrive at four possible answers:

1. *P* is not given among the religions.
2. *P* is given among the religions, but only once.
3. *P* is given among the religions more than once, but with only one singular maximum.
4. *P* is given among the religions more than once and without a singular maximum.

These four answers are comprehensive, because they are fully disjunctive: Either *P* is given or not. If *P* is given, it is given only once or more than once. And if *P* is given more than once, it is either with or without a singular maximum form (see Figure 2–1).

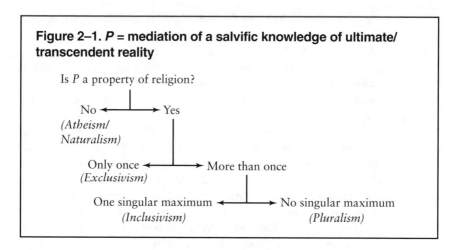

Figure 2–1. *P* = mediation of a salvific knowledge of ultimate/ transcendent reality

Is *P* a property of religion?

No ← → Yes
(Atheism/ Naturalism)

Only once ← → More than once
(Exclusivism)

One singular maximum ← → No singular maximum
(Inclusivism) *(Pluralism)*

Hence we have four different options with the following definitions:

(0) *Atheism/Naturalism:* Salvific knowledge of a transcendent reality is mediated by none of the religions (because a transcendent reality does not exist).

(1) *Exclusivism:* Salvific knowledge of a transcendent reality is mediated by only one religion (which naturally will be one's own).

(2) *Inclusivism:* Salvific knowledge of a transcendent reality is mediated by more than one religion (not necessarily by all of them), but only one of these mediates it in a uniquely superior way (which again will naturally be one's own).

(3) *Pluralism:* Salvific knowledge of a transcendent reality is mediated by more than one religion (not necessarily by all of them), and there is none among them whose mediation of that knowledge is superior to all the rest.

Let me add a few further comments on this interpretation of the typology and the definitions involved.

1. Because the four options form a fully disjunctive and therefore logically comprehensive classification, every option within the theology of religions, as far as it entails an answer to the opening question, can be subsumed in one of the four definitions. There is no further option. However, every option is so defined that it covers a range of sub-forms. *Inclusivism*, for example, includes options that see an element of P in all religions or only in some, and it allows for various forms of grading P. What is crucial is that it allows for only one maximum instantiation of P. Similarly, my definition of *pluralism* encompasses options that would accept a maximum instantiation of *P* in only a few religions (at least two), or in a larger group of religions (theistic, or non-theistic, or the major world religions, and so forth), or even in all religions. And if not the equality of *all* religions is postulated, then there can be a range of different versions: A *pluralist* might consider some religions as totally lacking *P* (that is, taking an exclusivist stance toward them) or as inferior realizations of *P* (that is, taking an inclusivist stance); such a person is still a *pluralist* as long as he or she regards some religions as equally high in their realization of *P*.[31] What distinguishes a pluralist from an inclusivist is the acknowledgment that there is no singular superior instantiation of *P* but rather several.

2. The validity of this formal reinterpretation of the classification does not depend on how the maximum of the instantiation of *P* (and accordingly the superiority or inferiority of *P*) is exactly understood. This may vary. Some may be inclined to understand the "maximum" in an absolute sense so that it does not permit any further potential increase, while others might feel that "mediation of salvific knowledge" allows for future improvement of, for example, quality, depths, width, and would perhaps argue that, precisely through constructive interreligious encounter, religions can grow with re- gard to *P*.

3. As the logical comprehensiveness of the typology entails that there is no further option, it would be a waste of time to look for a new option. The theological/philosophical debate can concentrate on the reasons that speak

---

[31] These are not purely abstract possibilities. John Hick, clearly one of the most prominent representatives of a pluralist approach, takes an exclusivist stance toward certain destructive cults or sects and an inclusivist one toward (quasi-religious) hu- manism. See John Hick, "A Concluding Comment," in *Faith and Philosophy* 5 (1988), 453; Hick, "Reply (to Mesle)," in *Problems in the Philosophy of Religion*, ed. H. Hewitt (Houndmills, UK: Macmillan, 1991), 83; Hick, *The Rainbow of Faiths* (Lon- don: SCM, 1995), 81.

for or against each of the four basic options and its possible sub-forms and should try to refine them. But in the end one has to choose one of them.

4. The first option—*atheist/naturalist*—can be excluded as a religious or theological option. It is a logical possibility (and, no doubt, one that can be supported by respectable arguments), but since it rests on the denial of a transcendent reality, it cannot be a religious and theological option. Therefore a theology of religions has to decide among the three remaining options of *exclusivism, inclusivism,* and *pluralism.*

5. In principle, every religion can define its relationship to the other religions by one of the three remaining options, that is, the typology is not exclusively linked with a Christian theology of religions.

6. However, as a classification of Christian theological options, it would look somewhat like the following:

- Christian *exclusivism* would mean that saving revelation is found only within Christianity and not within any other religion. This does not necessarily entail that all non-Christians are lost. Soft or moderate exclusivists could hold that there are ways by which God could save non-Christians *as individuals* (for example, through a postmortem encounter with the gospel). But, according to the definition given above, Christian exclusivism would deny any positive salvific role for other religions.

- In contrast to this, Christian *inclusivism* would hold that non-Christian religions sometimes entail elements of revelation and grace that are capable of supporting a salvific life. But since—according to Christian inclusivism—all salvation is finally through Christ, the revelation to which Christianity testifies is in a unique sense superior to any other form of knowledge of God, which in comparison with the Christian revelation remains necessarily fragmentary, incomplete, implicit, obscure.

- Christian *pluralism* would entail that some other religions—usually the major world religions (but perhaps only one other religion)—are in a theological sense on a par with Christianity. According to Christian pluralism these other religions testify to the same ultimate transcendent reality despite the different forms this testimony takes, and they do so with the same genuine authenticity and an equal salvific potential.

CLARIFICATION

Let me now add some clarifying remarks concerning the names used in this tripolar classification of theological options. Even though it is the options themselves, and not the names, that are essential, still, I believe that these particular three names are appropriate. And yet, because these names are used as specific indicators and labels outside the theology of religions, they frequently give rise to confusion and misunderstanding.

- Thus, within the reinterpreted version of the typology, *exclusivism* does not denote *any kind* of exclusivist claims. Every truth-claim is in a sense exclusive, for it excludes the truth of its logical opposite. To criticize such an exclusivism would amount to intellectual suicide, for a proposition that would not exclude anything would no longer have any specific meaning and would therefore become unintelligible.

- In the context of this typology, *inclusivism* does not denote a position that emphasizes that all statements or judgments about another religion are expressed from within the framework of concepts and values and terminology of one's own religion. It is true that the serious study of another religion may lead to a significant widening and transformation of one's own religious horizon and hence may introduce a new terminology within one's own religion. But it seems to be an inevitable hermeneutical law that in every process of understanding something new has to start from one's own conceptual framework.

- *Pluralism*—as the term is used here—does not denote the simple fact that in our world, and increasingly in each of its societies, there is a plurality of religions. And it should not be confused with *pluralism* in the sense of a socio-political theory that conceptualizes and calls for societies that can accommodate ideological, religious, and cultural diversity. In order to defend a pluralist society in this sense, there is no need to hold a pluralist theology of religions. Apart from adequate political mechanisms, the defense of a pluralist society is ultimately based on the acceptance of human rights and the virtue of tolerance. And again, tolerance does not require a pluralist theology of religions. On the contrary, tolerance is required for what we disapprove of, while the pluralist option within a theology of religion is not about tolerating what we don't like but about giving due theological recognition to what we appreciate.[32] Therefore, the pluralist option neither substantiates nor substitutes toleration. Tolerance is simply something different and rests on different grounds.

  Moreover, as defined here, *pluralism* does not imply the relativistic feeling that all religions or indeed all world views or value systems must be equally good (or bad), because if it did, there would be no way of making any universal judgments at all. In contrast, here the pluralist option is precisely understood as a value judgment on other religions— a judgment that acknowledges theologically their equal value as ways of salvation.

So, within this reinterpretation of the threefold typology, the understanding of the pluralist option has a very precise form. Pluralism does not mean a vague or emphatic approval of interfaith dialogue. To some extent the value of interfaith dialogue can be affirmed by naturalists, exclusivists, inclusivists, and pluralists. Nor does pluralism mean the readiness to acknowledge elements of

---

[32] See Perry Schmidt-Leukel, "Beyond Tolerance: Towards a New Step in Interreligious Relationship," *Scottish Journal of Theology* 55 (2002), 379–91.

saving knowledge outside one's own tradition, for this is also possible for inclusivists (as they are defined here). Additionally, for a pluralist position (as understood here) it is not sufficient to accept other religions as "independently authentic contexts of salvation/liberation."[33] This would still allow for the possibility of regarding one's own tradition as being in an objective sense superior. Not independence but equality (in the sense of an equal quality of salvific knowledge of transcendent reality) is crucial—or, in a slightly softer version, abandoning the claim to the unique superiority of one's own tradition.

REAFFIRMATION

In order to reaffirm the usefulness of the typology (in its reinterpreted form) I now briefly respond to the eight major objections as they were listed above.

1. The typology has an inconsistent structure because the positions are not of the same genre and do not address the same questions (Tilley, Markham).

Response: This objection may or may not be valid with regard to one or the other of the many existent versions of the tripolar classification. But it easily can be seen that the objection does not hold for the reinterpreted version suggested here. In its reinterpreted form the typology has a consistent structure and a single focus. All of the four definitions refer to *religions or religious traditions,* not to individuals or the fate of individuals within these religions or religious traditions. The single focus rests on the religions' *claim to mediate salvific knowledge of a transcendent reality.* This claim combines a soteriological (salvific) and an epistemological (knowledge) element. But if this combination is understood in the broad sense in which it was introduced above, then it seems to be typical for religious claims.[34]

2. The typology is misleading, because it obscures or misses the real issues of a theology of religions (Tilley, D'Costa, DiNoia).

Response: Of course, everyone is free to construct a theology of religions as he or she likes. But if one takes the claims of other religions seriously, and if these claims amount in one or the other way to the mediation of a salvific

---

[33] John Hick, as quoted in Markham, "Creating Options," 34. However, in most places Hick gives a definition of religious pluralism that entails the crucial element of equality or non-superiority. The affirmation of religions as *independent* soteriological contexts should be seen as an implication of the pluralist denial of the Christian inclusivist claim that the salvation which is mediated through non-Christian religions was brought about and thus depends on the redeeming work of Christ.

[34] I entirely agree with John Hick's view "that in fact the truth-claim and the salvation-claim cohere closely together and should be treated as a single package." John Hick: *Problems of Religious Pluralism* (Houndmills, UK: Macmillan, 1985), 46.

knowledge of a transcendent reality, then the typology in its reinterpreted form is not only not misleading but directly touches the core of a theology of religions. Moreover, because of the logical comprehensiveness of the classification, it is ultimately inevitable.

3. The typology is too narrow. There are more than three options (Ogden, Grünschloß, Markham, Knitter, R. Plantinga).

Response: Due to the comprehensiveness of the logical reconstruction of the typology, there is no further option. Any "further option" would turn out either to fall under one of the four classified options (as in the case of S. Mark Heim, whose recent suggestions are clearly and explicitly inclusivist[35]) or to repeat one of these options in a different mode (as in the case of S. Ogden, who does not introduce a new option but repeats the pluralist option in the mode of potentiality[36]) or from a different perspective (for example, A. Grünschloß, whose "inferiorism" is nothing else than affirming inclusivism from a different angle[37]), or it turns out to entail no answer to the basic question of a theology of religions at all, so that there is nothing to be classified (as in the case of J. Fredericks).

Since in its reinterpreted form the typology does not leave any further option, it forces the scholarly discussion to focus on the arguments for and against each of the three viz. four positions. The typology thus focuses, sharpens, and thereby helps the discussion.

4. The typology is too broad. There are not really three options but only one or two (D'Costa, A. Plantinga, von Brück, Bernhardt).

Response: This objection is based on the broad range of potential meanings of the names. It does not apply to the strict definitions of the three options as they are provided in the reinterpreted typology. That is, if someone understands exclusivism in the sense that any truth-claim necessarily excludes the truth of the exactly opposite claim (D'Costa and A. Plantinga), then all of the three or four options are exclusivist in that sense. But this does not entail that option (0), (1), (2), and (3)—as defined above—would collapse into option (1).[38] Or if someone understands inclusivism in the general hermeneutical sense that any assessment of another religion will be made from the perspective of one's own religion and therefore inevitably draws upon its own concepts (Bernhardt and von Brück), then once again each of

---

[35] "I am a convinced inclusivist." S. Mark Heim, *The Depth of the Riches: A Trinitarian Theology of Religious Ends* (Grand Rapids, MI: Eerdmans, 2001), 8.

[36] The same objection to Ogden can be found in Hick, *The Rainbow of Faiths,* 19; and Hüttenhof, *Der religiöse Pluralismus als Orientierungsproblem,* 54.

[37] A Christian who would affirm the superiority of Islam (with regards to the salvific knowledge of transcendent reality) would not instantiate a new option but simply hold an Islamic inclusivism and consequently, I presume, convert. If someone sees another religion as superior to his or her own with regard to only some specific aspects, the resulting question is what this implies for the basic and central assessment of the ability of both religions to mediate salvific knowledge of transcendence.

[38] For a similar refutation of this objection, see David Basinger, *Religious Diversity: A Philosophical Assessment* (Aldershot: Ashgate, 2002), 4–5.

the three (or four—in an analogous form) options will be inclusivist. But within such a *hermeneutical inclusivism* there are still significant differences among option (0), (1), (2), and (3), and they do not all collapse into option (2). Therefore, it is indeed possible to state something like a "mutual inclusivism" in a hermeneutical sense (which is, in fact, a good description of what is actually the case between the religions), but it would not be possible to claim a "mutual inclusivism" in the sense of option (2) as defined above. It is logically impossible that of two religions each is objectively superior to the other in precisely the same respect—as it is impossible of two siblings that each of them is one year older than the other. That religions mutually claim their superiority is the problem for the theology of religions, not a valid solution.

5. The typology is too abstract and sterile. It does not do justice to the more complex reality of the living theologian (Ariarajah, Tilley, Skunks).

Response: This objection overlooks the important difference between a kind of phenomenological typology (which would not seek logical comprehensiveness but simply describes and classifies certain existent theological approaches) and a formal, logically comprehensive classification. The latter does neither purport nor intend to represent an exact description of the opinions of certain theologians, but to clarify which in principle possible options we have with regard to a particular problem. If such a classification is constructed properly but does not cover the views of a specific theologian or philosopher, the reason will be that his or her views simply do not entail an answer to the specific problem that is the focus of the classification. If they do, they can be subsumed among one of the classified options because the typology is comprehensive. It is important to keep in mind, however, that in its reinterpreted form the typology allows for a number of sub-forms and variants of the three basic options as they are defined above. And it is also true, as Hick and Race have observed, that "sometimes . . . people say that they do not fit into any of these categories,"[39] but "when they submit their own positive proposals, [they] turn out to exemplify one of the three positions."[40]

Additionally, there is also the possibility that theologians are sometimes too ambiguous or inconsistent in their statements so that for this reason a clear classification of their position is not possible. This, of course, would not be the fault of the typology but of the respective theologians. The typology can help to detect such ambiguities or unclarities in their work—and thereby once again help to clarify the conversation.

But what if a theologian takes different options with regard to different aspects; for example, if the theologian takes a pluralistic viewpoint with regard to soteriology but an exclusivistic or inclusivistic one with regard to epistemology? In that case—I suggest—one has to see whether in the end this does not amount to an overall assessment that is either pluralist, or inclusivist,

---

[39] Hick, *The Rainbow of Faiths*, 18–19.
[40] Race, *Interfaith Encounter*, 36.

or exclusivist—or whether the different choices may eventually lead to in-consistent conclusions.

6. The typology is misleading, because it does not do justice to the radical diversity of the religions (Heim).

Response: It is not the typology that is misleading, but rather Heim's sub-mission that it rests on an "unequivocal" concept of salvation. In its reinter-preted form it rests on the fact that the religions themselves make claims to a salvific knowledge of transcendence. The typology does not prejudge how these claims—and thus the nature of salvific—are understood and evaluated. This is precisely the point of difference and controversy among the defenders of an exclusivist, inclusivist, or pluralist approach. Nor has this anything to do with the acknowledgment of real difference. For example, consider a Christian exclusivist who believes that the Buddhist path—because it differs from the Christian one—does not lead to salvation. Would such an exclusivist exhibit a clearer acknowledgment of or higher esteem for difference than a Christian pluralist who also believes that the Buddhist path is different but nevertheless also leads to salvation, not despite being different, but simply in its difference? Why should only those count as accepting real otherness who identify otherness with falsity? Not the acknowledgment of otherness is at stake but its evaluation. While the exclusivist and the inclusivist judge the otherness of other religions by definition as something negative—as a devia-tion from, or a deficient form of, the only or full truth that their own religion embodies—the pluralist enjoys the flexibility to assess some forms of reli-gious otherness as false, some as inferior and some, despite and in their oth-erness, as equally salvific.

But what about Heim's particular suggestion that the various religious paths lead to different but nevertheless real eschatological ends? Would such a theological construct fall out of the tripolar classification? Not at all, for the crucial question is still, how—as in the case of Heim—the Christian theo-logian would assess these different salvations and the correlative fulfillments in relation to the Christian goal. For Heim these salvations are by no means all of same rank—not even some of them. Since the real God is the trinitarian God of Christianity, only Christians enjoy the eschatological vision of the ultimate truth. Thus, despite being real, the soteriological goals of the other religions remain deficient and inferior, being at best related to some particu-lar aspects of the comprehensive reality of the Trinity. While the Christian way thus leads to the highest heaven, other religious paths lead only to inferior ends;[41] or even to a hell-like state.[42] And thereby Heim implicitly reaffirms the

---

[41] See Heim, *The Depth of the Riches*, 271–96.

[42] See Heim, *Salvations*, 163: "From a Christian perspective this requires the some-what unfamiliar admission that other religious fulfillments may be both distinct and quite real. At the same time Christians may rightly continue to view the achievement of these alternative religious ends as something to be avoided, even in cases carrying some measure of the meaning of 'damnation.' That is, they are not positive evils (though such evils may be live possibilities), but they are aims different than the best that Christians know and hope for."

tripolar typology. He himself holds an inclusivism of the less generous sort,[43] not allowing the non-Christian religions to lead their adherents to the highest eschatological fulfillment, or in total to a sort of hell, but to a new, postmodernist kind of pre-modern limbo.

7. The typology is offensive (Neuhaus).

Response: No one should be offended by the names of the options, but if so, there is no reason why the same option should not be given a different name (as some exclusivists have preferred to refer to their own position as *particularist*). However, I think that none of the names is in itself offensive. In common language each of them can have positive overtones (as, for example, in "exclusive shops" or "exclusive service"; "inclusiveness" can mean a welcoming openness). Some exclusivists are therefore quite happy to accept the typology together with its usual labels.[44]

8. The typology is pointless, because we cannot make any of these judgments and therefore have to refrain from all of these positions (Fredericks, von Stosch).

Response: The options classified in the reinterpreted version of the typology can be avoided only if one avoids the basic questions to which the options relate: Are the central claims of other religions true? Do they really mediate salvific knowledge of a transcendent reality, as they claim? Avoiding those questions, I suggest, means not being seriously involved in the business of a theology of religions. I cannot see how those who are propagating *comparative theology* as an alternative to the *theology of religions* are able to enter genuine *theological* comparison (as distinct from a purely phenomenological one) without arriving at exactly the types of questions that are treated in the theology of religions.[45] Doing comparative theology is not an alternative to the theology of religions but should be an integral part of it, preventing us from aprioristic and apodictic judgments so that we arrive at our various positions cautiously and tentatively, always open to critical objections and potential revision. After all, the theology of religions, whether exclusivist, inclusivist, or pluralist, is still theology—a form of human reasoning based on faith and not a form of absolute, infallible knowledge.

---

[43] See John Hick's review of Heim's *The Depth of the Riches* in *Reviews in Religion and Theology* 8 (2001), 411–14.

[44] For example, Harold Netland, *Dissonant Voices: Religious Pluralism and the Question of Truth* (Grand Rapids, MI: Eerdmans, 1991), 8–35; Paul Eddy, *John Hick's Pluralist Philosophy of World Religions* (Aldershot: Ashgate, 2002).

[45] For a similar critique, see Knitter, *Introducing Theologies of Religions*, 236–37.

3

Is the Pluralist Model a Western Imposition?

A Response in Five Voices

PAUL F. KNITTER

If critics can be considered a blessing that indicates one is being taken seriously, then the pluralist model is greatly blessed. Critics abound. For a variety of reasons, both academic and religious leaders are taking very seriously and are greatly concerned about proposals that call upon all religious persons to lay aside their claims of superiority, recognize their mutual validity, and engage in a new kind of relationship in which all can learn from each other and work together for the benefit of all.

One of the sharpest and oft-repeated of these criticisms is that the pluralist model is a cleverly camouflaged but ultimately exploitative Western imposition. Let me try briefly to unpack that statement, in order to understand it and to take it seriously.

First is the claim that the pluralist model is an *imposition*. It's an imposition, fundamentally, because it forgets or ignores *the reality of language*. As postliberal theologian George Lindbeck has reminded us, language both defines and confines us. Language not only *expresses* what we think about; it *determines* and therefore *limits* what we think about. Our thoughts do not exist in some thin air, naked; they always come dressed in some language. Furthermore, though we certainly can learn many languages, we can speak only one of them at a time. That means that when we speak about other languages or religions, we're doing so in one particular religious language. This means, furthermore, we're always understanding and judging other religious languages from one religious language, our own. Just as we cannot speak in a universal language, so we cannot be religious, or understand religion, in one universal religious language. That's the problem with the pluralist model, the critics say—it tries to find a common language within

28

all religions. But in doing so it ends up imposing its own language on all the others.[1]

The fundamental problem with pluralists, the critics conclude, is that they really don't want to be pluralists. Pluralism means accepting not just that religions are *many* but that they are *different*—so different that they can't be boiled down to a system, or common essence, or common ground. Nor can one religion be evaluated on the basis of another religion; in fact, there is no universal criterion by which all religions can be weighed and sorted out. And this is what pluralists refuse, or are unable, to accept—that although religions can and should be tolerant of one another, although they can cooperate on humanitarian projects, they remain more different than they are similar.[2] Any effort to assemble them or connect them on the basis of some common essence or common "Ultimate Reality" ends up imposing "my" Ultimate Reality on yours. As William Placher puts it: "They [pluralists] cannot accept the possibility that there may be just different, even conflicting religions and no point from which to evaluate them except from within some one tradition or another."[3]

Second, the critics continue, the pluralist imposition of one religious language on all the others is seen today as the imposition of a *Western* language. This criticism can be verified both phenomenologically and politically. Just look at the originating, motivating ideals of pluralism; they were all originally packaged in the European Enlightenment—universal truth linked to the universality of reason, evolution toward ever greater unity, *e pluribus unum* (out of many, one), liberal democracy. Even more tellingly, look at the primary propagators of pluralism (and at the organizers of the conference behind this book!); they are predominantly Europeans and Americans, and mainly male.

Granted, these "fathers of pluralism" are not evil-minded imperialists out to lure other cultures and religions into a Western cage. Still, in the present *political* context of the world they may, warn the critics, be doing just that. Just as the persistent calls for globalization—that is, for a worldwide economy that will connect and gather all nations around the table of a common market—can serve, and is serving, to consolidate the dominance of those economies who built and control the table, so too can calls for a new pluralistic

---

[1] See George Lindbeck, *The Nature of Doctrine: Religion and Theology in a Postliberal Age* (Philadelphia: Westminster Press, 1984); William Placher, *Unapologetic Theology: A Christian Voice in a Pluralistic Conversation* (Louisville, KY: Westminster/John Knox Press, 1989); J. A. DiNoia, "Pluralist Theology of Religions: Pluralistic or Non-Pluralistic?" in *Christian Uniqueness Reconsidered: The Myth of a Pluralistic Theology of Religions*, ed. Gavin D'Costa (Maryknoll, NY: Orbis Books, 1990), 119–34.

[2] The most elaborate and careful argument for the dominance of the diversity of religions over any possible unity is made by S. Mark Heim in *Salvations: Truth and Difference in Religion* (Maryknoll, NY: Orbis Books, 1995) and *The Depth of Riches: A Trinitarian Theology of Religious Ends* (Grand Rapids, MI: Eerdmans, 2001).

[3] Placher, *Unapologetic Theology*, 144.

community of religions turn religion and religious dialogue into a tool that serves the agenda of the powerful. To call for a pluralistic "equality of religions" in a world in which there is no economic-political "equality of nations and peoples" is at best naive, and at worst dangerous. As Sheila Greeve Davaney puts it: To foster a true pluralism of religions it is necessary to address "those dynamics of power that invest some perspectives with great legitimacy while dismissing others. It does little good to advocate a position that calls for open debate, inclusive of multiple voices, while ignoring the mechanisms by which many are rendered invisible, denied legitimacy, or so thoroughly located at the bottom of a hierarchy of values that their reality counts for little in the evaluative equation."[4]

These are deep-reaching, sobering criticisms. In this essay I want to respond to them and to show that, ultimately, they are ill-founded. But to do that, I have to take them seriously. Indeed, I believe that we pluralists can advance our project only by learning from the warnings and accusations of these critics. There are real dangers lurking out there on the other side of what John Hick and I, back in 1986, called the Rubicon.[5] If the pluralists' move represents as decisive a turn for religious traditions as Julius Caesar's crossing of the Rubicon did for him and Rome, then pluralists better be wary of pitfalls and precipices as they plot their new paths in new territory. The critics, I believe, offer us pluralists warning signs of just where the pitfalls and precipices lie.

But ultimately I believe they are warning signs, not roadblocks. To accept these postmodern criticisms of the pluralist model uncritically is to be caught behind a roadblock to what many feel is the possibility, if not the necessity, of a new kind of relationship between the religious traditions of the world— a relationship of shared understanding and cooperation that will promote not just the well-being of the religions but also of the planet.

So in what follows I hope to offer not just a response to these critics but, by taking them seriously, a defense and further clarification of the pluralist project. I hope to show that this project is *not* a Western imposition. I'll try to do so by drawing on different voices—five in all—of persons who take religion seriously, either as practitioners or as scholars. What these different voices, coming from different religious traditions, have to say can, I believe, be accepted and affirmed by people within all religions. These voices will either clarify or confirm essential ingredients in the pluralist perspective on religious diversity and dialogue, and by doing so they will make evident, I trust, that these ingredients are not just "made in the West." Though some of the elements of the pluralist model may come in Western wrappings, their contents are drawn from multi-religious sources.

---

[4] Sheila Greeve Davaney, *Pragmatic Historicism: A Theology for the Twenty-First Century* (Albany: SUNY, 2000), 162.

[5] See the Introduction to John Hick and Paul F. Knitter, eds., *The Myth of Christian Uniqueness: Toward a Pluralistic Theology of Religions* (Maryknoll, NY: Orbis Books, 1987).

THE VOICE OF RELIGIOUS BELIEVERS AND TEACHERS:
EXPOUNDING UNIVERSAL TRUTH

Religious truth is universal truth. This is what we hear from and see in religious believers and in their teachers. The truth they know or have experienced, while it is certainly meant for them, is meant not only for them. It is also for others; it can also touch and transform the lives of others. Minimally, we can say the meaning and power that individuals experience within their own religion is also felt to be relevant for others; it can have powerful meaning for others and enrich their lives. Maximally, some religious believers will go further and say not only that the truth they have discovered or been given is relevant for others but also that it is necessary for others. Without this truth others cannot be "saved" or come to the fullness of truth. But I suggest that such a maximal claim is but a further theological elaboration of the fundamental belief that my truth is relevant also for you. What a religious person feels, naturally and necessarily, is that what is good for me can also be good for you. The corollary—that what is good for me is not only good but *necessary* for you—is more a matter of what religious believers have been taught, not what they really *know* in the marrow of their religious bones.

The point to note is that every religious believer is naturally a religious teacher or preacher; all religious believers want to share what they have been given. So we should not be surprised that many religions are self-confessed missionary religions. Some are more missionary than others; Christianity, Islam, and Buddhism stand at the top of the list of those communities that have sent forth believers (*missionaries* are literally the "sent ones") to tell others about the truth of the gospel, the Qur'an, the Dharma. But even those religions that are not distinguished by sending missionaries are ready to accept converts; Hinduism and Judaism, for example, have received into their communities many who have been moved by an attractive truth that radiates from such communities.[6]

But my point is not to compile a missionary scorecard to grade the various traditions. Rather, it is to bring to the surface a reality that I believe stirs in the depth of all human experience: If something is really true and important, it cannot be true just for me. If it's not also true for others, I have reason to question its claim on me. This is especially the case for those truths that constitute the bedrock and the daily energy of our lives—religious truths.

In a certain sense, then, all religious believers are *inclusivists*. All of us experience, understand, and judge other religions from the perspective of our own religion. And we do so not just because that is the human condition in which it is impossible to find a point outside of culture to look at all

---

[6] Only the indigenous religions, with the strong place-bound, geographically determined quality of their experience and beliefs, seem not to be eager or ready to seek or accept converts.

cultures objectively. We are inclusivists also because we believe that where we stand gives us the ability to see elsewhere; it enables us to understand others. Even more, religious beliefs lead us to suspect, or even assert, that if the others stood where we stand, they would understand themselves better!

This "universal understanding power" that religious believers feel they have makes for a sharp contrast, if not contradiction, between postmodern assertions and religious experience. Postmodernists insist that meta-narratives, or universal truths, are impossible (and dangerous). Religious believers, by the very nature of their experience, make such universal claims (though often they are not sufficiently aware of the dangers of doing so). George Lindbeck may overstate his case, but I think it is still a fundamentally accurate case, when he claims that all religious people and communities believe they have and can offer others "a totally comprehensive framework, a universal perspective" for understanding what humanity is all about and where it might go.[7] So even though not all religions are explicitly missionary and in search of new members, all, or most, religious communities hold that what they see enables them not only to see beyond their own borders but to understand and "put in order" what they see out there. In different ways and to different degrees religious truth is other oriented. All religions make universal truth-claims.

And this is something that we pluralists can recognize, even though we have not always done so with sufficient clarity. In pressing the case for throwing out the "bath water" of absolute truth-claims and intolerance, have we perhaps also thrown out the "baby" of universal claims? In our efforts to dismantle doctrines that devalue other religions, have we perhaps also dismantled religious beliefs that can challenge other religions? And so we have been accused, perhaps rightly so, of imposing a definition of religion that muffles the universal assertions that religious people naturally make. We have been accused of relativism and of opening the door to the view that every religion has its own truth and should not question the truth of others. What's true for you is not true for me. So be it. The pluralist view that *many* truths must be recognized has been understood to mean that *every* truth must be recognized. That becomes, in effect, the position that *no* religious assertion can be taken seriously.

But in order to clarify for our critics—and perhaps for ourselves—what we pluralists are about, I want to say loudly and clearly that the pluralist model can, and must, affirm not just the reality but the value of universal religious truth-claims. There is nothing contradictory between *plurality* and *universality*. Here, I believe, we can note a sharp and revealing difference between what is called the postliberal view of religious diversity and the pluralistic view. In affirming the value of many religions, but also in insisting that each religion is a cultural-linguistic system unto itself, postliberals like George Lindbeck and William Placher (perhaps also S. Mark Heim) end up isolating each religion in its own dogmatic and conceptual backyard with no

---

[7] Lindbeck, *The Nature of Doctrine,* 49.

exigency or possibility for dialogue with people in other backyards. Pluralists, by contrast, try to hold high the value of many religions but at the same time bring them together into relationships of mutuality. (Which is why, for me personally, *mutuality* is a better name for our model than *pluralism*.)[8]

Pluralists do not want simply to affirm the diversity and the value of many religions; the pluralist agenda is also the attempt to bring these many and different religions into conversation. And in order to have a conversation, all those involved have to feel that what they want to bring to the conversation is something that everyone else can and perhaps even must listen to and potentially learn from. By learning from others, dialogue partners do not need to convert to the other religion, but their own religious self-understanding and practice will be different, deepened, maybe even transformed for having learned something from the other. Without participants bringing challenging truth-claims to the conversation, dialogue becomes only a clarifying exchange of information about each other (valuable, certainly, but not yet dialogue).

So if I may resort to a simple syllogism: if all religious believers make universal truth-claims, and if pluralists acknowledge and affirm the value of such claims, then at least on this score, pluralism can be endorsed by believers of all traditions.

THE VOICE OF RELIGIOUS MYSTICS/TEACHERS: ABSOLUTE MYSTERY

But while pluralists affirm the validity of universal claims, they resolutely oppose the validity of absolute claims. A pivotal piece in the pluralist perspective, one might say, is precisely the distinction between making universal and absolute truth-claims. While all absolute truths must be universal, universal truths need not be absolute. This is the pluralist challenge to traditional religious believers: you can and should continue to go forth to proclaim what you know to be true and good, but you cannot legitimately proclaim that this is the only word, or the last word, on what is true and good.

And here's the rub—where, according to the critics, pluralism flies in the face of what all religions naturally do. Religions, throughout history, *have* made absolute claims; that is, they have announced that they have the only, or the final, or the superior truth revealed by God or available to humanity; or they have presented themselves as the one source of the truth and salvation available to all peoples and tribes. So, the critics point out, when pluralists come along and deny the possibility of absolute claims, such pluralists become an example par excellence of Westerners imposing a tenet of the

---

[8] See Paul F. Knitter, *Introducing Theologies of Religions* (Maryknoll, NY: Orbis Books, 2002), 109–49; Knitter, *One Earth Many Religions: Multifaith Dialogue and Global Responsibility* (Maryknoll, NY: Orbis Books, 1995), 23–25.

Enlightenment on all religions—namely, the Enlightenment belief that all truth is historically conditioned and therefore relative.

Pluralists have to agree that many if not most religions have made absolute claims and in one form or another put themselves at the head of the list of religions. But to challenge such beliefs is not, pluralists would further claim, simply a Western imposition. Rather, it is a rediscovery of what mystics and teachers in multiple religious traditions have always maintained, but what has too frequently been forgotten or ignored. If many religions make absolute truth-claims, all religions contain a critique of such claims. Stated simply and provocatively, according to the mystico-theological traditions within all religions, absolute claims can be made only in a qualified manner.

Among mystics and teachers (theologians) across the traditions, there is broad agreement that what the religions are seeking is beyond human comprehension and that therefore all human speaking about it can never be more than "relatively adequate." In different ways and in different contexts, religions recognize that what they are after they can never fully find. Yes, they find something, and that something transforms their lives, but they never find everything. Religion deals with that which can never be totally known or definitively grasped by human beings. So if religious practitioners can be utterly certain that they have experienced God or Truth or Enlightenment, they also are utterly certain that this Reality is *more* than what they have experienced. It is just as much (or more) "beyond" as it is "here"—just as transcendent as it is immanent; even those religions, such as Buddhism, that affirm the utter immanence or "suchness" of Nirvana or *Sunyata*, recognize that its immanence is more than—transcends—their experience and understanding of it. In Christian terms, God names a mystery that is incomprehensible, and therefore the *apophatic* (affirming, positive) quality of every doctrine must be held in dynamic tension with the *kataphatic* (denying, negative) quality of every doctrine.

Whether a religion understands the object of its quest to be a being, or truth, or an experience, it recognizes that there is always more to come. One never fully arrives, or one is never fully in the present moment. Religions deal with more—more to know, more to experience, more to appropriate. Such a "more" is often understood horizontally, that is, temporally or eschatologically, but it can also be grasped vertically, as having to go more deeply into what is already there. Even the fully enlightened are never finally enlightened.

Mystics announce this persistently, and teachers or theologians recognize it: religions deals with Mystery. And therefore the language that most religions feel they must use to speak about their experience and to pass it on in the community can never say it all. Even the religions of the book, though they hold up their books as God's truth for all peoples, admit that no book can hold the totality of divine Truth. Though Christians affirm that God's very Word was incarnated in Jesus, Jesus (in the words of John's gospel) reminds them that "the Father is greater than I." And though Muslims announce to all that Allah's truth is, as one scholar puts it, "enlibricized" in the

Qur'an, they also recognize that if their text contains "one-fourth" of divine Truth, "three-fourths" remains mystery.[9] This distinction between God/ Truth as *really* known in religious experience but never *fully* known—or as Panikkar puts it, the distinction between *pars* and *totum* (the part and the whole)—echoes like a parental admonition throughout all the religious traditions: yes, you know something, but don't get smart and think you know everything.

In an exchange of emails in preparation for the conference that is the basis of this book, John Hick made a succinct observation and admonition: "In Christian terms [the distinction is made] between Godhead and God (Meister Eckhart), in Hindu terms between *nirguna* and *saguna* Brahman, in (Mahayana) Buddhist terms between the *Dharmakaya* and its manifestations in the Buddhas, in Jewish and Muslim mysticism between *Ein Sof* and *al-Haq* and the God of the scriptures."[10] Such distinctions between what we *do* and *do not* know all point to the ineffability of the Ultimate or Ultimate Truth—that is, to the sobering fact that, as Aquinas put it, "the divine substance surpasses every form that our intellect reaches."[11] So, to Lao Tzu's admonition that "the Tao that can be named is not the eternal Tao," Aquinas echoes, "He knows God best who acknowledges that whatever he thinks or says falls short of what God really is."[12]

If all religions recognize the *ineffability* of God or Truth, they all implicitly but necessarily recognize the *non-absoluteness* of all their own claims and beliefs. In this sense, all religions can accept the pluralists' invitation to come to the table of dialogue without claiming to have the full, final, or definite hold on revelation or truth. Or to phrase this invitation in more inviting terms, there is the suggestion of John B. Cobb, Jr. (who does not call himself a pluralist) that there is "one relatively objective norm" that all religions can affirm—namely, the forthright and "humble" admission that they always have *more to learn*.[13] Following Cobb, even if a particular religion (I think of my own Catholic tradition) feels it cannot abandon its centuries-long belief that it has been given God's full and final revelation, it can still admit that it has more to learn about what this fullness really contains. All Catholics, even the pope, is still "on the way" to understanding the "finality" or "absoluteness" of their God-given revelation. Such recognitions indirectly but effectively relativize a religion's absolute claims.

---

[9] Huston Smith, *The World's Religions* (HarperSanFrancisco, 1991), 232.

[10] From a July 2002 exchange, partially represented in Hick's essay in this volume. For references and further citations, see John Hick, *An Interpretation of Religion* (New Haven, CT: Yale Univ. Press, 1989), 236–40. Critics of Hick would add that where he is clear about what we do not know of Ultimate Reality, he might be clearer on what we *do* or *can* know.

[11] Aquinas, *Summa contra Gentiles*, I:14:3.

[12] Lao Tzu, *Tao Te Ching*, 1; Aquinas, *De Causis*, 6.

[13] John B. Cobb, Jr., "Beyond Pluralism," in D'Costa, *Christian Uniqueness Reconsidered*, 86–87.

So we draw a conclusion: if all religions recognize the absolute mystery of what they have discovered or had revealed to them, no religion can claim to have absolute truth. This plank of the pluralist model, therefore, does not seem to be an imposition. Rather, it grows out of a respect for the humanity everyone has in common with everyone else and the limits of finite human existence.

THE VOICE OF RELIGIOUS PHILOSOPHERS: DIFFERENT AIMS

If pluralists can be commended for reminding all believers that no religion can have the final or full word, they perhaps need to be chided for not recognizing how different these words can be. As already indicated above, this is presently the most oft-repeated and the sharpest critique of the pluralist model. It comes especially from philosophers of religion who say that the differences among the religions are profound and persistent—yes, even *incommensurable*. We cannot use the concepts or language of one religion to measure or understand the concepts or language of another.

To make a sharp criticism even sharper: if no religious claim can be absolute, differences between the contents of the claims may be absolute. This possibility or probability, as we heard from William Placher earlier, doesn't seem to register on the consciousness of pluralists.

Still, it has registered on some pluralists. In an earlier collection of Christian pluralist voices, *The Myth of Christian Uniqueness*, Raimon Panikkar warned his fellow pluralists of making a "universal system" out of the pluralist model, a system that would drown real differences in a sea of shared validity. In Panikkar's understanding, "pluralism . . . accepts the irreconcilable aspects of religion . . . [and] defends the pluralism of truth because reality itself is pluralistic."[14] John Cobb pushes Panikkar's admonitions even further when he makes a suggestion that would seem to be a square peg in the round hole of the pluralist model: the starkness of religious differences implies that the Ultimate is not one but many![15] But the most elaborate case that the differences among the religions are more radical than any pluralist can imagine or accept is put forth by S. Mark Heim. Drawing on both philosophy and trinitarian theology, he argues that we can most accurately and honestly deal with the plurality of religions by admitting that fundamentally most religions are *going in different directions*! The "ultimate aims" of the religions, he suggests, are not the same. They are not seeking salvation but *salvations*. That's why the religions are incommensurable, why one can't be judged on the basis of the other. The religions are not only *conceptually* and

---

[14] Raimon Panikkar, "The Jordan, the Tiber, and the Ganges," in D'Costa, *The Myth of Christian Uniqueness*, 109–10.

[15] John B. Cobb, Jr., *Transforming Christianity and the World: A Way beyond Absolutism and Relativism,* ed. Paul F. Knitter (Maryknoll, NY: Orbis Books, 1999), 113–27.

also *metaphysically* incommensurable. They have different goals. Therefore, if I, the Christian, am going to Boston, I can't give you, the Buddhist, any advice on how to get to San Francisco![16] So the popular image of many religions, each following its path to the same mountaintop, has to be reworked; each religion is heading up a different mountain!

Though talk of multiple ultimate ends and multiple Ultimates may ruffle the sensitivities of most pluralists, the concerns of such talk must be taken seriously by anyone working within the pluralist model. I confess that in my eagerness to bring my fellow Christians to recognize the validity of other religions, in my efforts to find common ground for a more authentic dialogue of religions, and in my way of speaking of the Ultimate Reality that connects the different religious families, I did not make sufficient room for the real, deep, distinctive, perhaps irreducible differences among the religions. We pluralists have not sufficiently listened to the question critics ask of us: Whose common ground, or whose Ultimate Reality are you talking about? Perhaps, as well, we have not been sufficiently sensitive to the fears of ordinary believers that in the pluralist approach their distinctive identities will be swept under the rug of commonalities.

But what we have not done in the past, we can do now. And that's the key point I want to make in this section of my essay. There is no intrinsic contradiction between the pluralist model and real diversity. One can speak, as pluralists do, of the validity of many religions, and at the same time affirm the distinctiveness of each of them. One can indicate, or search for, what the religions have in common without ignoring or hiding differences. At least that is what I believe pluralists can and should do—affirm the possibility of unity without jeopardizing the reality of diversity.

To go a step further, I believe that pluralists can even recognize with Heim that religions are pursuing goals that are genuinely and intractably different from each other. The bottom line of Heim's case is that, in the final analysis, the religions of the world are more different than they are similar. As I think will become clearer in the next section of this essay, such an assertion is not inherently at odds with what the pluralists are saying. More colloquially, people traveling to San Francisco and people heading to Boston can have something to say to each other. If differences are the prime matter of dialogue, then the deeper and more stubborn the differences, the more exciting and challenging will be the dialogue. If religious differences won't go away, we'll always have something to talk about. The issue then becomes, How should we manage our differences? How can we make genuine connections in the midst of real differences. How can we measure incommensurables?

Even Cobb's articulate proposal for multiple Ultimates need not put pluralists on the defensive. If Panikkar is right that "reality itself is pluralistic" and that the Ultimate Reality or Truth includes difference and diversity, then we have to find ways of speaking about the "manyness" contained in the Ultimate. Maybe "many" Ultimates is one way of so speaking, paradoxical

---

[16] See Heim, *The Depth of Riches*, esp. 209–39.

as it is and has to be. We see this struggle to speak of "one" and "many" at the same time in many of the religious traditions.[17] Again, in recognizing the manyness of the Ultimate—or many Ultimates—we face the challenge of how these Ultimates can still connect with, speak to, or, as Christians say about the three Persons in the one God, how they can "dance with" one another.[18] Such questions are addressed by the last two voices we will be hearing from.

THE VOICE OF RELIGIOUS FRIENDS: SHARED AIMS

In this section I want to draw on experiences (my own and those of others) that can help us grasp how people from differing religious traditions can and do interact—how they can understand one another despite their differences. You might say that these experiences are *hermeneutically instructive* in the encounter of religions. I'm talking about the experience of people who have become friends across their religious boundaries. Interreligious friendships can tell us much about the nature of religion.

Friendships incorporate a beautiful, paradoxical blending of differences and commonalities. Friends recognize and affirm how genuinely different they are, but they also feel the possibility of connecting with each other despite these differences. They are not out to convert one another, but at the same time they feel the need to explain their deepest religious convictions in a way that will enable the friend not only to understand but to affirm the beauty or the value of such a belief. Friends feel the need, and in their relationship find the means, to develop a language that will translate, as it were, between the two very different religious language games that each lives in. Among friends, different ultimate aims, maybe even different Ultimates, can connect, communicate, and clarify one another.

How this happens is difficult to describe clearly. Let me give a concrete, personal example drawn from my conversations with a Buddhist friend in Cincinnati, Michael. I recognize his reluctance to speak about any kind of an Ultimate Being or Reality, and I certainly don't want to turn him into a theist. But neither is it sufficient for me to lay things out intellectually so that he can grasp how belief in God makes sense within my Christian world view. I want him to see how it is good for me to have such a belief, to believe in God—and how it is also good for the world. *I want him to be glad that I'm a theist, though he remains a non-theist.* To do this, we have to search for

---

[17] Hinduism holds to thirty-three million Gods all manifesting the one Brahman, Christianity insists that God is both one and three, Islam insists that the one Allah must have ninety-nine names.

[18] The Greek word used by the fathers of the church is *perichoresis*.

new language, new ways of speaking that will respect and not denigrate our differences and at the same time will somehow bridge them.

What I think I'm describing is how interreligious friendships can both affirm and then bridge the gulf of incommensurability. Michael and I remain very different in our fundamental philosophical and religious world views, but we can talk to each other and connect those differing views of the world and ultimacy. Friends can understand each other even when they speak two different religious languages. And as this happens, their languages grow, are enriched with new vocabulary, new poetry. Here is where such conversations not only communicate, but also clarify, even transform. In trying to communicate to Michael why it is good for me and for the world that I believe in God, I've had to use new words, new combinations of words, new images. And in so doing, not only does he understand me more clearly, I understand myself—and my tradition—more appropriately and engagingly.

Friends from different religious histories and experiences discover in their conversations that no matter how different they truly are, they can talk to each other. They can communicate. And if there is anything to the old Latin dictum *Ab esse ad posse valet illatio* (from reality we can infer possibility), then perhaps we can conclude from what friends *do* that there is something that makes it *possible* for them to communicate with each other. And this "something" exists between them or among them. Their particular differences are somehow contained within, or connected by, this larger, transcendent-immanent reality. Maybe the image of Ultimate Reality is an appropriate "finger" to use to point to the "moon" of a Universal Mystery that enables connection and communication.

So to the insistence of scholars like Heim and Cobb that religions are pursuing different ultimate ends, interreligious friends—and advocates of the pluralist model—might add: "Yes, but these ends are not independently ultimate; they are, rather, interrelatedly ultimate. That means that they are really and irrevocably different, but at the same time they are able to and need to connect with one another." And this implies that there is something within and beyond them that functions as the ground or matrix of their connection. We may not want to call this "something universal" the common *essence* of religions, or even their *common ground*; we may be wary of speaking of an Ultimate Reality. But at the same time, interreligious friends know that there is something common, something universal, something more than just our differences.

The pluralist model wants to recognize this "something" between and within the religions. But so do the religions themselves! This is what we heard above in the section on the voices of religious believers and teachers. All religions claim to have experienced or discovered something that is universal—which means something that is potentially meaningful for others, able to connect with them, something that cannot be contained fully in any one language or culture. It is this "something," this mystery for which we will never find the "right" name or symbol that, according to Levinas, gives the "face of the other" its power and its attraction over us.[19] In the otherness of my religious friend I find differences that I will never be able to include neatly in my limited categories, but at the same time I can talk with, learn from, and respond to this stark otherness. In the face of the religious other I see or sense the face of the Other that shines within and beyond us all.

Pluralists affirm this. And I trust that persons in all the religious communities of our world can affirm it as well.

THE VOICE OF RELIGIOUS ACTIVISTS:
COMMON CONCERNS

Over the past few decades I detect something else going on in the world of religions and of interreligious relations, something that urges and enables religious people to realize that as different and as unique as they truly are, they must set aside their claims to have the only or the best way, and cooperate and communicate between their differences. The operative word in that last sentence is *cooperate*. Interreligious friends are becoming interreligious activists. Perhaps better, the shared need to act is becoming the occasion to form or deepen friendships. This has been exemplified in recent meetings of the Parliament of World Religions. There, countless men and women from religious communities seek to respond to the challenges facing the earth and all its inhabitants. They sense that their *religious* response, if it is to be meaningful and effective, must be *interreligious*. No matter how different they are, religious must "get their act together" in order to act together.

To expand on Levinas's imagery, the "face of the other" that today challenges and appeals to men and women of all religious traditions is not just the face of the religious or cultural other; it is also, perhaps even primarily, the face of the *suffering* other. A growing number of people in *all* religious communities (which does not mean *all* people in *all* communities) find themselves called to do something about the immense amount of unnecessary suffering that afflicts so many human and other sentient beings. They feel this call precisely because they are religious. Call it compassion, call it charity, call it interconnectedness, in a variety of ways, religion sensitizes people to the suffering of others. This call, I believe, is today being heard not within the religions individually but among them collectively.

Although the proposed solutions for alleviating this suffering often differ vastly, still, the call to respond to earth's suffering ones is the same. And that means that the different solutions must be shared and learned from. The suffering others of this world, therefore, can be seen as mediators among the various religious communities, calling them together to work and talk with each other for the relief of suffering and the promotion of peace.

---

[19] For an insightful review of Levinas's thought and its implications for Christian theology of religions, see Mervyn Fredrick Bendle, "The Postmetaphysics of Religious Difference," *Pacifica* 11 (1998), 1–26.

So if the voices of interreligious friends tell us that the religious families must talk about and learn from their differences, the voices of interreligious activists suggest where they can start their conversations, or what the focus of their discussion of differences might be. In holding up suffering as a common cause for interreligious encounters, activists are suggesting that our interreligious dialogue and search for the true and the good can best begin in the ethical realm. This is not the place to make a philosophical case that we best know the truth by doing the truth, and that therefore we can share the truth by trying to do it together.[20] Rather, I appeal to what has been happening over the last two or three decades. People from a wide variety of religious traditions are coming together to act and talk with other religious people in order to do something about hunger, poverty, violence, and sickness on our planet. Whatever the complexities and dangers in present-day efforts to come to some kind of an interreligious global ethics, the effort to alleviate suffering brings people together and makes clearer than ever the need for religious people to talk and act together in order to meet the ethical challenges that all of humanity faces.[21]

I need to end this section with a more specific and more relevant suggestion: Since the events both on and after 9/11—both the attack on the United States and the response of the American government—there is a particular kind of human suffering that calls all religions together for joint analysis and response. I refer to the suffering caused by religiously motivated violence. The religious traditions of humankind must give an example of united protest based on common guidelines rooted in shared religious values that will provide a counter force to the way religion is being used by *all* parties in these conflicts. Rabbi Jonathan Sacks offers an eloquent and urgent call:

Religious believers cannot stand aside when people are murdered in the name of God or a sacred cause. When religion is invoked as a justification for conflict, religious voices must be raised in protest. We must withhold the robe of sanctity when it is sought as a cloak for violence and bloodshed. If faith is enlisted in the cause of war, there must be an equal and opposite counter-voice in the name of peace. If religion is not part of the solution, it will certainly be part of the problem.

Religion can be source of discord. It can also be a form of conflict resolution. We are familiar with the former; the second is far too little tried. Yet it is here, if anywhere, that hope must lie if we are to create a

---

[20] For a clear and challenging summary of how such a case can be made, see Lisa Sowle Cahill, "Toward a Global Ethics," *Theological Studies* 63 (2002), 324–44; see also Knitter, *One Earth Many Religions,* esp. chaps. 4–7.

[21] As Cahill puts it: "Global ethics does not stand or fall with a universal set of specific moral prescriptions which few today would defend, but with the idea that there are after all some moral nonnegotiables and some clearly identifiable injustices to which all cultures and religions should be responsive for humanistic reasons" (Cahill, "Toward a Global Ethics," 328).

human solidarity strong enough to bear the strains that lie ahead. The great faiths must now become an active force for peace and for the justice and compassion on which peace ultimately depends.[22]

What I am calling the voices of religious activists offer, I believe, the clearest indication that the pluralist model, far from being an imposition, is actually being implemented by a growing number of followers from all the religions. In this kind of dialogue and cooperation of religions, in which the primary incentive and goal is to relieve suffering and promote peace, it is assumed by all that all the participants can make valid, important contributions and that no single tradition religion has a monopoly on intelligent insights into how suffering can be alleviated and peace established.

I hope that the different voices I have tried to bring into relief help both critics and proponents of the pluralist model to clarify and perhaps to correct their understanding of what the pluralist model is and why it can be endorsed and developed by believers and seekers from multiple traditions.

---

[22] Jonathan Sacks, *The Dignity of Difference: How to Avoid the Clash of Civilizations* (New York: Continuum, 2002), 9, 4–5.

PART II

Hindu and Sikh Perspectives

4

Mahatma Gandhi

A Prophet of Pluralism

K. L. SESHAGIRI RAO

For most, if not all, of us who are exploring what is called a pluralist model in order to make sense of the incorrigible reality of religious diversity, our motivations are not simply, or even primarily, academic. Yes, in contemplating the splendid, often contrasting, variety of religious beliefs and practices, we find ourselves overwhelmed by swarms of intellectual, philosophical, and theological questions. Religious diversity both delights and bewilders. But it also sometimes frightens. And here, the reality of the many different religions becomes not just an intellectual but a moral issue. Today, with particular urgency, we are realizing that the religions, in their splendid diversity, must not only *exist alongside one another,* but they must *live together with one another.*

When they don't, we have problems. When religious people are not able to recognize the value of other religious people, when they cannot affirm the possibilities of not only living next door to each other but cooperating for the benefit of each other, then the immense potential within religion for good becomes a directly proportional potential for evil. Swami Nikhilananda's observation is as harrowing as it is accurate: "On the one hand, they [religions] have contributed greatly toward peace and progress, building hospitals and charitable institutions, promoting art and literature, and conferring many other blessings on humanity; on the other hand, in the name of religion, people have waged wars, persecuted their fellow beings, and destroyed monuments of human culture."[1]

To avoid religious conflicts, to prevent the use of religion for violent ends, to tap the peace potential of religion—these are some of the principal

---

[1] Nikhilananda Swami, *Hinduism: Its Meaning for the Liberation of the Spirit* (New York: Harper, 1983), 185.

motivations for trying to develop what we are calling a pluralist model for understanding and living in a world of many religions. The traditional exclusivist perspectives, in which one religion is held up to be singular or superior to all others, seem to us to be inadequate, if not downright dangerous. Attitudes toward other religious beliefs that regard them as intrinsically erroneous, or inadequate, or in need of fulfillment in one's own religion do not encourage—perhaps they do not permit—differing religious communities to live side by side in friendly cooperation.

So if religions are going to be part of the solution, rather than part of the problem, in humanity's efforts to avoid a "clash of civilizations" and bring about a "community of civilizations," religious believers have to learn to regard each other as neighbors, not competitors. They have to learn to affirm each other, not replace each other. They have to find in their own history and tradition the resources and guidelines for a more authentically pluralistic and dialogical understanding of religious differences.

Mahatma Gandhi found himself facing the very same challenge. In his efforts to nonviolently dispatch the colonialists, he also had to fashion a new nation out of India's diversity of cultures and religions. He too realized that religion can be as much a part of the problem as of the solution. Drawing on his Hindu culture and beliefs, on the diversity that India has always not only tolerated but lived from, and on his own personal spirituality and wisdom, Gandhi proposed an understanding of and challenge for religious diversity that can direct and inspire us today. That is the claim of this essay. Gandhi was, and remains, a prophet of pluralism.

AN INDIAN/HINDU PROPHET

Gandhi lived and died vindicating moral and spiritual values against the forces of materialism, parochialism, and violence. He believed that if human beings are to grow in peace and understanding, they must relate to other human beings with fearlessness and friendliness, irrespective of religious or national affiliations. As he pointed out, dialogue is essential for progress. The different communities and their leaders need not only to communicate and cooperate to make the world a better place, but also to fashion an open environment in which to pursue truth. Growth in spiritual life, he held, will develop in people the capacity for humanity, charity, and tolerance and enable them to build a new civilization based on justice and moral regeneration.

Gandhi was in the thick of religious plurality and dialogue from the early years of his life. Among his father's friends were a good many Muslims, Parsis (Zoroastrians), and Jains, as well as Hindus; they gathered frequently in his house for religious discussions. The young Gandhi eagerly listened to their conversations. This experience impressed on his mind the problem of religious diversity and the need to find a way of understanding that diversity that would foster unity rather than conflict among the followers of different faith communities.

This religious quest was further stimulated by his Christian friends in England and South Africa. In London he spent a large part of his time in religious discussions. The literature of the Theosophists introduced him to the movement for the unity of religions. Sir Edwin Arnold's English version of the *Bhagavad Gita* stirred him so deeply that for the rest of his life it became his constant guide. He also read *The Light of Asia* and *The Sayings of Zarathustra* with great interest. He was moved by the teachings of the New Testament, especially the Sermon on the Mount. The verse "But I say to you, Do not resist an evildoer. But if anyone strikes you on the right cheek, turn the other also" (Mt 5:39) went straight to his heart. The personality of Jesus held a fascination for him all his life.

Gandhi also read Carlyle's *Heroes and Hero-Worship* and learned from it of Muhammad's "greatness, bravery, and austere living." Washington Irving's *Life of Mahomet and His Successors* raised the prophet in his estimation. The prophet's austere life and profound teachings influenced him a great deal. C. F. Andrews observes:

> Gandhi's profound admiration for the character of Prophet Muhammad as a man of faith and action, and also for his son-in-law Ali, as a man of tender love and suffering, deeply affected him. He was impressed to a remarkable degree by the nobility of the early caliphate and the fervent faith of the first followers of the prophet. The bare simplicity with which they lived, their chivalrous devotion to the poor, their intense belief in God's overruling majesty, all these things had a great effect on him.[2]

DIALOGUE WITH OTHER RELIGIONS

The Mahatma pursued religious dialogue on two levels: theoretical and practical. At the theoretical level his objective was sympathetic understanding of the living world religions. Ignorance about the faiths of other people, he realized, gives rise to prejudices and misrepresentations resulting in unwillingness to accept the integrity of the followers of other traditions. People quarrel about religion only when they lose sight of the human dimension of all religions. It is lack of sensitive understanding of others' faith that has often led the practitioners of religions to mutual recrimination and bloodshed.

Religious believers generally have insufficient opportunities for and interest in knowing about the values and insights of other believers; indeed, there

---

[2] C. F. Andrews, *Mahatma Gandhi's Ideas* (London: George Allen and Unwin, 1931), 62.

is a pervasive ignorance of the creative principles of all faiths, including one's own. Whatever the reason for such a state of affairs in the past, Gandhi felt that it could not be allowed to continue. Modern men and women need to expand their religious consciousness by understanding in depth the spiritual truths revealed in religions other than their own. If anything like a pluralist model for the interaction of religions was to be possible, it had to be based, according to Gandhi, on accurate knowledge that each religion has of the other.

Gandhi therefore believed that education without the study of the religions is incomplete. Religious study is not only a legitimate intellectual pursuit but a vital aspect of human culture and civilization. It relates to the wellsprings of individual and social life and deals with the central questions of human life and destiny. One neglects the study of religions at the risk of failing to understand humanity and history. Reminiscing about his early life, Gandhi expressed much regret at the lack of facilities to study religion at his school. He discussed this predicament in his autobiography: "I am Hindu by faith, and yet I do not know much about Hinduism, and I know much less of other religions. In fact, I do not know what is and what should be my belief. I intend to make a careful study of my own religion, and as far as I can, of other religions as well."[3] This he did later on, devoting a good measure of his time to the study of comparative religion, which exercised a profound influence on his life. He became convinced that the study of the different religions would contribute to a healthy religious pluralism.

Gandhi would not make qualitative or evaluative comparisons between religions. Indeed, he saw no use in such an endeavor. To him the main point was not how palatable or unpalatable one religion was to the followers of another religion but the fact of its profound influence on its own followers. "As we wish the followers of other religions to appreciate us, so ought we to seek with all our hearts to appreciate them. Surely, this is the Golden Rule."[4] Gandhi was humble and eager to learn from other traditions and their followers. He believed that there was good in all traditions and went straight to their best, purest, and noblest elements with a view to benefiting from them in his own life.

His study of the religions revealed that every religious tradition had its periods of growth and decline, and that no religion, insofar as it was historical, was perfect. He saw that each religious tradition has needed purging of old abuses at one time or another and that each religion has had its band of reformers and saints. He considered it misguided, therefore, for any tradition to fasten on itself or on others the crudities of a bygone age. Recognizing that each great religion contained numerous elements, tendencies, and movements, he refused to characterize a religion on the basis of a single sect or movement.

---

[3] M. K. Gandhi, *Autobiography* (Boston: Beacon Press, 1983), 120.

[4] Quoted in K. L. Seshagiri Rao, *Mahatma Gandhi and C. F. Andrews* (Patiala: Punjabi University Press, 1978), 43.

Gandhi's approach was to encourage the purification of religions rather than to seek their replacement. He believed that a knowledge of other religions makes Hindus better Hindus, Muslims better Muslims, Christians better Christians, and all humans better members of the world community. Interreligious dialogue, he saw, offers help in refining and developing neglected dimensions of each religious tradition. The insights of different religions belong to all peoples. The truths revealed to the Christians should become precious to the followers of other faiths, and vice versa. Religious dialogue also makes people of different backgrounds sensitive to one another. No religion should, therefore, bar its followers from studying other religions or supplementing their own spiritual knowledge and discipline. In all this he was fashioning the foundation stones for what today we are calling the pluralist model of religious diversity.

But Gandhi also saw limits to the embrace of other religions. Ready as he was in acknowledging his deep debt to other faiths, he also insisted that while we should throw open our windows for fresh breezes from different directions, we should refuse to be swept off our feet. He developed a capacity for assimilating insights of other traditions and thus enriching his own. In a revealing conversation Gandhi told Mrs. Henry Polak in South Africa: "I did once seriously think of embracing the Christian faith. The gentle figure of Christ, so patient, so kind, so loving, so full of forgiveness that he taught his followers not to retaliate when abused or struck, but to turn the other cheek—I thought it was a beautiful example of a perfect man." "But you did not embrace Christianity, did you?" she asked. "No," replied Gandhi thoughtfully. "I studied your scriptures for some time and thought earnestly about them . . . but eventually I came to the conclusion that there was no need for me to join your creed to be a believer in the beauty of the teaching of Jesus or try to follow his example." And then from the depth of his Hindu sensitivities, he added: "If a man reaches the heart of his own religion, he has reached the heart of others too. There is only one God, but there are many paths to Him."[5]

PRACTICAL DIALOGUE

Religious dialogue, for Gandhi, was not just a theoretical or academic matter; it had an existential, practical dimension. He put more emphasis on the practical aspects of religion and inward life. He said, "Divine knowledge is not borrowed from books; it has to be realized in oneself." His teaching is put very simply, "My life is my message."[6] Because he was not interested in dogmas, he was able to cooperate with the adherents of other religions in

---

[5] Quoted in Krishna Kripalani, *Gandhi: A Life* (Calcutta: Calcutta Press, 1978), 25.

[6] Quoted in Homer Jack, ed., *World Religions and World Peace* (Boston: Beacon Press, 1969), 125.

realizing the higher ideals of life. As a result, members of different races and faiths worked and struggled together in his movements for freedom and justice in behalf of oppressed groups in South Africa and in India. The Indian National Congress, which spearheaded the nonviolent freedom struggle under the leadership of Gandhi, included Parsis (Zoroastrians), Hindus, Muslims, Christians, Buddhists, and followers of other religions. He did not think that any theological consensus was a prerequisite for working together for human justice and freedom. Participants in his movement were reminded, however, that all religions emphasized each person's responsibility for other human beings and were urged to follow the highest vision of their respective faiths.

Gandhi's ashrams both in South Africa and in India were outstanding examples of the kind of harmonious cooperation that the pluralist model seeks to facilitate. They were the "moral laboratories" where his experiments with truth and nonviolence were conducted in the living of daily life; there were no dividing lines of class, nationality, or creed. The inmates of his ashrams belonged to different religions and races and lived a life of voluntary poverty, simplicity, purity, and service. In the community life of the ashrams Gandhi gave first place to the culture of the heart and training of the spirit. "To develop the spirit is to develop character and to enable one to work towards a knowledge of God and self-realization," he said.[7]

Gandhi helped and encouraged the inmates of his ashrams to keep their respective religious observances. For example, he took care to see that the Muslim young people in the ashram community offered their *namez* (prayer) and observed their Ramadan fast. He also encouraged the Hindu members to observe *pradosha* (fast until evening), and the Christians their Lent. The result of the practices was that all the inmates became convinced of the value of fasting and self-denial. These practices led to fidelity in the observance of the different religious customs and festivals and demonstrated the unity of the ashram community despite the members' differences in beliefs and practices. When the South African courts, practicing religious discrimination, refused to recognize marriages performed according to non-Christian rites, the entire ashram community—Hindus, Christians, Parsis, and others—took it as a serious affront to the sanctity of Indian married life and struggled nonviolently, under Gandhi's leadership, until the South African government repealed the discriminatory religious treatment.

Offering an example of just how inclusive his model for religious pluralism should be, Gandhi invited an "untouchable" family to his ashram in Ahmedabad. This stirred up a mix of ambivalence and even opposition among his followers. Many of them became disgruntled; they did not want to live with the untouchables, and some left. Even his wife objected at first. Monetary support to the ashram from the public stopped. But Gandhi would not

---

[7] Quoted in Waren Lewis, ed., *Towards a Global Congress of World Religions* (New York: Rose of Sharon Press, 1979), 59.

give in; it was a matter of religious principle with him. He was prepared to move into the untouchable quarters of the city and, like an untouchable, live by manual labor. An unknown person came up with help, and in a short period the opposition died down; even the orthodox changed their minds. Further, Gandhi adopted the daughter of an untouchable family, Lakshmi, as his own daughter.

Gandhi was and remained a religious Hindu, and a *sanatani* or orthodox Hindu at that. He was relentless, however, in his criticism of the excrescences that had accumulated in Hinduism through the ages. He exposed the evils in the Hindu social and religious structure and campaigned publicly for their removal. Through his efforts for the transformation of Hindu society and for the setting of new moral standards, he changed the lives of millions of people. He worked for the redemption of the outcasts, the emancipation of women, basic education, cottage industries, prohibition, and like causes. Religion and interreligious dialogue, for Gandhi, were never detached from social and political realities.

We might list the intended, and achieved, results of interreligious dialogue for Gandhi as follows: (1) mutual learning, (2) sensitive awareness of other religions, (3) deepening of this awareness into respect, (4) a progressive reinterpretation of one's own life and traditions, and (5) mutual cooperation for the common objectives of truth and justice.

TRUTH: THE CONTENT AND GOAL OF RELIGION AND DIALOGUE

The most remarkable aspect of Gandhi's life and work was his dedication to the search for truth. "Truth became my sole objective," he said. "It began to grow in magnitude every day and my definition of it has been ever widening."[8] While he started with the conviction that God is truth, later he declared that truth is God. This meant that, for him, truth included more than mere truthfulness; it signified eternal being. It embraced what is true in knowledge, what is right in conduct, and what is just and fair in human relations. Therefore, even when Gandhi appeared to be engaged in struggles that were not explicitly religious in character or in movements connected with social reform and justice, his dominant motive was still religious:

> Man's ultimate aim is the realization of God, and all his activities, social, and religious, have to be guided by the ultimate aim of the vision of God. The immediate service of all human beings becomes a necessary part of the endeavor, simply because the only way to find God is to see Him in His creation and be one with it. This can be done only by service to all. I am part and parcel of the whole and I cannot find Him apart from the rest of humanity. . . . If I could persuade myself that I

---

[8] Gandhi, *Autobiography,* 34.

could find Him in a Himalayan cave, I would proceed there immediately; but I know that I cannot find Him apart from humanity.[9]

In seeking truth within humanity Gandhi did not stop at intellectual or verbal agreements; he also sought to establish truth in terms of justice and fair play for all. He stressed, therefore, that the only means of attaining truth in life is *ahimsa*, nonviolence, which is nothing less than the "ability to love the meanest of creation as oneself."[10] It is in this unique way that Gandhi brought home to everyone the spirit and practical content of religion and of interreligious dialogue, not in heavy theological language, but in the language of daily life and truthful living. Here he foresaw the ultimate aim of the pluralist model: religious diversity can become interreligious conversation and cooperation.

Indeed, Gandhi's purpose in calling for religious dialogue was not the elimination of religious differences but an appreciation of one another's faith and practice that would lead to cooperation in the moral and social spheres. He sought to understand both the similarities and the differences. He was impressed by the fact that moral and spiritual values are stressed by all religions. The Golden Rule in one form or another and the injunction to transcend the ego are present in all of them. All preach that peoples' relations to one another are more important than their relations to material things. All religions teach that service to the poor, the sick, the helpless, and the oppressed is service to God, or a necessary expression of Enlightenment. For Gandhi, therefore, in the eternal struggle between good and evil, or between ignorance and authenticity, all religions are called upon to take sides with the good and raise humanity to a higher moral level. In this sense the success of any religion is the success of all religions.

Gandhi was aware, on the other hand, of the differences among the great religions arising from historical and cultural backgrounds. The different traditions do not all have the same beliefs and doctrines; they do not prescribe the same rituals or prayers or subscribe to the same kind of myths. He believed that any attempt to root out these differences not only is bound to fail but is a form of sacrilege. Since differences are important, and in some cases unbridgeable, he discouraged uncritical syncretism. Actually, he welcomed the enrichment that comes with religious diversity. He wanted people from all religions to maintain their special symbols of identity. The need was not for a new religion but for respectful dialogue among the adherents of different religions. Here he previewed the emphasis of the pluralist model that a greater unity among the religions does not exclude—indeed, it presupposes—the abiding diversity of religions.

So Gandhi did not look upon eclecticism with favor. He did not approve of the abdication of one's own religion and its heritage. On the contrary, he

---

[9] *Harijan*, August 29, 1936.

[10] K. L. Seshagiri Rao, *Mahatma Gandhi and Comparative Religion* (Delhi: Motilal Banarasidas, 1990), viii.

advocated firm adherence to one's own tradition. Eclectics do not go deeply into any religious tradition; their approach is superficial and fails to grasp the distinctive message of each tradition. According to Gandhi, to call a person eclectic was to say that he or she had no firm, focused faith. So Gandhi advocated religious harmony, not a blending of all religions into a uniformity of faith and practice.

On the other hand, he realized that to be too firm and focused on one's own religion can easily lead to sectarian trends and loyalties—to what in India is called communalism. He cautioned that it was dangerous to humankind as a whole today to overemphasize the parochial. He urged all people to look at things from a larger context and from a human perspective. While individual identity is precious, it is always part of a larger picture. The parts are necessary to make the whole, but the whole is somehow larger than all the parts put together. Here, too, Gandhi was pointing to essential concerns and values in the pluralist model for religious diversity. Each religion must be what it is, but it can be what it is—and grow into what it can be—only in relationship with other religions.

HIS LASTING IMPORTANCE

In India the problem of interreligious relations has engaged the attention of thinking persons for over three thousand years. In his own day Gandhi was confronted with strained relations between Hindus and Muslims. Hatred and suspicion had poisoned the atmosphere. Bloody religious riots were frequent. The growing tension between the two communities distressed Gandhi a great deal. He deplored these riots and believed that both Hindus and Muslims could and should live and work together for the common good. He pleaded and prayed and fasted for religious harmony. In fact, during the last decades of his life his major preoccupation was harmony between Hindus and Muslims.

Gandhi was a Hindu who advocated the rights of the Muslims. He pleaded with the Hindu majority to treat the minority with justice and fairness. He went from place to place, meeting Hindus and Muslims and proclaiming the fatherhood of God and the brotherhood/sisterhood of all peoples. He said to the people: "God is one. Allah and Rama are his names." In the midst of pervasive darkness, Gandhi served as a beacon of light. He sought to heal the wounds that people, in their religious frenzy, were inflicting upon themselves. He worked miracles. Lord Mountbatten, the last viceroy of India, described the situation in this way: "While the 55,000-man boundary force in the Punjab was swamped by riots, the one-man boundary force brought peace to Bengal."[11] A fanatic Hindu, however, believing that Gandhi was disloyal to Hinduism, assassinated him. Even in his death he achieved something remarkable; his martyrdom shamed his people out of the hysteria of hatred and

---

[11] Kripalani, *Gandhi*, 185.

fratricide and helped the country consolidate its constructive and democratic forces.

Gandhi wanted harmony and friendship to be established not merely between the Hindus and Muslims of India, but among the adherents of all the great religions of the world. "Hindu-Muslim unity means not only unity between Hindus and Muslims but between all those who believe India to be their home no matter to what faith they belong."[12] The problem of the mutual relationship of religions is worldwide today. What is going on in Ireland, the Middle East, Cyprus, the Indian subcontinent, and elsewhere in the name of religion is most distressing and depressing. The exaltation of terrorism in the name of religion is tragic. In the words of Gandhi, "To revile another's religion, to make reckless statements, utter untruth, to break the heads of innocent men, to desecrate temples or mosques is a denial of God."[13]

Gandhi's interreligious dialogue authentically represents the Indian attitude of respect for all religions. The idea that "truth is one: sages call it by different names" has been alive in Hinduism since the time of the Rgveda. Because of his great concern for truth, Gandhi was inwardly receptive to the currents of truth coming from other religions. To ignore any of them meant to ignore God's infinite richness and to impoverish humanity spiritually. Gandhi wanted all religions to revive their pristine past and develop their traditions. "I ask no Hindu or Mussalman to surrender an iota of his religious principle. Only let him be sure that it is religion. But I do ask of every Hindu and Mussalman not to fight for an earthly gain."[14]

Although Gandhi insisted that each religion must hold firm to its principles and distinctive differences, he was clear that no religion can hold up these principles and differences as superior to all others. In questioning absolute truth-claims, he resonates with a core content of the pluralist model. Here religious believers, or especially religious leaders, can learn from the scientists. The sciences, which study the natural world, do not claim "any monopoly of wisdom for their own particular branch of study nor quarrel about the superiority of one science over the others."[15] In a similar way, Gandhi held that each religion must bring its individual contribution to humanity's understanding of the spiritual world and not quarrel about the superiority of one religion over another, for God's love embraces the whole world. He believed that all the world religions are God-given and that they serve the people to whom they are revealed. They are allies engaged in the common cause of the moral and spiritual uplift of humanity. In the context of the emerging world community, all the great religions are useful, necessary, and complementary to one another as revealing different facets of the one truth.

---

[12] *Young India,* April 16, 1931.

[13] Andrews, *Mahatma Gandhi's Ideas,* 208.

[14] Ibid., 308.

[15] R. B. Lal, *The Gita in the Light of Modern Science* (Bombay: Somaiya Publications, 1971), 9.

The problems that threaten the world community are not merely political or economic; they arise as well from certain basic religious and spiritual attitudes. If the faith and integrity of other persons are not respected, genuine communication and consequent world community will be at best a dream. Arnold Toynbee, after surveying the history of the entire human race, has made the following significant observation:

> At this supremely dangerous moment in human history, the only way of salvation for mankind is the Indian way—Emperor Ashoka's and Mahatma Gandhi's principle of nonviolence and Shri Ramakrishna's testimony to the harmony of all religions. Here we have an attitude and spirit that can make it possible for the human race to grow into a single family—and, in the Atomic Age, this is the only alternative to destroying ourselves.[16]

---

[16] See *Bhavan's Journal* (Bombay) 28, no. 2 (1982): 27.

5

Can There Be More Than One Kind of Pluralism?

ARVIND SHARMA

The standard pluralist model in the study of religion and in the philosophy of religion is easily summarized.[1] It pertains to the assessment one religion makes of another in terms of its salvific potency. If one religion thinks that it alone constitutes the road to salvation and the other religion simply doesn't, the position is described as exclusivist. If one religion continues to think that it alone constitutes the path to salvation but admits that other religions also go part of the way but not the whole way, which it alone does, then the position is described as inclusivist. If, however, one tradition thinks that all other traditions also constitute valid paths to salvation, along with itself, then the position is described as pluralist.

TOWARD CULTURAL PLURALISM

The argument could be diagrammatically represented as follows, with the arrows indicating the direction of increasing salvific potency conceded to the other tradition:

$$\text{exclusivism} \longrightarrow \text{inclusivism} \longrightarrow \text{pluralism}$$

The point to note for the ensuing discussion is that pluralism stands here as a position distinct from and in contrast to the other two positions.

---

[1] See, for example, John Hick, *Philosophy of Religion,* 4th ed. (Englewood Cliffs, NJ: Prentice-Hall, 1990), chap. 9; William A. Young, *The World's Religions: Worldviews and Contemporary Issues,* 2nd ed. (Upper Saddle River, NJ: Prentice-Hall, 2005), 387–90.

But what if the pluralist position were made to include the other two positions? Books on American constitutionalism, for instance, speak of three approaches to the American Constitution: the intentionalist, the originalist, and the pluralist, adding that *the pluralist includes the other two*. Is it then possible to construct a pluralist model in the study of religion that will *include* rather than *exclude* the exclusivist and the inclusivist positions?

This seems to be a distinct possibility if the argument is developed as follows. The standard pluralist model uses the willingness to accept the salvific potency of all religions as its criterion. If, however, this criterion were changed to "absence of coercion" in disseminating one's point of view, then it might be possible to include both exclusivism and inclusivism within a pluralist model rather than keeping them out. It has been pointed out, for instance, that nothing is really wrong with exclusive claims as such (for they could be true). They become misguided when an effort is made to enforce them on an individual or a community through the use of coercion (for those who so enforce them could be in the wrong about that of which they seem so certain). Similarly, it could be argued that there is nothing wrong with inclusivism as such—for inclusivists could be right too. It is the attempt on their part to coerce people into accepting their position that would be wrong—for they too could be wrong. *Similarly, even pluralists would cease to be so if they began to exercise coercion and forced the exclusivists and the inclusivists to accept the pluralist position.*

On the basis of this distinction, the first model of pluralism could be described as one of *soteriological pluralism* and the second one as that of *ethical pluralism*. It now seems possible to suggest that if both these models are combined, then one obtains a model of *cultural pluralism*.

THE EXAMPLE OF HINDUISM

Hindu culture might provide an illustration of such a possibility. There are, for instance, clearly exclusivist elements present within Hinduism. Klaus K. Klostermaier writes:

> It is India as a geographic entity that offers the occasions of sanctification; only in India are cows, snakes, rats, and vultures sacred; only in India do ascetical and religious practices lead to salvation. Ancient India singled out *madhyadesa*, the heartland of India, as the really holy land; beyond its boundaries salvation could not be gained.[2]

Similarly, the medieval Hindu scholar Madhusadana Sarasvata argued that non-Hindus could not be saved because they could not even possess an adequate soteriological formulation and that Advaita Vedanta represented

---

[2] Klaus K. Klostermaier, *A Survey of Hinduism*, 2nd ed. (Albany: SUNY Press, 1994), 43.

the complete truth.[3] The most developed version of these positions has been offered by Wilhelm Halbfass as follows:

> The Indocentrism developed in "orthodox" Hindu thought transcends by far what is ordinarily called "ethnocentrism." It is not simply an unquestioned perspective or bias, but a sophisticated theoretical structure of self-universalization and self-isolation. Seen from within this complex, highly differentiated structure, the *mlecchas* [non-Hindus] are nothing but a faint and distant phenomenon at the horizon of the indigenous tradition. They do not possess an "otherness" against which one's own identity could be asserted, or in which it could be reflected. They are neither targets of possible conversion, nor sources of potential inspiration. The "otherness" is a negative and abstract one; it does not contain any concrete cultural or religious challenges. Classical Hindu thought has developed an extraordinary wealth of schemes and methods of religious and philosophical subordination and coordination, of inclusion, hierarchization and concordance of worldviews. But in this process, it has developed a complex, internally differentiated framework of orientation, a kind of immanent universe of thought, in which the contrasts of the "indigenous" and the "foreign," of identity and otherness, seem a priori superseded, and which is so comprehensive in itself that it is not conducive to any serious involvement with what is different and apart from it—i.e., the "other" in its otherness.[4]

Alongside such exclusivistic tendencies, inclusivist tendencies are also found as is illustrated by the following passage:

> One curious and symptomatic passage occurs in the conversation between Bhcgu and Bharadvaja which is contained in the *Santiparvan* of the *Mahabharata*. This discussion begins by asserting that the differences between the castes were not originally present and that the existence of the three lower castes may be explained through their neglect of *dharma* and fall from the brahmnic state. Following this, reference is made to monsters and spirits *(pisaca, raksasa, preta)*, while "barbaric tribes" *(mlecchajati)* are named whose knowledge and reason was lost and whose behavior was governed solely by their desires *(svacchandacaracestita)*. For the orthodoxy represented by the Mimamsa, however, the original unity and affinity which such models insinuate played no role.[5]

---

[3] K. Satchidananda Murty, *Revelation and Reason in Advaita Vedanta* (Delhi: Motilal Banarsidass, 1974), 293.

[4] Wilhelm Halbfass, *India and Europe: An Essay in Understanding* (Albany: SUNY Press, 1981), 186–87.

[5] Ibid., 332.

Even such an allegedly conservative text as the *Manusmrti* contains the following passage:

> [238] A man who has faith may receive good learning even from a man who is lower, the ultimate law even from a man of the lowest (castes), and a jewel of a woman even from a bad family. [239] Ambrosia may be extracted even from poison, and good advice even from a child, good behavior even from an enemy, and gold even from something impure. [240] Women, jewels, learning, law, purification, good advice, and various crafts may be acquired from anybody. (II-238–40)[6]

It should be noted that the text allows for accepting even *dharma* from wherever one might. The *Manusmrti* also contains the following pluralistic verse in its last chapter:

> Some say he is fire, others that he is Manu, the Lord of the Creatures, others Indra, others the vital breath, others the eternal ultimate reality. (XII-123)[7]

The following famous verse translated by P. V. Kane and found in the *Subhasitaratna Bhandagara*, and also found inscribed on a temple wall in South India, broadens the scope of the underlying pluralism even further:

> May Hari, the Lord of the three worlds, bestow on you the desired reward, whom the *Saivas* worship as *Siva*, Vedantins as *brahman*, the Bauddhas as Buddha, the Naiyayikas proficient in the means of knowledge as the Creator, those devoted to Jain teachings as Arhat and Mimamsakas as Yajna.[8]

The logician Udayana, who composed his well-known work *Nyayakusumanjali* in AD 984, spreads the net even wider to include Carvakas and even craftsmen, who worship the supreme as the "all-maker" *(visvakarma)*.[9] This is tantamount to including Marxism and producerism (consumerism) among liberating world views in a modern context.

HINDUISM AND CULTURAL PLURALISM

As a culture Hinduism has allowed all these positions to coexist. Now the question arises: Which is the best way of describing this state of affairs, for

---

[6] Wendy Doniger and Brian K. Smith, *The Laws of Manu* (New York: Penguin books, 1991), 42–43.

[7] Ibid., 290.

[8] P. V. Kane, *History of Dharma-Shastra* (Poona: Bhandarkar Oriental Research Institute, 1977), vol. 5, part 2, p. 1624.

[9] Ibid., n2609.

the situation could easily be related to Hinduism's tradition of nonviolence or tolerance. In other words, is Hinduism nonviolent, tolerant, or non-exclusive?

Our first reaction to this question could well be—is there a choice involved? Is it not all three?

I submit that a choice is indeed involved if the matter is considered carefully. Hinduism is in favor of nonviolence on the whole, but while it avoids violence it does not rule it out. Similarly, while Hinduism is tolerant, it is intolerant of intolerance. Were this not the case, why would it find Christian proselytization offensive?

No such reservations characterize its description as non-exclusive. Note that it is non-exclusive to the point of even accepting exclusive claims as *claims* as long as they are not imposed on others. And its comprehensiveness even allows for the consideration of the possibility that exclusive truth-claims may be true, like non-exclusive truth-claims. But it must function basically from within a non-exclusive framework because such a framework allows for the coexistence of both exclusive and non-exclusive claims in a way not possible within an exclusive framework. Thus the encyclopedic imperative of Hinduism—that is, its ambition to be all things to all human beings—requires that it stick to a non-exclusive orientation, because non-exclusive orientation allows room for both exclusive and non-exclusive claims to coexist.

Hence, Hinduism may be more accurately described as a non-exclusive rather than as a nonviolent and tolerant tradition, although these are also acceptable descriptions. A point of some subtlety is involved here. No definition of Hinduism can be final, because within it no religious or philosophical theory or practice can be final—including this one. This is probably where it goes beyond Buddhism, which is said to assert that the absolute truth is that there is no absolute truth. But back to Hinduism. The Hindu view—that no position within it can be final—including this one—produces an important consequence in the present context. As no philosophical position can be final, including this one, its pluralism allows room for absolutism within it, and room for exclusivist sects as some forms of *Vaisnavism*, and even for claims of philosophical supremacy, such as those made by *Vedanta*, and more specifically, *Advaita Vedanta*. Yet such absolutism within it is the result of its own self-relativization, whereas the absolutism of the Abrahamic religions—and I have particularly Christianity and Islam in mind here—involves the relativization of others. Or, to put it another way, even the intolerance of Hinduism is an expression of its tolerance, while even the tolerance displayed by most forms of Christianity and Islam is a kind of intolerance, a temporary reprieve until one joins the Christian or Islamic fold. Other religions insist on making themselves the criterion; Hinduism is willing to be a sample along with them.

A MORE EMBRACING PLURALISM

From a Hindu perspective, then, the tendency in much of modern religious and philosophical discourse to identify pluralism only with *soteriological pluralism* obscures the fact that other forms of pluralism, which were identi-fied in this paper as *ethical pluralism* and *cultural pluralism*, can also be identified and that their identification, far from being merely an academic exercise, has important implications for our understanding of *pluralism as such*, namely, whether it has to be exclusive of exclusivism and inclusivism in keeping with the common assumption or whether it can be of a kind that is also capable of being hospitable to even exclusivism and inclusivism within certain limits, a possibility generated by the Hindu perspective on it. These limits, of course, would involve ways of preventing the freedom provided to exclusivism and inclusivism from undermining the very structure that makes the coexistence of both of them within a pluralist framework possible.

6

Sikhism and Religious Pluralism

DHARAM SINGH

Religious pluralism as a fact of human existence is as old as the religious history of humankind; the founders of almost all the major world religions were born and lived in pluralistic situations. In spite of this, we can still call it a newly experienced reality because in the past people lived secure in their own tiny and isolated religious camps, unconcerned with the issue of plurality of religions and the allied theological and social problems. Today, however, the world has become physically one—what some have called a global village. In this practical situation we cannot run away from or wish away the social reality of religious pluralism and the social and theological issues arising from it. In the modern-day world we must realize that "the religious life of mankind from now on, if it is to be lived at all, will be lived in a context of religious pluralism. This is true for all of us."[1]

What constitutes a pluralist society? John Furnivall calls it a "medley of peoples," for they mix but do not combine. Each group holds by its own religion, its own culture and language, its own ideas and ways. As individuals they meet, but only in the market place, in buying and selling. This is a pluralistic society, with different sections of the community living side by side, but separately, within the same political unit.[2]

NEEDED: A RELIGIOUSLY GLOBAL VILLAGE

Unfortunately, however, in today's pluralistic global society, each faith community is not in harmonious relationship with the others. This has been due mainly to the fact that each religious community is overly zealous in

---

[1] Wilfred Cantwell Smith, *The Faith of Other Men* (New York: Harper and Row, 1962), 11.

[2] J. S. Furnivall, *Colonial Policy and Practice: A Comparative Study of Burma and Netherlands* (Cambridge: Cambridge Univ. Press, 1948), 304.

underrating the ideology and culture of the others. And this excessive zeal usually stems from the way leaders of each religion claim a monopoly of truth for their faith. To them, only their religion, or only their prophet, can lead people on the path to God-realization and self-realization. Other religions are declared inferior, or inauthentic, or "pagan." This exclusivist attitude is doing much damage to our social fabric;[3] religious people and their leaders have the responsibility to address and try to rectify this problem.

What we need, I suggest, is a religiously global village. And to achieve this—to enable different faith communities to live harmoniously and peacefully—we need something like the pluralist model we are exploring in this book. In this model the value and validity of multiple religious communities are recognized. Religions, in the pluralist perspective, do share something in common; they make common reference to, or presume, a single, transcendent reality.[4] Still, they have genuine differences, for each religion is a different historical manifestation of that reality, and it presents visions of God, world, and humanity from a localized, historically particular perspective. In other words, it can be said that the essence of divine revelation is universal but when shared by the receiver-prophet with humankind in a mundane language in a specific historico-religio-cultural context, it acquires limitations as well as differentiation.

To affirm the fact of diverse religions as finite manifestations of one Infinite is in no way to diminish the significance of any particular religion; rather, such diversity reveals the richness of eternal and infinite truth. One must try to understand and appreciate the religious beliefs and practices of one's neighbor. No doubt, one cannot put one's faith in parenthesis while trying to understand and examine the faith of the other; yet, one must listen attentively to the faith of the other as this is witnessed to by the believer, without prejudging that faith and without abandoning one's own commitment. This, as M. A. C. Warren reminds us, is a very delicate undertaking: "Our first task in approaching another people, another culture, another religion is to take off our shoes, for the place we are approaching is holy. Else we may find ourselves treading on men's dreams. More serious still, we may forget that God was here before our arrival."[5]

---

[3] For an understanding and detailed discussion of the terms *exclusivist, inclusivist,* and *pluralist,* see Alan Race, *Christians and Religious Pluralism* (London: SCM, 1983). This phraseology was used by Alan Race for the first time and was subsequently supported by John Hick (*The Rainbow of Faiths* [London: SCM, 1985]). It was later criticized by Ian Markhan in "Creating Options: Shattering the 'Exclusivist, Inclusivist, and Pluralist' Paradigm," and defended by Gavin D'Costa in "Creating Confusion: A Response to Markham," both in *New Blackfriars* (January 1993).

[4] This is a general statement. A caveat to this claim must be entered in the case of certain traditions that tend to deny that religious language points to anything real, for example, the *sramanic* Indian traditions.

[5] M. A. C. Warren, "General Introduction," Christian Presence series (London: SCM, 1959).

Religious pluralism cannot be confined to the knowledge of other religious systems and their doctrines and teachings. This would mean trying to confront a religious truth in the abstract. Pluralism presumes the effort to know and appreciate the historical-cultural context and the people who make up other faith communities. This will require no small effort, for although our earth has been transformed economically, politically, and informationally into a global village, many of us still prefer to remain in our own small, individual villages. We have become neighbors with people of different races and religions, yet we still prefer to call and consider them alien.

We can lead meaningful, satisfying—and today we can add *safe*—lives only if we work out a more dialogical relationship with our neighbors, who may not necessarily be of our own race or color or religious persuasion. We must not only live with our religiously diverse neighbors, but we must also talk with, work with, and learn from them.

India encountered religious pluralism as a social reality in the ancient past; the West did so only in the nineteenth and the twentieth centuries. With the growing awareness of the fact of religious pluralism,[6] the earlier view of Christian missionaries has for several reasons undergone a sea change, leading to the reinterpretation and restating of Christian theology.[7] The early Muslim theological stand was that other religions are deviations of the one primordial religion, while "Islam was the full revelation and therefore the norm of all religion."[8] It is difficult, however, for contemporary Muslims who find themselves in minority positions in alien cultures to adhere to this view. Hinduism in the Indian context enjoys a unique position insofar as it is theoretically pluralist, but practically it has always endeavored to assimilate religions of Indian origin unto itself without conceding an independent status to any of them.

For many people today it appears more and more difficult to hold to such exclusivist or inclusivist models for understanding religious history. This history indicates, rather, that there can be no one way to the realization of God and that there are many paths and many saviors to help people in their efforts

---

[6] This awareness came during what is called the European Enlightenment in the seventeenth and the eighteenth centuries, when there developed a realization that Christianity was part of a much larger human world. Changing patterns of mobility also shattered the old conceptions of religious history. The explosion of information in the West about the religions of the world during the twentieth century also helped change the earlier ill-informed and hostile stereotypes of other faiths. Also, the earlier exclusivist attitude had begun to poison relationships between Christian minority and other majority communities in some countries of the world. For details, see Race, *Christians and Religious Pluralism*; Hick, *The Rainbow of Faiths*; John Hick and Paul F. Knitter, eds., *The Myth of Christian Uniqueness: Toward a Pluralistic Theology of Religions* (Maryknoll, NY: Orbis Books, 1987).

[7] This does not mean that all Christian theologians tend to be pluralists; many still hold to either the exclusivist model or the inclusivist model.

[8] Harold Coward, *Pluralism in the World Religions: A Short Introduction* (Oxford: Oneworld Publications, 2000), 81.

to pursue truth and meaning. Further, these many ways cannot exist in isolation from one another, and they cannot possibly remain intolerant of or indifferent toward the others. The neighbor can no longer remain a stranger. It is necessary for different religions and faith communities to meet one another and relate to one another, the objective being not to absorb or obliterate the other but to help and learn from each other. This has become obligatory for humanity today because pluralism is no more only a textbook issue; it has become a human existential problem.

A YOUNG AND WORLD-AFFIRMING RELIGION

The Sikh faith is one of the youngest of the major world religions, and as such it can also be called a later stage in the history of the evolution of human religious consciousness. It originated with Guru Nanak (1469–1539) in a northwest province of India but has since spread throughout the world despite the fact that it is not a missionary faith. No doubt the expansion of the Sikh community is mainly due to the Sikh Diaspora, but dissemination of knowledge about the Sikh faith has also helped in this expansion, though in a limited way. Chronologically, the fifteenth century, when the Sikh faith originated belongs to the medieval period of Indian history. An in-depth study of the faith, however, reveals its critical attitude toward the medieval spirit and its responsiveness to modernity.

In the modern-day circumstances outlined above, the Sikh religion can play a crucial and constructive role, mainly because it has evolved an interreligious theology. The Sikh faith accepts plurality, but this acceptance is not passive; it is, rather, critical. This critical spirit is quite explicit on at least two vital points. First, the Sikh Gurus are highly critical of any religion and tradition that sanctions and safeguards hierarchical social structures. The idea of inequality by birth among people is not acceptable to them. There are many hymns in the Sikh scripture that criticize the spirit and philosophy of the Vedic tradition, which classifies humans into different *varnas* or castes and denies many rights to those born in the lowest *varna*. In Sikh theology, all humans are equal, no matter how different they may appear externally. All humans are, in essence, one with, and before, God, and that makes them equal among themselves. In one of his hymns Guru Nanak sided with the lowliest among the lowly and also states these so-called low castes and the poor are God's favorites.[9]

Second, the Sikh faith opposes a religion that mobilizes mass support in the name of religion in order to serve the interests of a ruling political class. The Sikh Gurus were well aware of the danger of religion becoming an instrument of political dominance in the hands of a select few. Therefore, in their hymns they criticized the Hindu and the Muslim clergies for their role in misusing religion for the purpose of oppressing certain classes of society.

---

[9] Guru Granth Sahib, I, 15.

Before the origin of the Sikh faith, the Hindu clergy denied the Sudras, the lowest caste in the Hindu social order, the right to enter a place of worship or to read or listen to a scripture being read; they had no right to progress in the realms of spirituality and thus attain salvation. To achieve this ultimate end of human life, they were supposed to serve the higher-caste people well during this lifetime and thus earn their next birth in a higher caste. Thus, the clergy in a way tried to retain the status quo in society and keep these Sudras in a position of perpetual subservience. The Sikh Gurus changed the very concept of religion by first denying any place in the new faith to clergy and by eradicating all distinctions of high and low between one human being and another. On the other hand, the Muslim clergy during the Muslim rule in India tried to interpret scriptures to justify even many of the unjust actions of the rulers performed by them not out of any religious obligation but out of pure political expediency.[10] As we said earlier, the Gurus in their professions and practice sided with the lowly, the oppressed, and the suppressed. Thus, the Gurus used religion to do away the evils of injustice, oppression, and exploitation; they used it as an instrument for social change.

The Sikh faith integrates the world and worldly life with the idea of divinity. It rejects asceticism, but at the same time it is also highly critical of a hedonistic way of life. These two extremes both are rejected in Sikhism. Also, the Sikh concept of social action is marked by boundaries of morality. In Sikhism, Khalsa-Panth,[11] as created by Guru Gobind Singh in fulfillment of Guru Nanak's mission, is the agency to which the task of social transformation has been endowed. The Khalsa, as an individual, stands for a realized self and, in its collective sense, represents the classless and casteless social structure of the Gurus' vision. The scripture, on the other hand, renders the general framework in which the task of social transformation is to be accomplished.

---

[10] Ibid., I, 951.

[11] The creation of Khalsa-Panth refers to a very significant development in Sikh history. Every Sikh, in growing up, is supposed to receive the baptism of the double-edged sword and thus become a member of the Khalsa-Panth. The origins of this baptismal ceremony go back to the Vaisakhi day (March 30) of AD 1699, when Guru Gobind Singh, the tenth Guru of the Sikh faith, summoned a huge gathering of his followers at Anandpur. While addressing the gathering, he asked if anyone from among the gathering was ready to offer his head to the Guru. A Sikh got up and came to the Guru, who took him to the adjoining enclosure and came back with a blood-smeared sword. He repeated the demand five times and the five Sikhs thus selected became the nucleus of the Khalsa-Panth. First, the Guru administered the baptism of the double-edged sword to these five Sikhs who are known in the Sikh tradition as the Five Beloved Ones. Then the Guru himself received baptism from these five, thus declaring the Khalsa equal to the Guru. The Khalsa-Panth is a casteless and classless social ideal of Sikhism.

Also, the word *khalsa*, of Arabic origin, was used for the crown lands, that is, the lands under the direct suzerainty of the king. The Khalsa in Sikh tradition is directly related to Guru/God and needs no mediator. For details, see Prithipal Singh Kapur and Dharam Singh, *The Khalsa* (Patiala: Punjabi Univ., 1999).

In other words, the scripture is a sort of constitution that lays down the structures according to which one must live one's social and religious existence, while the Khalsa-Panth must not only live that kind of life but also create conditions conducive for that kind of life. Both the structure and the agency, however, must function in harmony to bring about peace and coexistence, love and compassion, equality and justice in society.

In Sikh belief, God both creates and permeates the entire phenomenal world. This understanding of God as both transcendent creator and immanent presence lends relative reality to the finite world. This world cannot be considered simply to be sinful or mere *maya* (delusion, not real) or primarily a place of suffering; it is, rather, the dwelling place of the Divine. As the residence of the Lord God, the world need not be renounced; on the contrary humans must strive to fashion the world into the kingdom of God. In this process, for Sikhs, the spiritual is socialized, and the secular and social are spiritualized. Ethics, therefore, is central to Sikh belief and practice; Sikhs are called to an active and righteous participation in family and social life. The ideal religion for Sikhs calls upon people to perform concrete good deeds in this world but at the same time constantly to remember the Divine Name. "The best religion amongst all the religions is one that asks man to remember God's Name and do noble deeds," says the Sikh scripture.[12]

RELATIONS WITH OTHER RELIGIONS

The lives of the Sikh spiritual teachers, the message of the Sikh scripture, and Sikh tradition and history all stand witness to the constructive and positive Sikh response to interfaith relations. For example, if we look at the life of the founder of the faith, Guru Nanak, we learn that after he received the revelation, he went on four preaching odysseys in four different directions to share this divine message with the people at large.[13] In the south, he traveled to Sri Lanka; in the east, he went to Dhaka now in Bangladesh; in the west, he passed through Rajasthan, Gujarat, and proceeded to Baghdad and Mecca; and in the north, he traveled deep into the Himalayas. During these odysseys he seems to have made it a point to visit any place of pilgrimage or importance to either Hindus or Muslims. At such places he would call on the holy men who might be living there and have a spiritual discourse with them. Instead of thrusting his view of truth on anyone, he would listen to them and

---

[12] Guru Granth Sahib, V, 266.

[13] For details, see the Bein episode in the *janam-sakhis* (the traditional life accounts of Guru Nanak) wherein Guru Nanak, after leaving the house at Sultanpur where he was living with his sister and brother-in-law to carry out his usual morning routine of bathing in the Bein rivulet, does not return and is missing for a number of days. It is believed that during those days he remained in meditation, during which he was summoned by Nirankar (God), who offered him a cup of nectar and directed him to go into the world and spread his message.

also share with them the revelation he had had. The Sikh tradition does not support polemics but instead recommends a meaningful and constructive dialogue in which one must listen to the other's viewpoint and then offer one's own witness. Such a dialogical relationship with other faiths leads to a much-needed deeper understanding and appreciation of other religions.

The Sikh scripture calls for respect for all religions, tolerance for religious pluralism, and understanding and cooperation among different faith communities. It is quite explicit in its statement that revelation cannot be religion specific, region specific, or caste specific and that the claim to truth cannot be a monopoly of any one particular religion, caste, class, or region. Since each expression of revelation is considered an attempt to encounter and understand the Real One in a particular localized context, we must respect other religions, notwithstanding our disagreements and differentiations in regard to outward symbols and rituals. That is why the Sikh Gurus advised everybody to be true to his or her faith: a Muslim should be a true Muslim, and a Hindu should become a true Hindu. There is no instance in Sikh history or tradition of exhorting anybody to convert to Sikhism because it was, so to say, a better faith than any other. Also, Sikhism seeks to unite people belonging to different religious traditions into a broader unity. Sikh theology holds that the object of religion is not to divide humankind but to unite it; "not to act like scissors and tear asunder the social fabric, but to act like a needle and sew it together."[14]

The Sikh scripture was compiled by Guru Arjan (1563–1606), the fifth spiritual preceptor of the Sikhs, in 1604;[15] the collection included hymns of his own and of his four predecessors, as well as hymns coming from the Hindu and Muslim traditions that had been selected on the basis of their resonance with Sikh beliefs. No change has since been made in the contents of the scripture except that Guru Gobind Singh (1666–1708), the tenth Guru, added to it the hymns of Guru Tegh Bahadur, his spiritual predecessor, some time before he bestowed upon the scripture itself the office of Guru; in Sikh tradition, the Word, or more precisely the Word as contained in the scripture, is equated with the Guru. *Granth* or the Word as contained therein is revered as the living Guru or the Guru Eternal. The Word in it is taken as the spirit-incarnate of the Gurus. As it is, all the hymns contained in the scripture are of equal significance and reverence for a Sikh. For example, a hymn of Kabir, Ravidas, or Farid is as sacred to a Sikh as that of Guru Nanak. Thus, the holy Granth Sahib provides a unique example of negating the idea that revelation is religion specific; rather, it shows respect for religious pluralism and tries to bring together the essential message of religion as communicated by holy people from different traditions.

Furthermore, these holy contributors to the scripture come not only from different religious backgrounds but also from different castes and different

---

[14] *Varan Bhai Gurdas*, XXXIII.4.

[15] The work on the compilation of the Sikh scripture was completed in 1604—the same year work began on the Authorized or King James Version of the Bible.

regions. For example, Kabir is a weaver, Ravidas is a cobbler, Namdev a calico-printer, and Dhanna a peasant; all this might sound absolutely normal to a Western reader because these words stand for different professions, but in the Indian context, especially of those days, they signified the castes *(varnas)* to which these holy men belonged.[16] Interestingly, most of these holy men belonged to the so-called low castes (Sudras) and oppressed classes (Dalits). Thus, the medieval Brahmanic view that barred this lower strata of society from religious enlightenment was soundly rejected. Sikhism discards the caste system in social relations and declares all social and religious offices open to all those who deserve them. The Sikh scripture says that one becomes a Brahmin not by being born in a Brahmin family, as the *varna* system suggested, but by reflecting on Brahman (God)[17] and that it is not the prerogative only of the Kshatris/Khatris to rule, but rather only the deserving should sit on the throne.[18] The Sikh shrines are open to all, irrespective of caste, class, or creed. All the devotees in a *gurdwara* sit together on the same floor, and any true Sikh can read the scripture and say the *ardas* or prayer.[19] It is not one's caste or creed but the good deeds done during one's lifetime that earn one a place in the Divine Court.[20]

These contributors to the Sikh scripture do not belong to any particular region, rather they come from very far off and different places in India. For example, Namdev comes from Maharashtra (South India), Jaidev from Bengal (East India), Kabir and Ravidas from Uttar Pradash (North India), Farid and Dhanna from Rajasthan (West India), and the Gurus themselves belonged to Punjab in the northwest of India. Thus, in the Sikh viewpoint all spiritual preceptors of the world belonging to different places and countries of the world are equally holy and venerable. Again, we see that the Sikh scripture strongly affirms that truth or revelation is neither religion specific nor region specific nor caste specific.

Similarly, Sikhism also rejects the idea of only one Savior. The idea that my prophet or my spiritual teacher is the only Savior to lead humanity on the road to salvation is alien to Sikhism, which takes different religions as divine revelations made known by the prophets or spiritual preceptors at different times in different spatio-cultural contexts. It accepts each one of the prophets

---

[16] The horizontal division of the Hindu social order into four *varnas* was rather strict, and the low-caste Sudras were denied any right to spirituality. Several of these holy men from Hindu tradition whose hymns find a place in the Sikh scripture happen to be Sudras. The Gurus, by including their hymns in the scripture, suggested that revelation is not caste specific and that no one on the basis of caste can be denied the right to become liberated.

[17] Guru Granth Sahib, II, 512.

[18] Ibid., I, 1088.

[19] In the Sikh tradition, *ardas* is made to God in the presence of the Guru Granth Sahib; Sikhs do so after the morning and evening services in the *gurdwaras*. They also offer prayer to seek divine blessings any time they start a new venture or as thanksgiving after the successful completion of any job.

[20] Guru Granth Sahib, III, 514.

and the traditions founded by them as equally valid paths toward God-real-ization. In one of his hymns as included in the Guru Granth Sahib, Guru Amar Das, the third spiritual preceptor of the Sikhs, declares all religious traditions equally valid as he prays to Lord:

> The world is burning in the fire of passion
> Save it, O Lord, by Thy grace;
> Save it the way Thou consider best.[21]

There are several instances in the Sikh tradition where we find the Sikh Gu-rus advising their followers to give equal regard to the prophets and seers from all traditions. Sikhs must also not look down upon those who have a different form of worship. Such an attitude was much ahead of the times and can very easily be taken as a precursor to the modern-day pluralistic model. The oft-quoted example of this viewpoint is that of Guru Arjan, who was once visited by Bhai Gopi (a Bhardwaj Brahmin) and his companions, Bhai Vesa and Bhai Tulsia (also Bhardwaj Brahmins) and Bhai Bhiara. They were confused by the diverse incarnations in which God was worshiped. The Guru advised them: "All forms and attributes are God's, yet He transcends them. You should, therefore, worship only the Absolute One. At the same time, you must abjure rancor toward those who have a different way of worship."[22]

Lest this understanding and appreciation of other religions should remain an abstract idea, Sikhism seeks to promote a dialogical relationship between different faith communities. The Sikh scripture is quite emphatic in stating that "man throughout his worldly existence must seek to converse with oth-ers by first listening to others' viewpoint and then putting forward his own, for this is the only way to attain truth."[23] The notions of "listening to the others' viewpoint" *(kichhu suniai)* and "putting forward your own view-point" *(kichhu kahiai)* clearly urges fruitful dialogue aimed at searching for the truth. The Sikh scripture categorically rejects polemics, insisting, rather, that only after polemics have been set aside can the real search for truth begin and bear fruit.[24] Polemics and argumentation cause—and are also caused by—"the ego which in the Sikh scripture is referred to as a 'serious malady'";[25] but humility, a prerequisite for genuine listening to another, is the essence of all virtues.[26] There are innumerable references in Sikh scripture that stress the value of humility. Kabir humbly refers to himself as the worst and every-one else as good, and goes on to say that whoever believes in this dictum is his friend.[27] Shaikh Farid urges us to be as humble as grass on the pathway

---

[21] Ibid., II, 853.

[22] Bhai Mani Singh, *Sikhan di Bhagat Mala and Varan Bhai Gurdas*, XI.20.

[23] Ibid., I, 661.

[24] Ibid., I, 1255.

[25] Ibid., II, 466.

[26] Ibid., I, 470.

[27] Guru Granth Sahib, Kabir, 1364.

that is trodden under the feet of many,[28] while Guru Arjan teaches that those who humble themselves are to be exalted.[29] Thus, Sikh scripture clearly teaches that we are to cultivate humility and share our own views while we listen to the views of others, for only so can we all progress on the path to truth.

The best example of interfaith dialogue in the Sikh scripture is Guru Nanak's *Sidh Gosti,* which is a sort of spiritual dialogue on the Sikh philosophy of life vis-à-vis the philosophy of yoga. In this composition the yogis put searching questions to Guru Nanak, who answers them with courtesy and confidence. The dialogue is held without hurting the feelings of any of the participants, ever retaining serenity and sobriety and aiming at realizing the truth. This is the basis as well as the ideal of interfaith dialogue in Sikhism. Other examples of dialogue can be found within the hymns of Sikh saints. Certain *slokas,* especially of Kabir and Farid, frequently have been held up and commented upon by the Gurus for the way they make use of dialogue rather than polemics as a means for clarifying or expanding God's message to humanity.

The vision of religious tolerance and the affirmation of religious pluralism that are found in the message of the Gurus as contained in scripture are embodied in the lives of the Gurus themselves and in Sikh tradition in general. This is evident in the way Guru Nanak was revered not just by Sikhs but also by Hindus and Muslims. And Guru Arjan was recognized by the Emperor Jahangir for the way his message and conduct brought Hindus and Muslims together to converse with him. Guru Tegh Bahadur went even further and laid down his life to protect religious freedom, offering himself for sacrifice in order to stop the Muslim ruler of his time from forcing the conversion of Hindus to Islam. It was clear that he would have done the same for Muslims had they found themselves in the same situation under Hindu rulers. When Guru Gobind Singh took up the struggle against the deceit and decadence of Hindu Rajput chiefs and against Mughal oppression, he could count many Hindus and Muslims standing at his side. One of the most moving Sikh affirmations of the value of other religions can be found in Bhai Kanahaiya, as he looked out over the slain and wounded soldiers on the battlefield of Anandpur and honored the same divine essence in all of them, no matter what their religion.[30] Treating all human beings as spiritually one and ethnically equal no matter what their religious beliefs is the prerequisite for maintaining harmonious relationship among different faith communities.

---

[28] Ibid., Farid, 1378.

[29] Ibid., V, 266.

[30] Bhai Kanahaiya was a devotee of Guru Gobind Singh; during a battle the Guru had to fight against the Rajput hill chiefs and the Mughal imperial forces, the Bhai served water to the wounded soldiers. One day it was reported to the Guru that the Bhai served water to the wounded soldiers of the enemy camp as well. The Guru sent for him and asked him to explain. He told the Guru that he saw the same divine image in each face irrespective of the camp he belonged to. The Guru, on listening to this, was highly pleased and urged him to tend to the wounds of all.

LOOKING AHEAD

If we want a world free from the prevalent distrust and disharmony, oppression and violence, we must be able to see others as our brothers and sisters. This means that we have to discover how to affirm our own identity without threatening the identity of others.[31] And we have to recognize and feel in our religious awareness that when we revile another's religion or desecrate another community's place of worship, we revile or desecrate the divine Presence itself.

The central message of the teaching of the Sikh faith is that if we truly believe in God's love for all beings, we must affirm and value the others in their otherness. The Sikh religion considers all religions and their revelations to be valid; while affirming other faiths, it also urges dialogue as a means of recognizing and learning from our differences. Within such dialogue Sikhs see the love of God as the energy for love of humankind; they express this love through *seva* or voluntary service rendered unto others and other such philanthropic activities. Sikhs are in full agreement with St. James's assertion that "faith without works is dead" (Jas 2:20); with their ethics of creative activism, they seek to realize the Gurus' vision of a society based on faith, love, and justice. This is the need of our contemporary, threatened world—that we do not limit ourselves to words alone but try to actively to turn religious words into reality in our social lives.

---

[31] Marcus Braybrooke, "Sikhism: A Religion for the Third Millennium," in *Perspectives on Sikhism* (Patiala: Punjabi Univ., 2001), 15.

PART III

Buddhist Perspectives

7

Excuse Me, but What's the Question?

Isn't Religious Diversity Normal?

RITA M. GROSS

I am of two minds about philosophical and theological discussions of religious diversity.[1] On the one hand, I have devoted a great deal of my life working to make people more comfortable with and accepting of religious diversity. That was one of my major aims in the countless sections of the course "Introduction to the Religions of the World" that I taught for almost thirty years. For two reasons, I did not see the course as merely a neutral, information-dispensing way to provide some humanities credits in a college degree program. First, I gave up on the notion of academic neutrality long before it became fashionable to do so under the label of post-modernism. As a female scholar focusing on women's lives and religious issues, the academy treated me in anything but a neutral manner, making it difficult for me to take claims about its neutrality seriously. Second, I know the attitudes toward religious diversity with which many of my students entered the classroom because I had been brought up just as they had been, in a conservative and not very diverse part of the country (northern Wisconsin,

---

[1] The terms *diversity* and *pluralism* are both regularly used in discussions about the variety of religions found in the world. It is important to distinguish between the *fact* that there are many religions, and the *value* placed upon the multiplicity of religions. It has become common to use the word *diversity* to refer to the simple fact that there are many religions in the world, and *pluralism* to refer to a specific theology of religions, a theology that evaluates this diversity positively and regards all religions has having some validity. In this essay I have chosen to follow this usage very precisely. Thus, *diversity* and *pluralism* are not interchangeable in my usage.

USA). Most of them had been taught exclusivism,[2] and many of them believed it.

I knew from personal experience how such religious indoctrination can wound young people and what a struggle it can be to pull away from such indoctrination, especially if one is not taught about any alternatives. When I was twenty-one, I was excommunicated for the heresy, among others, of being unwilling to affirm that people of other faiths went to hell. A few months after that, I began graduate studies in the comparative and cross-cultural study of religion. Part of my delight in that field is due to the endlessly diverse and interesting religious phenomena one can investigate, but I also intended to use my training in the field to help other students think past religious exclusivism into something more humane and dignified. In those days (mid 1960s), the divide between descriptive and normative inquiries into religion was much stricter than it is today. Therefore, such motivations could not then be part of my public persona, but in retrospect, it would be dishonest to claim otherwise.

On the other hand, I sometimes get frustrated by the continuing need to reflect on theologies of religious diversity. After all, isn't religious diversity normal? Why should I expect anything else or feel uncomfortable with people whose religious beliefs may be quite different from my own (as long as they don't seek to impose their beliefs on me)? As far as the eye can see, religious diversity has been a fact of human existence. The more we learn about religion, the clearer that reality becomes. Nor is there any indication that religious diversity is ever going to disappear. So why is religious diversity ever an issue? I have been deeply aware of the normality and joy of religious diversity for so long now that it is almost impossible for me to imagine the feelings of someone troubled by religious diversity. Why not simply celebrate such diversity and learn what we can from and about each other, rather than trying to find theological validations of such diversity?

Nevertheless, demographics may force us to focus on delineating and defending pluralistic theologies, given that two populous religions with long histories of making exclusive truth-claims about their own relevance and

---

[2] For many years theological discussions of religious diversity claimed that there are three basic ways that religions have interpreted religious diversity. First is the exclusivist model, according to which only my religion is true and has value; all others are false and would not exist in an ideal world. Second is the inclusivist model, according to which other religions may contain partial or limited truth but will be eventually replaced by the truth of my religion. Third, the pluralist model claims that all religions have some validity, that religions could learn from one another, and most important, that members of one religion should not seek to convert others to their own religion. Recently, a fourth model, the acceptance model, has been suggested. According to this theology of religions, value judgments about the validity of various religions should be suspended in favor of learning more deeply what each religion is actually claiming. For a recent overview of all these positions, see Paul Knitter, *Introducing Theologies of Religions* (Maryknoll, NY: Orbis Books, 2003).

authority have a very strong grip on the intellectual and spiritual lives of large segments of humanity. One does not know whether to laugh or cry when looking at the almost identical content of their claims to possess the only true religion. "The deity gave us the final word; you are mistaken if you think you have it, and you will suffer for that belief."

When we discuss issues of religious diversity, are we discussing a truly interesting theological and philosophical issue, or are we only discussing something we must be concerned about because of demographics? Is religious diversity truly an interesting theological problem or only a very serious political problem? If anything, the question should be why diversity among the world's religions troubles and worries many people, rather than the question of how we find theological resources within our traditions to allow for the reality of religious diversity. Thus, I become annoyed sometimes with the continuing need to discuss the "problem" of religious diversity. I'm much more interested in the problem of how religions ever become so enamored of themselves that they think they hold a monopoly on relevance and the ability to help people negotiate life. I also think it is useful to point out that most of the theological literature dealing with religious diversity and pluralism stems from religions that historically have made exclusive truth-claims, a fact that colors the discourse and makes it difficult for those of us who simply don't operate with the assumption that religious diversity is anything other than the expected, normal course of events.

WHERE TO BEGIN

Training in the cross-cultural comparative study of religion is always useful, and I think some basic facts about how the reality of religious diversity has been handled in a variety of religions could prove instructive. Most people from religions that claim exclusive and universal truth for themselves assume that all religions make the same claim for themselves, a position that encourages both conflict among religions and disparagement of religions different from one's own. But many religions do not attempt to persuade others to join them, and many even disallow converts.[3] So much for the claim that

---

[3] Examples of religions that do not seek or encourage conversion are numerous. For most indigenous traditions, religion and culture are so intertwined that it would be impossible to convert to the religion. One could only be adopted as a member of the people. Many versions of classical Hinduism claim that one can only be born a Hindu; it is impossible to become one. Post-biblical Judaism gave up the quest to gain converts. Today, potential converts are initially discouraged and are told that Judaism does not accept converts. Though Buddhism is one of the world's most successful "missionary" religions, the Dalai Lama often suggests to people that they should find what they are looking for within their own traditions rather than becoming Buddhists.

everyone believes his or her own religion is the best and would be the only religion in an ideal world.

Another popular belief among those who make universal and exclusive truth-claims is that one must choose—multiple religious belonging is impossible. Try telling that to most traditionally religious people in East Asia. Why choose only one? Why not patronize, for now, the religions or denomination that really specializes in my problems? It is impossible for one perspective to be the best at everything![4]

From the perspective of the cross-cultural comparative study of religion, the fact of the matter is that the religions that are most strident about their claims to universal and sole relevance and most frightening in their vision of the ideal future share a specific theology combined with a political fact— monotheism and imperial success. To many it seems logical that monotheism implies a claim that X religion is the true religion. After all, they claim, if there is only one deity, then its religion has to be the true religion. This logic ignores the fact that the one deity created diversity as the most obvious fact about the world. If the deity intended species and cultures to be distinctive and diverse, then why not religions?

Regarding this theology, many versions of Christianity and Islam seem to be on a collision course; their claims to be the religion uniquely and solely preferred and created by the deity are so similar that, if there can be only one true religion, it is hard to imagine how these two religions will manage to coexist. One will not be absorbed by the other, and the results of their continued claims to possess unique and sole truth and relevance are only negative. The negative fruits of such exclusive claims are the strongest argument against their theological worth. A theology with such disastrous consequences cannot be true.

What Christianity and Islam share with each other but do not share with the progenitor of monotheism is imperial success—and that may be Judaism's saving grace. Theologically, it can seem that monotheism would be intractable—one deity, one religion. But contemporary Judaism has managed to avoid the fate of being a monotheistic, proselytizing religion proclaiming it

---

[4] Multiple religious belonging is much more common in East Asia than exclusive loyalty to one tradition. In Japan, most people patronize both Shinto and Buddhist temples and participate in festivals of both religions. This has led to a common explanation that Japanese people often consider that they are "born Shinto and die Buddhist." This does not refer to a change of religions during the life span, but to emphases that are more common at the beginning of life or at the end of life. For a good discussion of this pattern see Ian Reader, *Religion in Contemporary Japan* (Honolulu: Univ. of Hawaii Press, 1991). In China it was commonly assumed that "the three traditions" (Buddhism, Confucianism, and Taoism) should work together and not be in conflict. For a good discussion of this perspective, see Judith Berling, *A Pilgrim in Chinese Culture: Negotiating Religious Diversity* (Maryknoll, NY: Orbis Books, 1997). Multiple religious belonging is also becoming much more common among certain modern Westerners. Many people now claim to be simultaneously Buddhist and Christian.

deserves to be the only religion. Instead it has developed a theology of multiple covenants and an attitude of tolerance of other religions combined with internal fervor. Modern Judaism, though monotheistic, discourages conversion. Why? It had the good fortune to have any ambitions toward empire squashed relatively early in its history. Christianity and Islam were not so lucky. They both acquired empires early in their existence, and this experience seems to have given them a lot of confidence about their universal relevance. Perhaps the fact that empire seems to be more disastrous than monotheistic theology provides some hope.

Theologians may say that I am merely reciting information. But, in my view, information is always informative. People do not *have* to proclaim universal and sole relevance for their religion; it is merely the habitual pattern of *some* religions to do so. If theologians of all stripes were more informed of the data and variety of world religions, I believe we could avoid many useless theological controversies. But, more important, we might avoid much human suffering caused by religious claims of unique and universal relevance, for I contend that their potential to cause harm and suffering, rather than any possible intellectual error, is the main problem with exclusive, or even inclusive, claims about religious truth.

My other starting point is that I operate as a Buddhist "theologian." My engagement with issues of religious diversity stems from my pain as a victim of monotheistic (Christian) claims of exclusive religious truth and the resulting attempts made by that particular version of Christianity to instill scorn of religious others into me.[5] As a Buddhist, I do not have any significant issues with religious diversity, nor do I think Buddhism historically has regarded religious diversity as anything except a normal fact of existence. Buddhism has always existed in a multi-religious context, often as a minority religion and rarely as the majority religion. But Buddhism is also the only religion to spread worldwide without a strong imperative to become the world's sole religion. How this happened might be worth examining. The tradition of debate about the merits of various religious or philosophical positions is extremely strong in Buddhism, but I hope to show that such debate can aid rather than hinder us in a religiously diverse world. I know that on some occasions, versions of Buddhism have also become addicted to the notion that they are solely relevant, but this, I think, is a historical possibility for any religious perspective and that study of religion in cross-cultural and historical perspective is a safeguard against such hubris. However, I also think that basic Buddhist ideas have some resources that could prove useful in worldwide discussions of religious diversity.

---

[5] Rita Gross, "Religious Diversity: Some Implications for Monotheism," *Cross-Currents* 49, no. 3 (1999), 349–66; Gross, "Feminist Theology as Theology of Religions," in *The Cambridge Companion to Feminist Theology*, ed. Susan Frank Parsons (New York: Cambridge Univ. Press, 2002); Gross, "Feminist Theology: Religiously Diverse Neighborhood or Christian Ghetto?" *Journal of Feminist Theology* 16, no. 2 (2000), 73–78, 124–31.

From any perspective whatsoever I contend that discussions of religious pluralism should begin with religious diversity as a fact, as reality, as something that we must live with. That means that the primary question is how best to live with religious diversity, rather than where it came from, why it persists, whether or not it should exist, or even whether there is some convergence or underlying unity to religions. Of course, this is a standard Buddhist approach to things. Virtually any Buddhist manual will suggest that the first and most necessary step is to ascertain the reality of our situation and that speculating about who or what started things or how they will end or what imaginary world we would prefer to inhabit is a waste of time, though such speculation may be entertaining. Following this advice, Buddhists come up with the first noble truth of suffering, a non-theistic cosmology, and no evidence of personal immortality.[6] Buddhists make these claims, not to make fun of longings people commonly experience, but because if we do not, in fact, know what our situation is, we are helpless to know how to work with it or to change it.

The situation regarding diversity of religions is simple: there has always been religious diversity, and there is no reason to assume things will change, given everything we know about human behavior and reactions. Religious diversity does not have to be explained. Religious diversity is not a mistake to be undone in some future ideal world. It simply is the way things are. I think assimilating *this* fact, which is not really a theological issue at all, but simply a matter of observation, is the foremost agenda in discussions of religious diversity. Religions that make exclusive truth-claims and regard religious diversity as a mistake or a problem must come to terms with and acknowledge this fact. There is no other choice, just as there was no other choice than to accept that the sun does not revolve around the earth. Changing discourse about the diversity of religions from discussing the *problem* of religious diversity to the *fact* of religious diversity would, it seems to me, make a vast and profound difference to that discussion.

A second fact about religious diversity is also critical. The result of exclusive truth-claims is not religious agreement but suffering. The track record of religions that claim exclusive and universal truth for themselves is not praiseworthy or uplifting. How much empire building, how many crusades and religious wars, big and small, have gone on in the name of defending the "one true faith"? There seems to be a cause-and-effect link between claims of exclusive truth and suffering; or to say it more strongly, the main result of exclusive truth-claims has been suffering, not salvation.

---

[6] It is impossible in this context to give an overview of Buddhist teachings. For an academic overview, see Richard Robinson, Willard L. Johnson, and Thanissaro Bhikku, *Buddhist Religions: A Historical Introduction*, 5th ed. (Belmont, CA: Wadsworth/Thompson Learning, 2005). For a very readable insider's introduction to basic Buddhist outlooks, see Traleg Kyabgon, *The Essence of Buddhism: An Introduction to Its Philosophy and Practice* (Boston: Shambhala Publications, 2001).

HOW TO PROCEED

Then the primary question becomes, not the *truth* of religions—mine or others—but their morality, their/our treatment of ourselves and others. This could also be phrased as a concern with religions' *utility*, by which I mean their ability to effect meaningful transformation toward kindness, compassion, and non-aggression in their adherents. This question about religions' value and worth is also connected with what I will be discussing as Buddhist concern with *Method*, one member of the Buddhist pair—Wisdom and Method. This arena, Method, is the arena in which debate and contention are appropriate and fruitful—not the arena of non-empirical metaphysical or theological truth-claims. It seems to me to be a mistake to begin with questions about whether there is a universal religious truth, the truth of various religions, their partial truth in relation to mine, or how there could be more than one true religion.

For starters, if there can only be one true religion, then all of us, except for possibly one person, espouse untrue religions, since everyone's religious position is at least slightly different from everyone else's, and probably also different from that person's own position at a different point in life. Even within the various religions theologians have never been able to agree about what is true, so how could some cross-religious truth be derived? Furthermore, religions teach very different things, and I am extremely skeptical about the search for some convergence at a deep level. For example, the generic monotheism that often is acceptable to Jews, Muslims, and Christians is completely unpalatable to me, and it is by no means an inclusive position. Discussions of what religions teach is an integral part of interreligious dialogue, but it is not the place to begin to construct a pluralistic theology of religions.

It doesn't really matter what religious view people espouse if they mistreat themselves or others. No matter how lofty or orthodox their views may be, or how sophisticated their understanding of emptiness may be, their religion is not working properly, is a false religion, if it does not result in kindness and compassion. Thus, people who engage in strong-armed forceful missionary tactics, such as terrorizing people about what will happen to them if they don't convert, are not preaching a true religion, at least as it is being preached and practiced by those particular adherents. Another example of such ethical misconduct in the name of religion concerns those who insist on trying to make everyone in society adhere to their values, for example by trying to outlaw sexual behaviors disapproved of by their particular religion. This kind of attempt on the part of one or more of the existing religions to force universal religious behavior in a religiously diverse world is the only truly negative aspect of religious diversity. The mere existence of differing ideas about religious truth cannot be harmful; only the attempt to do away religious diversity is harmful.

If people are kind and compassionate to one another, to strangers, to animals, and to the environment, why should I worry about whether or not they believe in Jesus Christ as their only savior, regard the Qur'an as the deity's final revelation to humanity, or meditate correctly on emptiness? Would their kindness be improved if they changed their theology? Or, as I was told in my youth, is their kindness irrelevant because they will go to hell for having incorrect theological views and ideas? Mother Teresa and Albert Schweitzer were both headed there, I was assured. Thus we see how bizarre religion can become when doctrinal truth expressed in words takes on ultimate importance. Let us put aside, once and for all, the question of truth in our discussions of the basis for a pluralistic theology of religions. Let us center on questions of ethics not metaphysics; let us focus on the impact our theologies have on our lives rather than searching for a generic theology we can all live with or some wiggle room in our own doctrines that allow for the legitimacy of other religions. It is more important that we learn how to live together than that we all think alike religiously. And since we are never going to all think alike religiously, we must not pin peace and security on theological agreement. Theological agreement is irrelevant to building a better, more peaceful world.

FINGERS POINTING TO THE MOON: WORDS—WHAT THEY CAN AND CANNOT DO

It has always seemed to me that the main problem for people who are uncomfortable with religious diversity and feel that somehow things would be better if we could all agree about religion is that they do not understand what words and ideas can do and what they cannot do. They overestimate the ability of words to communicate the ultimate and the ability of ideas to reach the truth.

I propose that Buddhist methods of working with words and ideas can help us to a genuine theology of pluralism that does not have to smooth out the differences between religions, search for some basic convergence of view, or dream of a "good parts" version of all the available materials.

I begin with a discussion of Wisdom and Method in Buddhism. Wisdom is about how things are, about truth, and Method is about how to get from error to insight, about what works and what doesn't work. Method is the tool kit, the various ways to approach Wisdom. Wisdom and Method are not the same thing. One cannot do the job of the other, and both are always necessary. Furthermore, they must be perfectly balanced. One could have a lot of Wisdom but be totally ineffective due to deficiency in Method. One could have practiced many Methods, but not have a clue about how to use them due to deficiency in Wisdom. This relationship between Wisdom and Method is most often demonstrated by talking about wisdom and compassion. Without wisdom, compassion is easily misspent, but without compassion, wisdom is useless, even counterproductive. Finally, it is important in a discussion of religious pluralism to understand that, while it might seem that Wisdom should be some universal truth, Method is necessarily plural.

Where do religious teachings fit into this dyad of Wisdom and Method? The usual expectation is that religious teachings would have to do with Wisdom rather than Method, because religious teachings purport to be about reality, which would be in the domain of Wisdom. But this would not be the usual Buddhist assessment. Religious teachings are a Method for getting from point A to point B. One could call those points ignorance and enlightenment. What is difficult to understand is that, though one can specify the intellectual, doctrinal content of error, *enlightenment is not a matter of intellectual content, beliefs, words, or ideas.* Because enlightenment is not an intellectual understanding or correct apprehension of reality, there can be false religious beliefs, but there can be no absolutely true religious doctrines, including the Four Noble Truths, the most usual candidate for Buddhism's bottom line about how things are. Religious teachings, even Buddhism's most cherished verbal portraits of reality, are nothing more than a Method; they are not the Truth or the content of Wisdom.

This is the point at which Buddhists begin to talk about rafts and shores, fingers and moons, and so on. One classic, oft-quoted statement makes the analogy: "O bhikkhus, even this view which is so pure, so clear, if you cling to it, if you fondle it, if you treasure it, if you are attached to it, then you do not understand that the teaching is similar to a raft, which is for crossing over, and not for getting hold of."[7] The raft, the teachings, are a method for getting to the other shore, about which nothing is said because there is nothing to say. The famous Zen analogy compares the person who focuses on doctrines to the person who focuses on the finger pointing out the moon and doesn't see the moon. Religious teachings are not the ultimate or absolute truth; they are just pointers to the "moon," which again is not further specified. Unfortunately, it is extremely common for religious people to make the mistake of putting all their attention on the finger, thinking the truth lies there. The "moon" is an experience, not a set of teachings or doctrines, and Buddhist tradition is consistent in saying that while Reality can be experienced, there are no words for that experience. Therefore, Wisdom or truth is not contained in or transmitted by religious teachings, and all religious teachings are in the realm of Method. The Mahamudra and Dzogchen traditions talk of the experience of the "moon" as nakedly seeing the mind as it is.

When you rest in this experience of the mind, which is beyond extremes or elaborations, what is the experience of that like? It is characterized by a profound state of ease, which means an absence of agitation or discomfort. Therefore, the experience is comfortable and pleasant. The term *comfortable* does not indicate pleasure in the sense of something you're attached to, or the pleasure of acting out an attachment or passion. It is simply the absence of any kind of discomfort or imperfection in the nature of the mind

---

[7] Attributed to the historical Buddha and quoted in Walpola Rahula, *What the Buddha Taught* (New York: Grove, 1974), 11.

itself. Therefore, the experience of that nature is characterized by comfy bliss-fulness. This is as close as we can come in words to what you experience when you look at your mind. You can't actually communicate what you experience. It's beyond expression. . . . It is inexpressible, indescribable and even inconceivable.[8] Note the absence of any metaphysical or theological language when the moon of reality is pointed to by language. "Truth," as such, really isn't the issue. The issue is what Methods get one from point A to point B, from confusion to experience that is not confused or mistaken.

At this point, it is easy to see why attachment to views is considered to be such a serious problem by Buddhists. As is well known, attachment or cling-ing is considered to be the root of suffering in Buddhism, and attachment to views is as problematic as any other attachment. Incalculable human misery is caused by people's attachment to their views, their belief that their ideas are *correct*. In fact, it is a Buddhist commonplace to say that all human suffering is ultimately traceable to a thought, a view in someone's mind, which is why it is important to purify one's mind. But purification has much more to do with not being attached to views or doctrines than with getting the right words in our heads or out of our mouths.

In the lore of meditation teachers, there are numberless anecdotes about how much spiritual progress is impeded by views, ideas, concepts, and by the conviction that they are important and true. It usually takes significant time on the meditation cushion just to begin to see how painful, imprisoning, and useless our thoughts, beliefs, and ideas are, how much relief there is in expe-riencing our thoughts without having to believe in them. Thus, from this point of view, it is inconceivable that salvation could be a matter of having the right thoughts or saying the right words, that the sheep are divided from the goats on the basis of their words, thoughts, and beliefs. Words, thoughts, ideas, and beliefs just are not capable to taking us to the experience of Reality.

Therefore, a pluralistic theology of religions does not really need to deal with questions of the truth of the various religions, or worry about the fact that religions teach very different things. Given the limitations of words and concepts to portray Reality, it is completely unsurprising that there are many different verbal attempts to express what those who have seen deeply have experienced. To expect them all to use the same words or eventually to give up the words they have used all their lives in the face of a missionary's ex-hortations is like expecting that all artists would draw the same thing or write the same poem.

The different teachings are a problem only if one believes that the finger (words, doctrines) could actually grab the moon, rather than merely point to it. The moon can be pointed to by many fingers at once, and the fingers could look rather different from one another. (To say they are all pointing at the same moon, so there must be one ungraspable truth, is not the point of

---

[8] The Ninth Gyalwa Karmapa, *Pointing Out the Dharmakaya*, commentary by Khabje Khenchen Trangu Rinpoche (Crestone, CO: Namo Buddha Publications, 2002), 90.

the analogy. Some of the fingers could be pointing at a moon reflected in water, others at a moon in the sky, and still others at a picture of a moon.)

When working toward a pluralistic theology of religions, we should concern ourselves not with the truth of religious teachings but with their utility, with how well they function as Methods to get people from point A to point B. We cannot say much about the experience of Wisdom, but we can usefully say many things about Method. For the strong Buddhist condemnation of words and concepts only applies when words and concepts are mistaken for experience, which means we become the slaves of our words and concepts. Once we understand what they can and cannot do, then words and concepts become our delightful companions, the means for communication and community.

This takes me back to my initial comment that theologies of pluralism should focus on questions of ethics, on questions of how we treat ourselves and others, not on questions of metaphysics. What Methods promote decency and kindness? Which Methods detract from decency and kindness, and perhaps even promote hatred and discord? Since all religious beliefs, doctrines, and teachings are in the realm of Method, not the realm of Wisdom, we can now have a discussion of religious doctrines focusing, not on whether or not they are true (they aren't), but on whether or not they are useful.[9] Such a discussion would be long and fruitful, and would probably lead to the conclusion that most or all religions have some useful Methods, and most or all religions have at times fallen into Methods that promote suffering. When we put the debate on this plane, which is where I think it belongs, I doubt we will find absolute winners or losers.

Buddhism has always suggested that there are multiple Methods rather than only one way to go. In fact, most versions of Buddhism teach that there needs to be internal diversity within Buddhism, simply because people are at different stages of development and need Methods appropriate to their stage of development. The variety of Methods provided includes a variety of doctrines and religious practices. When used as Methods, doctrines can help a lot, and different doctrines provide for different needs. The same is true of various religious practices. Some people will never be good meditators, and others have a limited appetite for devotion. Phrased as the "84,000 dharma gates" or the "variety of skillful means like the rainbow," this multiplicity has not been regarded as a flaw, either in the religion or in the people who need different Methods from one another. I find no hint in Buddhist thought that in an ideal world there would only be one dharma gate and that everyone would practice and think in the same manner. (However, Buddhists have argued about whose list of 84,000 dharma gates is best. Buddhists of all stripes expect internal diversity, but they don't all approve of sectarian divisions within Buddhism.)

---

[9] For a very helpful discussion of which religious methods promote hatred and discord rather than peace and harmony, see Charles Kimball, *When Religion Becomes Evil* (San Francisco: Harper and Row, 2002).

Regarding the question of Buddhism's own attitudes toward other religions, I suspect most Buddhists historically have felt that Buddhism was the best choice to make. Indeed, I feel that way myself; otherwise, I wouldn't have made that choice. But I don't think that because Buddhism works well for me, therefore it is the best choice for everyone, and I suspect that a similar attitude has been common throughout Buddhist history. I don't think most Buddhists would ever have thought that only Buddhists could attain enlightenment, though I'm sure most thought it was easier if one had access to Buddhist teachings and practices. But since enlightenment is experiential rather than a matter of perfect understanding of Buddhist teachings, it would be illogical to hold the doctrinal opinion that others could not experience that state of being (though there have been Buddhists who have claimed that Buddhist *women* simply could not get there). I don't think most Buddhists would ever have had problems with what is generally called the inclusivist position in discussions of religious pluralism. In fact, many Buddhists throughout history have lived, in one way or another, with multiple religious belonging. Buddhism has rarely been the sole religious identity even of Buddhists, so how could they deny that there is value in other religions? (Notice how these common terms in discussions of religious diversity imply the monotheist model of rigid, impervious boundaries between religions.)

What of the position commonly called pluralism, which would claim that no religion has all the answers and that all the great religions could learn something from other traditions? Again, I suspect that in the broad sweep of Buddhist history, such pluralist learning has occurred, though usually not as the result of a conscious process. How much does the style of Zen Buddhism owe to Taoism? East Asian Buddhism even lost the heavy emphasis on rebirth within the samsaric six realms so dominant in Indian, Southeast Asian, and Tibetan forms of Buddhism. In the modern world, one of the most interesting pluralist conversations would be the conversation between traditions that emphasize justice and righteousness and traditions that emphasize compassion and kindness. In my own work, I have introduced the possibility of a "prophetic voice" within Buddhism.[10] This is certainly in line with pluralist projects, though many Buddhists have been unhappy with the suggestion.

CONCLUSION

In this essay I have tried to suggest that the most useful contribution Buddhists can make to the discussion of pluralistic theology of religions is to push the insight that words, thoughts, ideas, doctrines, teachings, and so forth are only and nothing more than fingers pointing to a moon. They are

---

[10] Rita M. Gross, *Buddhism after Patriarchy: A Feminist History, Analysis, and Reconstruction of Buddhism* (Albany, NY: State Univ. of New York, 1993), 132–35; and Rita M. Gross and Rosemary Ruether, *Religious Feminism and the Future of the Planet: A Buddhist-Christian Conversation* (New York: Continuum, 2001), 163–86.

very limited in what they can do. They should never be regarded as bearers of ultimate truth but only as possibly useful Methods for human transformation toward kindness and compassion. However, as Methods, their potential should not be underestimated. The focus of discussion should change from concern about truth in religion to usefulness in religion, defining usefulness as that which enables us to live more comfortably in an inevitably diverse world. Those most uncomfortable with religious diversity also have a very high opinion of what words and concepts can accomplish, so this discussion is vital. They tend to regard words as somehow conveying ultimate truths, which has led to a great deal of suffering.

If you say something different from me about deity, ultimate reality, what happens after death, or any other such weighty matters, where does the problem lie? If you say that my views, different from yours, endanger my ultimate well-being, how can you possibly give a demonstration of that? If your views promote hostility and hatred, that is a problem and must be dealt with. But if you believe that Jesus Christ is the only savior for all people, and I can't make any sense of that view, what's the problem? The only problem would be your trying to impose belief in Jesus on me in any form, however subtle, or my doing the same regarding my views.

The first agenda of pluralistic theology is to learn how to live comfortably, cooperatively, and without arrogance in a religiously plural world. Many religions still have a lot to learn on that score, and I think Buddhist analyses of what words and doctrines can and cannot do would help a great deal in that agenda. The second agenda is truly to appreciate and learn from one another, but that is more difficult when some traditions still overestimate the utility of their specific words and doctrines.

8

A Pluralistic View of Religious Pluralism

SALLIE KING

I am a Quaker, and I am a Buddhist. (For those of you not familiar with Quakerism, also known as the Religious Society of Friends, it is a branch of Protestant Christianity.)[1] In the mid-1990s I had occasion to give a lecture on Buddhism and Quakerism at an annual Quaker gathering. As I rose to speak, I saw about fifteen hundred Quakers, or Friends, as we call ourselves, in the audience, and I could not resist asking them this: "If you have taken Buddhism into your spiritual life in some way, would you please stand up." About 85–90 percent of the room stood up. So I am by no means the only one who feels a serious affinity between Buddhism and Quakerism and who has brought the two together. Many have done so, to some degree. However, not many go as far as I in claiming a double religious identity.

I have held this double religious identity for about the last twenty years. As this identity has evolved, my view of religious pluralism has evolved with it, drawing, primarily, upon the resources of both Quakerism and Buddhism that most significantly shape my religious thinking. I speak in this essay with this double voice.

I begin by reviewing my understanding of the kind of thing that religion is; much of my understanding of religious pluralism is implicit in my understanding of religion.

---

[1] Contemporary Quakerism has several forms. Throughout this essay, I am referring to the form of Quakerism associated with the Friends General Conference. This branch of Quakerism maintains the original Quaker practices of unprogrammed Meeting for Worship and eschewal of paid ministry.

RELIGIONS ARE TOOLS

This understanding I take from Buddhism. A prominent text in the Buddhist tradition is the "Parable of the Raft."[2] In this *sutta*, the Buddha compares the *Dhamma*—that is, his teachings, Buddhism itself—to a raft, something to take us from this shore of *samsara* (the realm of ignorance and suffering) to the other shore of nirvana (the realm of wisdom and freedom). A raft, as he points out, does not transport one passively but requires one to make an effort if one wants to reach the other shore. A raft, moreover, is of no use once one actually reaches the other shore; one should leave it aside and go on one's way. Just so, says the Buddha, Buddhism is a vehicle, a tool, for helping us to transport ourselves from our present condition to the condition of enlightenment. It is not the end, it is a means; it is to be left aside when one has realized the goal. That is, Buddhism relativizes itself; it subordinates itself to Truth. It declares categorically that it is not itself the Truth; it is a vehicle or tool for realizing Truth. From this starting point in early Buddhism develop such well-known Buddhist teachings as the Zen Buddhist declaration that all of Buddhism (and, implicitly, all religious teachings of whatever origin) is no more than a "finger pointing at the moon." What we seek is the moon. We are repeatedly advised not to mistake the finger for the moon.

Obviously, on the basis of this premise one could assert that Buddhism is the best tool for reaching the goal of enlightenment, and many Buddhists do so. It is rather difficult, on this premise, however, consistently to hold to the kind of exclusivist view that one can hold on the basis of a claimed divine revelation. Certainly the door is open, on the basis of this premise, to a pluralistic view that sees many religions as potentially usable vehicles to Truth.

Quakers do not generally explicitly speak of Quakerism as a method. One exception to this generalization comes from a classic study by Howard Brinton, who writes:

> Quakerism is primarily a method, just as science is primarily a method. Quakerism includes also a certain body of beliefs, as does science, but in both cases these beliefs are accepted because they have been arrived at by experts using the proper method. They can be modified by further use of the same method by which they were arrived at in the first place.[3]

While Brinton is one of the few Friends to have thought to put it this way, the reality behind his reference to Quakerism as a method is one that most

---

[2] *Alagaddupama Sutta, Majjhima Nikaya,* 228–29.

[3] Howard H. Brinton, *Friends for 300 Years* (Wallingford, PA: Pendle Hill Publications, 1952), xiii.

Friends would recognize: Quakerism is a form of practice that, Quakers believe, opens one to experience of the divine. Quakerism has no creed or particular theology and has, over the centuries, adamantly refused to define itself in this way. Instead, Quakerism is defined by certain core practices, the most important of which is the unprogrammed Meeting for Worship in which Friends gather in silence, still their thoughts, and open themselves to the leadings of the divine Spirit. Other Quaker practices such as Meeting for Business, worship sharing, clearness committees, queries, and so on are all methods by which Friends attempt to open themselves to be in touch with, and guided by, the divine. Thus Quakerism, too, is not an end in itself, not the embodiment of ultimate Truth, but a means, a method, a set of practices, the aim of which is to gain the individual (and, important in Quakerism, the group) access to the divine Spirit.

The point here is not to compare Quakerism and Buddhism. The point is to see how each tradition is open to religious pluralism. Inasmuch as both religions see themselves as means to an end, each implicitly relativizes itself. Neither is bound to claim for itself "possession" of ultimate Truth, much less exclusive possession of ultimate Truth. They do not think in those terms. They do claim that they are vehicles to such Truth—good, reliable vehicles. That, in itself, says nothing about whether others also may be such vehicles, but it does leave the door open to such a view. The Dalai Lama, for one, does draw the pluralist conclusion from the view that religions are tools:

> In my own case, I am convinced that Buddhism provides me with the most effective framework within which to situate my efforts to develop spiritually through cultivating love and compassion. At the same time, I must acknowledge that while Buddhism represents the best path for me—that is, it suits my character, my temperament, my inclinations, and my cultural background—the same will be true of Christianity for Christians. For them, Christianity is the best way. On the basis of my conviction, I cannot, therefore, say that Buddhism is best for everyone.[4]

For the Dalai Lama, since religions are tools, given that people differ in significant ways from each other, it is easy to see that while some religions will suit some people best, other religions will suit other people best.

THE UNIVERSAL PRESENCE
OF THE LIGHT/BUDDHA NATURE WITHIN

Mahayana Buddhists, such as myself, work with the teaching of the Buddha Nature, which states that "all sentient beings possess the Buddha Nature."

---

[4] His Holiness the Dalai Lama, *Ethics for the New Millennium* (New York: Riverhead Books, 1999), 225–26.

The Buddha Nature teaching arose in response to the question whether all people can and will, eventually, attain enlightenment. The answer that Mahayana Buddhism came up with was yes, all people (actually, all sentient beings) can and will eventually attain enlightenment, or Buddhahood, because their true nature is Buddhahood and this Buddha Nature is present in everyone.

This teaching means not only that all persons are *potential* Buddhas, but also that the "true nature" of humankind is a Buddha's nature. We have a Buddha within. That is, while on the surface we may manifest various degrees of ignorance, greed, fear, selfishness, and so on, we nonetheless have the nature of a Buddha—compassion and wisdom—concealed within us. Much Mahayana Buddhist practice is designed to get the Buddhist practitioner in touch with the Buddha within. Actualization of one's Buddha Nature is enlightenment. The contemporary Vietnamese Zen master Thich Nhat Hanh writes:

> As an historical person, the Buddha was born in Kapilavastu, . . . got married, had one child, left home, practiced many kinds of meditation, became enlightened, and shared the teaching until he died at the age of eighty. But there is also the Buddha within ourselves who transcends space and time. This is the living Buddha, the Buddha of the ultimate reality, the one who transcends all ideas and notions and is available to us at any time.[5]

Quakers have a remarkably similar teaching in the idea of the Light Within, or Christ Within. Quakerism heavily emphasizes this third Person of the Christian Trinity, the Holy Spirit, that part of the divine that, for Quakers, is present within every human being:

> The Religious Society of Friends holds as the basis of its faith the belief that God endows each human being which a measure of the Divine Spirit. The gift of God's presence and the light of God's truth have been available to all people in all ages. . . . The Divine Spirit, which Friends variously call the Inner Light, the Light of Truth, the Christ Within, That of God in Everyone, has power to reveal, to overcome evil, and to enable us to carry out God's will. Quaker testimonies arise from listening to and obeying this Spirit.[6]

This teaching is similar to the Buddhist teaching in being a principle of enlightenability and in being universal. However, in the Quaker case it is

---

[5] Thich Nhat Hanh, *Living Buddha, Living Christ* (New York: Riverhead Books, 1995), 34–35.

[6] Baltimore Yearly Meeting, *Faith and Practice of Baltimore Yearly Meeting of the Religious Society of Friends* (Sandy Spring, MD: Baltimore Yearly Meeting, 1988), ii, 12.

explicitly stated that this principle is divine, and moreover, the moral implications of the idea are drawn out.

Most significant for us is the fact that belief in this principle is the root of a prominent strain of religious universalism present in Quakerism since its origins. A famous statement from the early American Quaker John Woolman reads:

> There is a principle which is pure, placed in the human mind, which in different places and ages hath had different names. It is, however, pure and proceeds from God. It is deep and inward, confined to no forms of religion nor excluded from any, where the heart stands in perfect sincerity. In whomsoever this takes root and grows, of what nation soever, they become brethren in the best sense of the expression.[7]

Here John Woolman makes perfectly explicit the implication of the universality of the Light Within: since the Light Within is found in all persons of all places and all ages, it cannot be confined to any particular form of religion. Here the religious pluralism of Quakerism becomes completely evident.

In the ancient Buddhist texts such explicit pluralism is not found in connection with the idea of Buddha Nature but, again, the door is open to it, since what is needed for enlightenment is within and therefore not the exclusive possession of a religious institution. Some contemporary Buddhist leaders have become explicit in their pluralism. Thich Nhat Hanh sees Jesus in the same way that he sees the Buddha:

> As the child of Mary and Joseph, Jesus is the Son of Woman and Man. As someone animated by the energy of the Holy Spirit, He is the Son of God. The fact that Jesus is both the Son of Man and the Son of God is not difficult for a Buddhist to accept.[8]

For Nhat Hanh, there is a historical Buddha and a historical Jesus, a living Buddha and a living Christ. The living Buddha is the Buddha Nature, alive in us. The living Christ is the Holy Spirit, alive in us. On this basis he draws an explicitly pluralist conclusion:

> When we understand and practice deeply the life and teachings of Buddha or the life and teachings of Jesus, we penetrate the door and enter the abode of the living Buddha and the living Christ, and life eternal presents itself to us.[9]

Nhat Hanh does not hesitate to identify the living Buddha (Buddha Nature) and the living Christ (Holy Spirit), both the indwelling of Truth, of Life.

---

[7] John Woolman, quoted in *Faith and Practice of New England Yearly Meeting of Friends* (Worcester, MA: New England Yearly Meeting Friends, 1985), 91.

[8] Nhat Hanh, *Living Buddha, Living Christ*, 36.

[9] Ibid., 56.

RELIGIOUS TRUTH IS EXPERIENTIAL,
NOT DOCTRINAL OR DOGMATIC

Buddhist and Quaker teachings on the Buddha Nature and the Inner Light are important for the present purpose not only in that they are universal, but also in that they are the foundation of the two religions' view that religious truth is experiential, not doctrinal or dogmatic, much less creedal. In 1648, the founder of Quakerism, George Fox, wrote in his *Journal:*

> Now the Lord God hath opened to me by his invisible power how that every man was enlightened by the divine light of Christ; and I saw it shine through all. . . . This I saw in the pure openings of the Light without the help of any man, neither did I then know where to find it in the Scriptures; though afterwards, searching the Scriptures, I found it. For I saw in that Light and Spirit which was before Scripture was given forth, and which led the holy men of God to give them [the Scriptures] forth, that all must come to that Spirit, if they would know God, or Christ, or the Scriptures aright, which they that gave them forth were led and taught by.[10]

In this passage, Fox declares the authority of religious experience, that is, experience of the Inner Light, to be superior to that of scripture. While he is glad to find what he sees as confirmation of his experience in scripture, it is clear that what he relies upon is his experience. Scripture, he declares, is but an expression given forth from the Inner Light. It is more or less the traces left behind by the living Spirit.

In a similar vein, another early and esteemed Friend, Isaac Pennington, wrote:

> And the end of words is to bring men to the knowledge of things beyond what words can utter. So, learn of the Lord to make a right use of the Scriptures: which is by esteeming them in their right place, and prizing *that* above them which is above them.[11]

What is above scripture, and to be prized more highly than it, is, of course, the Inner Light and the illumination and guidance that it brings. Again and again Quakers declare that it is the Inner Light that is primary, all else being a manifestation of it.

That religious truth is experiential, rather than doctrinal, is foundational in Buddhism. The Buddha himself was a man who became the Buddha because of his enlightenment experience, a form of experience that both discloses religious truth and radically transforms the person. Buddhism is a

---

[10] George Fox, *Journal*, ed. John L. Nickalls (1952), 33.
[11] Isaac Pennington, *Letters*, ed. John Barclay (1828), 39–40; Letter XVI, undated.

method or path designed to lead its practitioners into this kind of experience. Buddhism is a religion whose approach is not faith but *ehi-passika*, "come and see," that is, come and see in one's own experience. The Buddha clearly differentiated between belief and knowledge, insisting upon the latter. In one famous exchange, a people called the Kalamas told the Buddha that they had heard many different teachings from many different itinerant religious teachers and did not know whom or what to believe. The Buddha's advice was this:

> Yes, Kalamas, it is proper that you have doubt, that you have perplexity, for a doubt has arisen in a manner which is doubtful. Now, look you Kalamas, do not be led by reports, or tradition, or hearsay. Be not led by the authority of religious texts, nor by mere logic or inference, nor by considering appearances, nor by the delight in speculative opinions, nor by seeming possibilities nor by the idea: "this is our teacher." But, O Kalamas, when you know for yourselves that certain things are unwholesome . . . and wrong, and bad, then give them up. . . . And when you know for yourselves that certain things are wholesome . . . and good, then accept them and follow them.[12]

In short, belief, respect, authority, tradition, inference have no spiritual value; only actual *knowledge* is of value, that is, indubitable knowledge based in one's own life experience. This kind of attitude, while sometimes neglected, has remained important in Buddhism to this day; experiential knowledge is what Buddhism is all about. In Zen Buddhism, Bodhidharma's famous saying that Zen is "not founded on words or scripture" and the famous painting of Zen monks gleefully burning books and scripture are dramatic ways of making the same point: truth is found in one's own experience; it does one no good to rely on the secondhand source of the traces of other peoples' experience, left behind in books. Thich Nhat Hanh writes:

> The Buddha did not present an absolute doctrine. His teaching of non-self was offered in the context of his time. It was an instrument for meditation. But many Buddhists since then have gotten caught by the idea of non-self. They confuse the means and the end, the raft and the shore, the finger pointing to the moon and the moon. There is something more important than non-self. It is the freedom from the notions of both self and non-self. For a Buddhist to be attached to any doctrine, even a Buddhist one, is to betray the Buddha. It is not words or concepts that are important. What is important is our insight into the nature of reality and our way of responding to reality.[13]

---

[12] *Anguttara Nikaya* (Colombo, 1929), 115, cited in Walpola Rahula, *What the Buddha Taught*, rev. ed. (New York: Grove Press, 1974), 2–3.

[13] Nhat Hanh, *Living Buddha, Living Christ*, 54–55.

There is an important corollary to the view that religious truth is experiential and not doctrinal: while both Buddhists and Quakers do, of course, speak, they are, at heart, suspicious of doctrinal formulations of religious truths. A twentieth-century Friend, celebrating the good relationship between Quakerism and science, wrote:

> Religious creeds are a great obstacle to any full sympathy between the outlook of the scientist and the outlook which religion is so often supposed to require. . . . It would be a shock to come across a university where it was the practice of the students to recite adherence to Newton's laws of motion, to Maxwell's equations, and to the electromagnetic theory of light. We should not deplore it the less if our own pet theory happened to be included, or if the list were brought up to date every few years. . . . So too in religion we are repelled by that confident theological doctrine which has settled for all generations just how the spiritual world is worked.[14]

The contemporary Zen teacher Thich Nhat Hanh composed a precept stating:

> Do not be idolatrous about or bound to any doctrine, theory, or ideology, even Buddhist ones. All systems of thought are guiding means; they are not absolute truth.[15]

With respect to religious pluralism, if religious truth is experiential, rather than doctrinal, then there will be no impulse to identify the particular verbal teaching of a particular religion as Truth itself, or belief in it as necessary for salvation. If religious truth is experiential, and especially if that religious experience is universally available, then it is not the possession of any religion and not under any religion's control. It is outside of all that, something that is available to human beings simply by virtue of our being human.

Moreover, given that Truth is experiential, another corollary follows: language that attempts to express religious Truth can never be fixed but is, on the contrary, in principle open to ongoing efforts to express the inexpressible. Quakers call this ongoing revelation or continuing revelation. This is the idea that just as, in the past, experience of the Spirit led to the composition of the Bible, Spirit continues to lead people today and throughout time in ongoing revelation just as valid and authoritative. George Fox is famous for having challenged the preachers in churches, saying, "You will say, Christ saith this, and the apostles say this; but what canst thou say?"[16]

---

[14] A. Stanley Eddington, *Science and the Unseen World* (1929), 88–91, cited in *Faith and Practice of New England Yearly Meeting*, 57–58.

[15] Thich Nhat Hanh, *Interbeing: Commentaries on the Tiep Hien Precepts*, ed. Fred Eppsteiner (Berkeley, CA: Parallax Press, 1987), 27.

[16] Testimony of Margaret Fell Fox, *Journal of George Fox*, II, 512, bicentenary edition, cited in Brinton, *Friends for 300 Years*, 16.

Thich Nhat Hanh puts together the language of religion as a method, of the divine within, of religious pluralism, and of ongoing revelation in the following Buddhist-Christian idiom:

> Jesus said, "I am the door." He describes Himself as the door of salvation and everlasting life, the door to the Kingdom of God. Because God the Son is made of the energy of the Holy Spirit, He is the door for us to enter the Kingdom of God.
>
> The Buddha is also described as a door, a teacher who shows us the way in this life. . . . But it is said that there are 84,000 Dharma doors, doors of teaching. If you are lucky enough to find a door, it would not be very Buddhist to say that yours is the only door. In fact, we have to open even more doors for future generations. We should not be afraid of more Dharma doors—if anything, we should be afraid that no more will be opened. . . . Each of us, by our practice and our loving-kindness, is capable of opening new Dharma doors.[17]

With the universal presence of the Spirit/Buddha Nature, ongoing revelation, or the opening of new Dharma doors, is the norm to be expected.[18]

EPISTEMOLOGICAL TRANSCENDENCE

It should be obvious by now but is still worth making explicit, that in this view, religious Truth is epistemologically transcendent. It cannot be conceptually known in any final or adequate way. There are two aspects to this understanding of epistemological transcendence. First, concepts are tied in

---

[17] Nhat Hanh, *Living Buddha, Living Christ*, 38–39.

[18] My readers might still want to challenge my double-voicedness, saying, Despite your views on religious language, these two paths are still incompatible, inasmuch as Quakerism affirms that, ultimately, there is something there (that you call Spirit), while Buddhists do not affirm that there is anything there, in any sense; there only is emptiness, an absence of something. While there is plenty here that philosophers, scholars, and theologians could discuss, at the end of the day I do not find an incompatibility here. If one held to a full-bodied Christian theology, there could be a problem. But Quakers have already taken a major first step. Many Quakers already shy away from unreserved affirmation of God as "a being," moving in the direction of a vague "Spirit." Quakers recognize many concepts of God in the Bible. Quakerism makes it possible to leave aside the God of classic theology understood as "a being" (though many Friends certainly accept that theology) and to embrace the God in whom we "live and move and have our being" (Acts 17:28). While Buddhism tends to take a resolutely apophatic path, a reality in which we live and move and have our being, or a reality that could be called Spirit, is not necessarily outside the pale of Buddhist thought, as is evident in the importance in Buddhism of Dhamma/Dharma (which means Truth and Reality, as well as the Buddhist teachings) and the great respect, in some branches, shown to something called Mind.

with language and culture. But Truth as revealed by the Inner Light or Buddha Nature is not of that nature. Therefore, language and concepts don't fit it well. Second, the Truth of the Inner Light or Buddha Nature is vast beyond our measuring. Whatever we might want to think or say with respect to it would be radically inadequate.

FORM AND EMPTINESS

The Mahayana Buddhist idea of form and emptiness is a useful tool for expressing the relationship between religious Truth and the effort of religions to express that Truth. When we say that that Truth is empty to us, we refer to its epistemological transcendence. The empty nature of Truth is its lack of a permanent, fixed absolute form that we can grasp, name, or say. Truth transcends our ability to definitively grasp, name, or conceive it. This we know. And yet, we believe that we have had a little experiential taste of that Truth. Therefore, we cannot resist pointing our finger at the moon. The urge to speak of it seems innate to us. We must manifest in some form our sense of our relationship with it, our sense of what it means to us. So we always, again and again, express the emptiness in some form, knowing always that none of those forms is adequate or ever can be adequate. This is the dialectic of our religious life. We know that no language, no ritual, no symbol, no form of any kind is an adequate expression of the Truth. Yet without some form we cannot open our mouths, we cannot support each other in our seeking, we cannot even point at the moon. So we do our best, again and again, to express emptiness in form. The danger is that we come to love our forms so much, we become so attached to them that we forget that they are not the Truth, not the moon, only the pointing finger.

As we have seen, both Quakerism and Buddhism see themselves as means to the religious end, not as possessors of the ultimate Truth. Maintaining a strong sense of the "unpossessability" of ultimate Truth, they require forms that can express this unpossessability. But does not a form, by its very nature, attempt to "capture" the Truth?

Quakerism's strategy for avoiding this problem is to strip the form down to its barest possible bones. Friends meet for worship in an unadorned room, or perhaps outdoors, in silence. They attempt to still their thoughts and open themselves to the presence of the living Spirit, "waiting upon the Lord." If anyone is moved by the Spirit to speak, he or she may do so; male or female, child or elder, the only stipulation is that no one should come to the Meeting for Worship intending either to speak or not to speak. If someone speaks, the others listen but do not respond. That is the entirety of the form. The idea is to avoid forcing the Spirit to take any particular form. "The wind blows where it chooses" (Jn 3:8), and Friends would not constrain it in any way.

In his classic history of Quakerism, Howard Brinton describes early Quaker worship. Though he speaks in the past tense, this form of worship is still practiced in Friends Meetings to this day:

Worship consisted in waiting upon the Lord to hear His voice and to feel His power. Rituals, books, words and songs which were at one time vital expressions no longer for the most part retained their vitality. They were not necessarily expressions of the experience of the worshiper. Quaker worship was designed to prevent the substitution of form for Spirit by omitting forms established in advance of the time of worship and presenting an opportunity, in the silence of waiting, for the Spirit to appear in whatever form it chose to take. What that form would be no one could predict.[19]

Of course, all of this is still a form, but a more bare-bones form is hard to imagine.

Buddhism's strategy is different. In its Mahayana schools, Buddhism has embraced the idea of *upaya*, skillful means. This is the teaching that one should adjust the form of the teaching, the form that Buddhism itself takes, as necessary in order to fulfill the Buddhist goal of assisting people's search for enlightenment. Explicitly devising and embracing this teaching is good evidence of how conscious Mahayana Buddhists were of the relativity of all religious forms, very much including their own, and how intentional they were in making the teaching of the relativity of all religious forms a central part of the Buddhist message. The *Heart Sutra* famously negates the foundational Buddhist doctrines in its awareness that they, like all religious forms, are only fingers pointing at the moon, only skillful means, not absolute Truth. It boldly asserts that this very act of negation is itself the "perfection of wisdom," thereby reaffirming freedom from clinging to views, even Buddhist views, as part of enlightenment.

Quakers and Buddhists, then, should, and often do, recognize that the words and actions of no religion possess the Truth and take all forms of worship, ceremonies, teachings, and so forth with a grain of salt, including their own. Since Truth cannot be contained in any form, what counts is results: Does this form of expression help people to actualize or to be in touch with the Truth that is within them? If so, it is of value. That is the sole criterion that is consistent with their core affirmations. It follows that they should recognize that in the forms of worship, ceremonies, teachings, and so forth of another religion there may potentially be something of value for them, a manifestation of emptiness or Truth that has the ability to speak to them. The Spirit "blows where it chooses"; one cannot know in advance where it might appear. As Brinton wrote, we cannot predict the form it will take. It might well take the form of a teaching from another religion. Thus we need to be open to learning from other religions.

Drawing upon this kind of awareness, twentieth-century Friend Douglas Steere urges Friends to engage in spiritual learning from persons of other religions in a practice that he calls "mutual irradiation." In this practice,

---

[19] Brinton, *Friends for 300 Years*, 16–17.

each is willing to expose himself with great openness to the inward message of the other, as well as to share his own experience, and to trust that whatever is the truth in each experience will irradiate and deepen the experience of the other.[20]

The Dalai Lama also advocates this kind of thing and has himself participated in some historic interreligious spiritual encounters. He writes that it is good

to meet genuine practitioners of different religions. Here you cannot really say "no" to the value of other religious traditions. According to my own religious experience and through personal contacts, my appreciation and knowledge about the deeper value of Christianity grew. These kinds of meetings can give a really powerful understanding about the value of other religious traditions.[21]

RELIGIONS ARE LIKE LANGUAGES

I am a Quaker and a Buddhist, but I do not want to say that these religions "say the same thing." They do not say the same thing; their forms—their languages, ceremonies, and so forth—are quite different. They are different life-worlds, internally quite consistent but, as forms, far apart. Yet, because of their core beliefs about religious experience and religious language, they do not contradict each other in any final way.

Living as a Buddhist and as a Quaker, I have come to see that religions are like languages. The world looks one way within one language and quite different within another. Languages are not really mutually translatable. They are not interchangeable. Something is always lost in translation. Living in the Quaker life-world, one is immersed in a world with a strong flavor of divine and human love; a world of biblical characters, hymns and symbols; a world in which one lives a kind of secular monastic life very much in the world; a world in which one is challenged to live up to the example of one's Quaker antecedents, who spoke truth to power and played major roles in shaping the social and political life of England and America. As soon as one says, "Christ Within" or "Inner Light," all this is implicit.

Living in the Buddhist world, one lives in the world of the serenely smiling Buddha; a world whose vista embraces lifetime after lifetime of countless rebirths held in tension with an invitation to complete selflessness; a world in which one strives to remove all "thought coverings," to erase everything

---

[20] Douglas V. Steere, *Mutual Irradiation: A Quaker View of Ecumenism*, Pendle Hill Pamphlet No. 175 (Wallingford, PA: Pendle Hill Publications, 1971), 8.

[21] His Holiness the Dalai Lama, "Dialogue on Religion and Peace," in *Buddhist Peacework: Creating Cultures of Peace*, ed. David W. Chappell (Boston: Wisdom Publications, 1999), 191.

and plunge again and again into vast emptiness; a world in which one feels one's connectedness with all things and has compassion for all beings, the insect as well as the human. Say "Buddha Nature" and all this is implicit. These worlds overlap, but they are not the same. They are two life-worlds, two languages. On some points they can understand each other deeply; on other points they elude each other. This is exactly why they can learn from each other.

WE KNOW THE PRESENCE
OF THE SPIRIT BY ITS FRUITS

While I do feel a great closeness between Quakerism and Buddhism, and while I do think it right, on principle, for members of the world's religions to learn from one another, I still think it necessary to put some limits on this sharing and mutuality. I don't necessarily want to learn from just anyone, only from those that I respect as expressions of the same Spirit that, I trust, is at work in the religions to which I am committed. Since anyone can start a religion for any reason, such a limitation seems to be necessary. Given my, and my religious traditions', mistrust of doctrine, it follows that I will look to the behavior of respected and revered persons in another religion to determine whether it seems to be a manifestation of the same Spirit by which I attempt to be led. We know the presence of the Spirit by its fruits in behavior. What particular behaviors do I look for?

1. Unconditional love, by which I mean a deep commitment to the well-being of all others, manifesting spontaneously in acts of gratuitous kindness, playing no favorites, except perhaps favoring the most needy.
2. Selflessness, or self-forgetfulness, putting oneself second and others first, manifesting in acts of generosity and perhaps of courage.
3. Nonviolence, gentleness, and kindness as a general rule. Nonetheless, sometimes one still must speak very directly, as when the prophetic voice is used.
4. Avoidance of rigid dogmatism. This is not to say that such a person does not have commitments and beliefs. However, those commitments will be worn with a smile, not a frown; they will not preclude friendship with persons of other beliefs.

In the presence of these behaviors, I know I am in the presence of the Spirit and I hope I am open to learn from the person who manifests them. The major (and, I am confident, many smaller) religions all have saints or the equivalent who manifest these kinds of behaviors. For those of us who believe in the universal presence of the Inner Light, this is no surprise. On the contrary, it is to be expected.

THE SUPREMACY OF SPIRIT

I close by letting my Quaker prophetic voice speak.

From a Quaker perspective, religious experience—the Inner Light—is everyone's most direct access to Spirit or Truth. I am greatly suspicious of any religious institution that uses exalted claims of its authority, its wisdom, or its paternal care that raise fear or use rewards or more subtle tools of influence and conditioning to insinuate itself between humankind and our own Inner Light, claiming, in effect, to speak for God. Any religious institution that claims "we alone possess the Truth; we alone possess access to salvation" errs gravely. The Truth, the divine, and the power of the divine cannot be possessed. To make such a claim is, at best, the sin of pride, the sin of idolatry, the sin of confusing oneself and one's human instruments with the divine. *This* is the true original sin. At worst, such a claim is no more than a cynical arrogation of power by a mere human institution putting itself in the place of the divine. What Quakers call the Inner Light and what Buddhists call the Buddha Nature has, in fact, been known experientially by people in all times and places. It is our most inalienable and precious gift as human beings. It is this that gives us our best access to God, Buddhahood, Truth. To interfere in any way with any person's accessing and actualizing that Inner Light is a grievous sin.

Only God is God. Only the Holy is the Holy. We dare not interfere. The divine of which I speak is radically and universally immanent. I can only celebrate it, wherever it manifests itself, in whatever form, under whatever name. I know for sure that it manifests itself in Christian, Muslim, Buddhist, Jewish, Hindu, Baha'i, indigenous, Taoist, Sikh, and countless other forms. That is in no way a problem. I can only regret, attempt to enlighten, or perhaps challenge any individual, or any institution—governmental, religious, or other—that attempts to control, stifle, suppress, or erase it, in whatever form, under whatever name it manifests itself.

We cannot possess the Truth. We cannot possess Spirit. Spirit possesses us. All religions are but forms attempting to manifest the vast emptiness. A religion is most skillful when it manifests in a way that allows Spirit to present itself but also remembers its own non-ultimacy, its own smallness and non-necessity. With the acceptance of one's own non-ultimacy comes the humility to accept that other religions can manifest Truth, too.

PART IV

Jewish Perspectives

9

Toward a Pluralist Theology of Judaism

MICHAEL S. KOGAN

From its inception, Israelite faith has been characterized by a balance between particularist and universalist themes. Abraham was called to be the
father of a "great nation," centered in a particular holy land. But the ultimate meaning of that nation's life was a universal one: "In you all the peoples
of the earth shall be blessed" (Gn 12:3). In different ages of its history, Israel
has stressed one or the other of these aspects of its divine commission. Today,
as we search for an understanding of Judaism appropriate to the contemporary world, we must revisit these ancient categories of thought, interpreting
them in new and enlightened ways. Conceived narrowly, Jewish particularism could lead us to conclude that God is interested exclusively in one "chosen people," while remaining indifferent to the rest of humanity. Similarly
considered, the universal theme of Israel's bringing blessing to all peoples
could be seen as a call for Jews to attempt to impose their faith on the whole
world. But, if we adopt, as we must, a broad pluralistic interpretation of the
particular and the universal in Jewish tradition, we arrive at a liberating
vision that will enable Judaism to live in a productive and mutually enriching relationship with its sister faiths around the world. Interpreted in the
pluralist spirit, Jewish particularism tells us that Judaism is the faith of the
Jewish people and has no mission to convert the world to its own religious
laws and practices. Similarly, the universal stress of our faith calls us to search
out the image of God in all human persons, to practice reverence for all life,
for all being, and to seek to make real the justice and love of God throughout
God's world.

Pluralism shows us the way to this higher vision. A responsible contemporary Judaism must develop its self-conception in the context of the global
consciousness that is affecting religion as well as all other aspects of world
culture. We must deal with and evaluate the truths revealed to others as well
as those we have had revealed to us. We must determine whether any of our

own claims must be given up in a pluralistic world. And we must decide what our role is to be in the new global environment as we continue to strive to live up to our divine calling to be a blessing to all the world's peoples.

JUDAISM AFFIRMS PLURALISM

Judaism is a faith that already contains elements of pluralism, for while Judaism views itself as the true faith of the Jewish people, it does not insist on a world in which everyone is Jewish:

> For all the peoples walk
>   each in the name of its god,
> but we will walk in the name of the LORD our God,
>   forever and ever. (Mic 4:5)

Judaism gladly accepts converts, but would-be converts are always told that they need not become Jews in order to live lives acceptable to God. The specific belief system and laws of conduct Judaism has developed are incumbent upon Jews only. What is universal in Judaism are certain ethical principles that are true for all peoples.

The *Tosefta*, a second-century rabbinic text, contains a universal moral code based on God's words to Noah's offspring following the flood. There were, of course, no Jews at Noah's time. The teaching was given for the guidance of all peoples. Its seven rules prohibit blasphemy, idolatry, murder, theft, sexual abominations, and cruelty to animals, and require all people to establish courts of law to govern their societies. Non-Jews can live lives pleasing to God by obeying these seven precepts. The requirements for a full Jewish life are much more stringent. One source lists 613 commandments given to Jews. Now, later Jewish sources may set much higher standards for Gentile conduct than these seven rudimentary laws, but the principle has not changed. There are two basic categories of revelation: one for Gentiles, one for Jews. Both are genuine revelations from God. Both are true. That is why Judaism does not actively seek out converts. Any religion that leads its adherents to live moral lives is, to that extent, true. Thus conversion to Judaism, while possible, is not necessary. Judaism believes in a universal ethic but not a universal theology. While holding that there is one God, Jews expect that different peoples will conceive of divinity in widely differing ways.

REVELATION IS BOTH PARTIAL AND REAL

This pluralist tendency, present in Judaism since biblical times, must now be developed further as we engage in full dialogue with those of other faiths. As we do so, we expect those of other religious communities to do the same. We are especially gratified to see Christianity moving in this direction.

There is no question that pluralism of some sort is exactly what Jews would like Christians to adopt. We hold that our covenant with God is eternal, unaffected (as regards the conduct and faith of Israel) by the coming of Jesus of Nazareth. Pluralists will recognize and respect our faith, in its own integrity, not subsumed under some larger Christian conception (inclusivism) or rejected as invalid since Calvary (exclusivism).

But, while Jews welcome such views, there is a problem with some pluralist interpretations of the world's religions. What is the origin of the world's faiths? Are all the great religions worthy of equal respect as noble products of elevated human imagination? Do communities of people develop religious systems in their attempts to conceive of what John Hick has called the "Real," the ultimate ineffable "isness" beyond all human conception?[1] Surely, this view is true in part. But it ignores the divine role in the establishment of religion.

Does any religion understand itself in exclusively human terms? Certainly, none of the Western religions does. Judaism, Christianity, and Islam are founded on *revelation*. This is not some out-of-the-way, trivial, or easily ignored claim; it is of the essence of these religions. It is among their central convictions. Judaism does not see itself as the product of a group of people who project their concept of God onto the void—or even the "Real." The faith of Israel stands or falls on the conviction that the God of Israel, who is the Lord and Monarch of the Universe, has elected this people to be God's witness in the world. Israel is to proclaim God's sovereignty, keep God's laws, and build God's kingdom on this earth.

The moral, ethical, and spiritual message Israel brings to a sometimes receptive, sometimes resisting world is the content of the revelation it has received from the Holy One. For not only does God reveal the divine existence to Israel, God also reveals commands, propositions, and goals. In short, revelation has a *content*; this content is found in scripture and is filtered through human responses down through the ages. Of course, it is human beings who hear the divine voice as they are able, and it is human language in which that voice is expressed. I am not propounding a biblical fundamentalism or denying the human element in the revelatory process. Tradition tells us that "the Torah speaks in the language of humanity."[2] But, at the same time, those humans who have received and passed on in human words the word of God have been acutely aware that what they were transmitting, they had *received*. God's word is not identical with the human words that express it, but it is borne aloft by them as they struggle to articulate the divine message. Religions based on revelation give up that self-understanding at their peril. Religious persons know that they are "addressed" by God, and they feel called upon to respond.

---

[1] John Hick, *A Christian Theology of Religions* (Louisville, KY: Westminster John Knox Press, 1995).

[2] Talmud: Berachot 31b.

Whether the command is "Thou shalt not murder" or "Honor the Sabbath day," whether they consider the election of Israel or the gift of the holy land, religious Jews feel in the very fiber of their being the summons of their God. The central command is "Hear, O Israel!" Israelites know themselves to be addressed, to be the object of God's attention, concern, and command. They understand themselves as being understood by God; they see themselves as being seen by God. They stand before God, and they know before whom they stand. This is the very essence of Jewish self-understanding. For believing Jews, their religion is not a human projection but the result of an original divine outreach to humanity. The God of the Bible is a God who reaches down to touch human creatures and make them subjects of God's earthly kingdom.

Some pluralists assert that Jews and members of other religious communities are only accidentally adherents of this or that faith. Essentially they are seekers of meaning and fellow travelers on the spiritual highroad to the "Real." But, for believers, their identities as Israelite or Christian or Muslim is no accident of time or place. Jews know that they were chosen by God as Israelites at Sinai, long before their individual births. Thus, from the perspective of Judaism, there is no such thing as a purely "cultural Jew" or "ethnic Jew." Every Jew is a Jew religiously, even those who do not practice their religion. They are Jews religiously because they have been chosen and commissioned by Israel's God to be among God's witnesses on this earth. "'You are my witnesses,' says the Lord" (Is 43:10). They may be good witnesses or poor ones, but they are witnesses nevertheless. What they do or do not do reflects upon the people Israel and its Heavenly King. Even the frenzied energy with which some Godless Jews proclaim their alienation from their people and its God and the Jewish apostate's frequent leadership of groups and movements devoted to removing God-consciousness from ever greater areas of human life attest to the power of God's call. Jews hear that call in their very marrow, and they respond with humble obedience or with energetic defiance. One only attempts to silence a voice that one has heard.

This compelling sense of being commanded by God and of being shaped and defined by that command is missing in much of the pluralists' writing on religion. It is, of course, correct that no faith tradition and certainly no individual can know God entirely as God is. No revelation can exhaust the inexhaustible. "You cannot see my face; for no one shall see me and live" (Ex 33:20), says the Lord. And yet God goes on to describe aspects of the divine life to Moses:

> The LORD, the LORD,
> a God merciful and gracious,
> slow to anger,
> and abounding in steadfast love and faithfulness.
>
> (Ex 34:6)

All of these terms are, to be sure, relational. They describe not the divine essence, but God in interaction with humanity. God is merciful—to whom?—to us! God abounds in steadfast love—for whom?—for us! All that we can say of God—can know of God—is revealed in the life God deigns to share with us, the creatures whom God loves. The divine totality is, of course, hidden from finite human beings. But that does not mean that we can know nothing of God or that all that we can know is a human projection. God is not wholly unknowable because God has chosen to reveal some aspects of the divine self to us. We only know of God what God has told us. This is not human speculation, but divine self-disclosure.

Revelation's content goes beyond commands and goals for human life. We dare to believe that the God of the universe has in some humanly unspeakable way invited us into the very divine life, has shared it with us insofar as we are capable of understanding it. What has been revealed may be only the tiniest fraction of the divine totality, but it is, nevertheless, as real a part of that totality as the inconceivably greater part that remains hidden.

This is what revealed religions claim, and those who call themselves theologians of these religions dare not dismiss these claims. If they do, they cease to represent the traditions they are attempting to articulate in new and creative ways. Theologians interpret the claims of their respective faiths. They may conceive them in radical formulations. But they may not simply ignore them any more than they may reject them outright. If they do, they become philosophers of religion engaged in free-lance theorizing, making their way through belief systems, accepting or discarding traditional doctrines as they will. But if they choose this path they have ceased to be theologians, properly so called.

Theology is not conducted in a vacuum or from some allegedly objective perch in the middle of the air. Theology must be grounded in a living faith tradition. To be part of a tradition does not mean that one must endlessly repeat the affirmations of one's forebears. It means, rather, that one must march forward in their name. But the steps one takes in this progressive journey must be along a path that is continuous with the one laid out by those who came before. Tradition is never a dead letter; it is a dynamic, growing reality. But new insights must emerge from the living fabric and deal with the categories of thought and experience that have given it its unique character and definition. Revelation need not be conceived as a literal voice from heaven. Nor need one identify the word of God precisely with the human words that bear it aloft. But to give up the sense of being addressed by a power beyond the human is to give up too much.

REVELATION IS BOTH PARTIAL AND UNIVERSAL

Can one be a pluralist while holding to the truth of the revealed nature of one's own faith? Certainly, as long as one makes room for revelation beyond the bounds of one's own group's experience. Jews are in possession of the word of truth through revelation, but that is not to say that theirs is the final word. Other traditions have an equal right to claim their own word of truth. We cannot judge their claims in advance. But we are called by our universal Creator to listen and evaluate and, perhaps, learn something new. It may well be that the God revealed to Israel has revealed other truths to other peoples through other means. The power of revelation is so great, its breadth so wide, that we dare not restrict it to a single word. We are called upon to proclaim with conviction and eloquence the truth that has been revealed to us, while listening to the equally impassioned (and perhaps equally valid) truths others claim to have had revealed to them. This is not simplistic relativism or unreflective universalism. It is an affirmation of the reality of a truth communicated by God combined with a humble admission that we may not be in possession of all of it. In fact, if we are limited human beings, we cannot possess a truth that, in its fullness, is in God alone. By definition, the finite cannot absorb the infinite.

Religious pluralists need give up none of their positive claims or traditional beliefs about what they have received. Only one claim must be surrendered: the single negative claim that there is truth to be found in no faith save our own. This pernicious attitude toward the religious other has been the source of the all-too-real negative tradition in religion, the dark side of the light of faith. Pluralist theologians can affirm a religion that is recognizable to the people in the pews while calling on them to transcend self-satisfied and self-congratulatory attitudes that contradict their own faith in a just and loving God who would not abandon most of the human race to darkness.

JUDAISM AVOIDS EXCLUSIVISM

Certainly Jewish pluralists must affirm the truth of what God has said to us while opening ourselves to the possible truth of others' claims. Such a theory of multiple revelations would be compatible with the views of pluralist Paul F. Knitter.[3] Jews would, in fact, be more open to this approach than would many Christians. Theoretically, at least, Judaism has been more tolerant of other faiths than has Christianity. The history of Jewish bigotry has been real enough, but it has told of a Judaism that has been intolerant primarily of deviations within the Jewish fold. Jewish authorities persecuted Christian sectarians as long as they claimed to be Jews, especially when they claimed to be the only true Israel (people of God). As it gradually became clear in the late first century that the Nazarene or Christian sect of Judaism had become a new Gentile-dominated religion—no internal threat to more traditional forms of Judaism—active opposition by Jewish authorities faded. Nasty remarks and negative evaluations of Christianity continued to be heard, but

---

[3] Paul F. Knitter, *One Earth Many Religions: Multifaith Dialogue and Global Responsibility* (Maryknoll, NY: Orbis Books, 1996), 8.

less and less frequently and with declining intensity. Jews simply assumed that Gentiles would believe strange things and took little interest. There were internal Jewish heresies to combat and sufficient opportunities to express negative impulses within the community.

Christianity, on the other hand, with its missionizing zeal, became obsessed with the Jewish other who refused to recognize the divinity of the Christian Messiah to whom Judaism had given birth. In time, Christian negative attitudes would be directed at Muslims and others, but the Jews were always the most unbearable other for their sister faith, whose universal claims seemed to be mocked by continued Jewish existence. How could the God revealed in Christ, the "universal savior," also will the continued existence of Jewry and Judaism? The monistic view fashioned by the church to deal with Jews became the model for Christian dealings with all other faiths. Henceforth, for Christians, the world would be divided between those already in the fold and those not yet brought to the one universal truth. Jews were seen as enemies of that truth and were consequently subjected to savage persecution by Christian authorities.

Jews, however, while assuming that their truth was incalculably fuller and richer than that granted to others, still recognized that God had spoken to and about Gentiles through those ancient universal ethical rules revealed to the sons of Noah. They never claimed that Israel alone had heard the word of God. No matter how rudimentary and partial God's message to the Gentiles had been, still it was a genuine divine communication. This view, as unsatisfactory as it may be in this age of dialogue, did prevent Jews from claiming the kind of revelatory exclusivism insisted on by Christians. Not only did Jews recognize that non-Jews could live by revealed ethical law, but they were also willing to see such a life as salvific for the religious other. "The righteous of all nations have a share in the world to come."[4] What was missing was any willingness to entertain the possibility that Israel's God may have revealed more to Gentiles than the Noahide laws. Christianity was never seen as having a divine source. Christians would be judged by God strictly in Noahide terms, as would all Gentiles. While no true Jewish theological evaluation of Christianity was attempted, nevertheless, as Gentiles, Christians and others could exist outside of Israel while remaining in touch with Israel's God who was always conceived as the God of all humanity. This is pluralism of a very rudimentary kind, but in proposing that God had spoken and continues to speak to non-Jews, it prevented Judaism from adopting a harsh exclusivism or a muddled inclusivism.

A JEWISH PLURALISM

If all this is true, then Jews will have fewer problems than will Christians in accepting a pluralist theory of multiple revelations. We already recognize

---

[4] Talmud: Sanhedrin 8b.

that God revealed to humanity guidelines for ethical life prior to the creation of the people Israel. And since Jewish tradition has continued to apply these standards to Gentile societies, we know that the revelations to Israel in no way superseded or invalidated the earlier more general revelation. Here the Jewish view of the continued applicability of the Noahide laws stands in contrast to the traditional Christian position regarding the pre-Christian revelations to Israel. Of course, all Christians recognize that the present validity of the New Covenant rests upon the prior validity of the Old. But it was usually assumed (following Paul's reasoning in Galatians rather than in Romans) that, with the coming of the new dispensation, the old had passed away. In contrast, Israel never held a similar view of the Noahide laws. They remained as valid for Gentiles after the creation and election of Israel as they had been before. They continue to offer minimum standards of conduct for Gentile societies.

Thus Judaism subscribes to a "double-revelation" theory that can now be expanded into a multiple revelation theory as we examine and attempt to evaluate the claims of other faith communities in all their particularism. Unlike Christians, who will have to think for the first time of another possible revelation (or revelations) existing side by side with Christianity, Jews have that thought structure already in place. But we now must apply it in ways we never have before, dealing for the first time with the specific claims of other faiths and their followers rather than simply lumping them all together as "Gentiles." Is it possible that the God who addressed the pre-Israelite world in Noah's day has also addressed the non-Israelite world with new revelations? This question cannot be answered a priori. But if we examine each of the great world faiths and find that it leads its followers to elevated lives of spiritual striving, ethical sensitivity, and moral conduct, then we must conclude that there is truth in it. And if its adherents claim that that truth has been received by them through divine disclosure through revelation, what reason would we have to dispute that claim? A pluralist theology of multiple revelations seems best suited to compassing the world's faiths, trying to see them as closely as possible to the way they see themselves.

CONCLUSIONS

At the beginning of the Israelite tradition, God calls Abraham with these words: "Get you out of your land and of your father's house" (Gn 12:1). Get you out! Get out of where you are and go to where you can be. This is a call to self-transcendence at the very beginning of the story of Israel and of the Western religious tradition. Get out of where you are, out into a wilderness, out into trackless desert. Abraham does not know where he is going; he goes by faith, and God says, "I will make you a great nation." Now this cannot mean a great nation in terms of numbers—the Jews are a tiny people—but a great nation in that Israel bears a great message into the world. Now Christians and Muslims are each more than 1.3 billion strong. If Christians and

Muslims take it into their heads to think that they are the only bearers of truth, they are narrow-minded and egocentric, but if we Jews, with at most 15 million people, insist that we are the only bearers of truth, not only are we narrow-minded and egocentric, but we are indulging in a kind of theological madness. Can we seriously entertain the notion that God, having created the 6 billion people now living on this earth, is concerned with the religious welfare of only 15 million? One is led to ask why God bothered to create the rest of them. But this question is ludicrous, as are the exclusivist assumptions on which it is based.

The God who is the loving parent of all people must have provided divine guidance to many cultures and societies in an effort to make the heavenly will known to all. Naturally, such words of revelation would be spoken to many peoples in many tongues, terms and symbol systems. Pluralism would seem to be the theory best suited to account for the wondrous variety of religions flourishing in the world. But what kind of pluralism are we talking about? There are many kinds. There is a plurality of pluralisms. I tend to do pluralism from the inside out, not the outside in. Rather than beginning with pluralist assumptions, I search for elements in our Jewish texts and traditions that are self-transcendent, that lead us inevitably beyond Judaism, out into the world of our sister faiths.

And there we find Christianity, with which we share a book; then Islam, with which we share a foundation of law and radical monotheism. And then beyond, to all the faiths with which we share a commitment to live the life of the spirit and to respect the dignity of every human being. Pluralist principles require self-transcendence and oppose egocentricity, whether an egocentricity of the individual or of the group. Religion in practice is, I think, both self-affirmation and self-transcendence. It calls the self to proclaim the truth it has received, but also to reach beyond the self, whether that self is individual or collective. We must take into account the religious beliefs and practices of others. It has been said that what people have in common is their uniqueness. There is no one theology for all. Every group's theology must recognize and make room for the theologies of others.

But, paradoxically, opposition to any universal theology seems to assume the upholding of a universal ethic. If there is no universally applicable ethic, how are we to distinguish between true religion and false religion, between the divine and the demonic? I accept the pluralist principle that a religion is "true" not because it accords with the true nature of God as God actually is (for who can know the divine nature in its totality?), but because that religion has the power to produce virtuous people. To say this we must hold to a standard of virtue that applies to everyone. So, if we are going to be safely relativist about theology, we must be universal in our ethics.

Jewish tradition teaches us to say in our prayers, "I am but dust and ashes, yet the world was created for my sake." We humans are finite creatures, limited in every way, except perhaps for our yearning, our yearning for the infinite. And this too leads us into pluralism, because our finite theories of the divine cannot compass the infinite divine itself, and yet we yearn to do so. Limited beings that we are, we turn to one another, and to one another's traditions to fill out what our particular visions lack.

Someone has said that all theology is local. In pluralist terms all theories of the divine are restricted by time and place, by language and historical experience. But if we allow these theories to meet, to talk to each other, to enrich each other, then the local begins to expand, ever growing, ever widening, until the vision of a new and wider world may emerge. With that vision, and bearing with us the wisdom we have gained from absorbing the teachings of other traditions, we may go back into our own communities to right wrongs, to smash the idols that isolated communities inevitably carve out for themselves from their fears and their need for ego-gratification.

Religious exclusivism is nothing more than corporate egoism of creed and community. Pluralism must include a humane prophetic witness, which will enable us to deal with our fellow beings of different faiths as well as with our own people, valuing distinctions of culture and belief rather than condemning or denigrating them. Pluralism offers us new structures of thought designed to do just that. How radically new are these structures? They are as new as the indefinite article in speech is unlike the definite article. Instead of being *the* chosen people, my people begin to see themselves as *a* chosen people. Instead of *the* true church, Christians come to see themselves as *a* true church. Nothing has changed in my devotion to my tradition. Yet everything has changed, because the world in which my tradition functions is recognized as filled with chosen peoples and true churches.

In other words, they are "chosen" and "true" in that they are communities that see themselves as chosen to seek out the truth. What a breath of fresh air all this represents! A new vision inspired by the infinite and the eternal to which we seek to draw near. In a world darkened by human self-isolation, by fear and distrust growing out of that isolation and ignorance of the other—the other who is in every case our brother and our sister—in the midst of that darkness pluralists say in the words that Jewish scriptures attribute to divinity itself, "Let there be light!"

There is a famous story in the Midrash, the ancient Jewish collection of legends, about Abraham and the idols. Abraham's father, says the story, was a manufacturer of idols. One day he went out, leaving little Abraham in the idol shop to watch the statues. Abraham had at that moment a revelation of the true God, and he took a club and smashed all the idols except the biggest one; he put the club in the hands of the largest statue. His father came home and said, "What happened here?! All my statues are smashed!" Abraham answered, "Well, they had a fight, and the biggest one killed all the others." His father replied, "What do you mean they had a fight? They are only statues." "Ah," replied Abraham, "then why do you worship them?"

There are idols of thought as well as idols of stone. John Calvin said that the human mind is a factory for the production of idols. And what is true for individuals is true for our religious communities; it is often the communities that produce the idols. Each faith community, I think, generates a particular kind of idolatry unique to it. Catholicism produces "ecclesiolatry," the worship of the church as an institution, rather than God. Protestants have their own form of idolatry. Karl Barth was speaking to a group of Protestants when he said, "You congratulate yourselves because you have no pope; but you have made the Bible into a paper pope." So Protestants produce "scriptolatry"—their version of idolatry, the absolutizing of the text. We Jews produce our own kind of idolatry, which is "ethnolatry"—the absolutizing of Jewish peoplehood, rather than God to whom we are called to witness.

What is idolatry? It is to put any earthly things in place of God. To put anything finite in place of the infinite. To put anything time bound in place of the eternal. A church, a book, a people. But God can also be an idol, if we mean by God only a human conception. Now we have to have human conceptions of God. If God is to impinge on our lives we must have such human conceptions, because we are human beings and we can have no other conceptions. And God must impinge on our lives if we are to call ourselves religious. I am a Jew. I worship the God of Israel. But that God can become an idol if I stop with it and imagine that I possess all of God. The idol is always opaque; the idol is always limited. However, that same conception of God can become a genuine revelation of God if we allow it to become transparent. True self-transcendent religion understands that the Holy One, the *Ein Soph*, the God beyond god, the Desert of the Godhead, the No-Thing, the Thou that cannot become an it, the Light Invisible is shining through the symbols and images revealed in our respective traditions.

Now what do I mean by revelation, how are these ideas revelations of God? Is revelation a truth that comes from God, or does it come from the human self? Well, it is both. It must be both, because the human, according to the scriptures, is created in the divine image. But what does that mean? In Judaism there can be no images of God; there can be no pictures of God. These are forbidden. I think they are forbidden because there already is a divine image and we are it. But surely we are not the image of God in a physical sense. God is imageless, and yet we are in the image of God. Thus humans are fashioned in the image of an imageless God. In Judaism the God who is imageless is also unnameable. We are forbidden to write or even to say the divine name. And yet we Jews know what that name means—God is called "The One who Shall Be" (Ex 3:14), in other words, the endlessly self-transcendent. That is the nameless name of the Eternal One.

If God is unnameable, indefinable, and irreducible to any image or any definition, then so are we, since we are earthly images of God. The human person is always more than any definition can name, always more. The higher religion should be an iconoclastic smashing of all the idols, of all the images that claim to be the totality of God, as well as images created of the human by the various disciplines that we have at all our universities.

Are we social beings? Sociologists say yes. They are right, but we are more. Are we sexual beings? Freudians say yes. They are right, but we are more. Are we economic beings? Marxists say yes. They are right, but we are more. Are we political beings? Yes, the political scientists are right, but we are more. It is the more that makes us human, as it is the more that makes God, God.

Alfred, Lord Tennyson put it well in his poem "In Memoriam":

> Our little systems have their day;
> They have their day and cease to be.
> They are but broken lights of thee,
> And thou, O Lord, art more than they.

Revelation is the breaking of the infinite into the finite to reveal to the finite the infinite life that was already there but in such a way that the finite was unaware of it. This is the infinite life within us, the *nefesh*, or soul. It is a reflection of the infinite life without, the *ruach*, the spirit of God. Revelation makes clear to us that this inner soul is the mirror of the universal spirit, that the infinite macrocosm is reflected in the finite/infinite microcosm. Thus we are introduced to our true nature by the revelation of God who is "more distant than stars yet nearer than the eye" (T. S. Eliot, "Marina").

One path to pluralism is to view all conceptions of God as merely human constructs. But this is only a partial truth. There must be something human in them or human beings could not receive them. But this is just the point. These concepts of God are received, not generated by people. If we insist that positive images of God are human creations and only human creations, we are denying the core experience of religious believers. That experience is of receiving a revelation of at least a part of the divine reality. Without revelation there can be no religion. Without revelation we are left with a form of human spirituality or self-transcendence that is crucial to religion but not sufficient. There must also be a breaking in from beyond the human, a communication from the divine. If theologians do not take this central experience of faith into account, or even deny it, then they will end up speaking for no one and speaking to no one. Our formulations are only valid if they reflect the lived experience of believers.

But it will be objected that the different revelations claimed by the various traditions sometimes contradict one another. How then could one divine reality be the source of them all? But why should God not use the varied languages and symbol systems of the world's peoples to reveal divine truths? Each age, each culture yearns to hear the voice of revelation anew. This is true even within a single faith in which a strong ongoing tradition still remains open to new insights from its transcendent source. If it does not cultivate such openness, it will soon cease to be a dynamic, living faith. Some examples may be of help here.

Jewish tradition insists that we never refer to "the God of Abraham, Isaac, and Jacob." No, we must always refer to the Lord as "the God of Abraham, the God of Isaac, and the God of Jacob." We must do this to remind ourselves that the Holy One is revealed to each new generation in new ways, ways that may be very unlike prior revelations. This does not mean that God changes in the divine essence or totality, whatever that may be. Rather it means that people and circumstances change, and so the divine messages must change so as to speak to those who need to hear them in the situations in which they find themselves. None of these revelations contains the totality of the divine. How could a finite message to finite human beings compass the infinite reality of God? Yet each message is true as a partial revelation of the One who, as infinite divine totality, is forever hidden from us.

In the "Hymn of Glory" chanted in the Orthodox synagogue at the end of the Sabbath morning service, God is described as imaged forth in many apparitions recorded in the Bible:

> I have not seen thee, yet I tell thy praise,
> Nor known thee, yet I image forth thy ways.
> For by thy seers' and servants' mystic speech
> Thou didst thy sov'ran splendor darkly teach,
> And from the grandeur of thy work they drew
> The measure of thine inner greatness too.
> They told of thee, but not as thou must be,
> Since from thy work they tried to body thee.
> To countless visions did their pictures run,
> Behold through all the visions thou art one.
> In thee old age and youth at once were drawn,
> The grey of eld, the flowing locks of dawn,
> The ancient judge, the youthful warrior,
> The man of battles, terrible in war,
> The helmet of salvation on his head,
> And by his hand and arm the triumph led,
> His head all shining with the dew of light,
> His locks all dripping with the drops of night. . . .
> His head is like pure gold; his forehead's flame
> Is graven glory of his holy name.
> And with that lovely diadem 'tis graced,
> The coronal his people there have placed.
> His hair as on the head of youth is twined,
> In wealth of raven curls it flows behind.
> Ruddy in red apparel, bright he glows
> When he from treading Edom's wine-press goes.

The hymn declares that, beneath all these images, God is One, and One who is revealed to God's children as they are able to receive the image that bears the message. To one seer God appears as a youth, to another, an "ancient of days," to a third, a judge, to a fourth, a warrior. And what of the greatest seer of all who saw in one encounter a burning bush, in another a cloud of smoke, and in a third, the back of a human figure? Did any of these sages doubt that it was the same One who was revealed in all these widely varied epiphanies? These images, all part of the Jewish tradition, have no more in common with each other than they do with apparitions of God found in the religious traditions of the East. Varied appearances do not necessarily imply varied sources. If this is true within one tradition, why should it not be true of the many traditions through which God speaks to humanity? To ask which of these appearances is "truest" is clearly to ask the wrong question. To hold that they are too different from one another to arise from a single source is to jump to the wrong conclusion. All come from God. They may seem contradictory, but all are partial but real experiences of an outreach from the divine to the human.

In his First Letter to the Corinthians Paul speaks of himself as having become "all things to all people so that by all means some might be saved" (9:22). With the Greeks he became like a Greek, with the Jews like a Jew. What he wrote to the Galatians was the virtual opposite of what he wrote to the Corinthians. Imagine the chaos that would have ensued if he had mixed up the letters and sent them to the wrong communities! Was Paul contradicting himself? No. He told each group what it needed to hear. Why cannot God do the same thing?

I offer the examples above to support the proposition that God has revealed different truths to different peoples at different times and places. All of them are partial truths designed to guide each group according to its needs. If this view can provide the basis for a pluralist theory of revelation, then pluralism need not deny the truth of revelation as it is experienced in the actual religious life of believers.

True pluralism calls on all the higher religions to recognize the power of revelation in the others. In other words, they come to see the religious other to be of God. God reveals and discloses. God introduces selves to themselves and to each other in all the great religious traditions. I start with Judaism, but from that perspective, Christianity is just here, just at the ends of my fingers, and just beyond is Islam, and then the other great faiths.

But if revelations of the divine and the human are also to be found in Buddhism and Hinduism and Jainism and Sikhism and Taoism, and so on, and so on, then all faiths are true that lead us from egocentricity to participation in the infinite life with all its ethical and spiritual blessings. The important thing is not to know Moses or Jesus or Buddha; the important thing, rather, is to know what Moses and Jesus and Buddha knew, and that is available to us in the contemporary world in a new way. Aided by modern communications and global consciousness we can learn what each of our traditions has to teach us to enrich our lives. When that happens, what those great sages knew is seen not just as human constructs in the earth-bound sense. They lead us from what human beings merely are to what human beings really are: finite bearers of the infinite life "in which we live and move and have our being."

10

Judaism and Other Faiths

DAN COHN-SHERBOK

Recently there has been considerable discussion in Christian circles about the relationship between Christianity and the world's religions. In contrast with such Christian exploration, contemporary Jewish thinkers have paid scant attention to the issue of religious pluralism. Though there is an interest in the development of Jewish-Christian dialogue as well as isolated instances of Jewish-Christian-Muslim encounter, the majority of contemporary Jewish thinkers have not seriously considered the place of Judaism in the context of humanity's religious experience.

A notable exception to this general neglect is a discussion by Jewish theologian Louis Jacobs in *A Jewish Theology*. In a chapter entitled "Judaism and Other Religions," Jacobs stressed that Judaism has always endorsed the view that there is only one God and that the Torah has not been superseded by any other religious tradition. Such a conviction, he believed, compels Jews to declare that the positions of other religions are false if they contradict the Jewish faith. "Far Eastern faiths are either polytheistic or atheistic. The Christian concept of God is false from the Jewish point of view. Judaism similarly denies that Mohammed received a revelation from God which made him the last of the prophets with the Koran in the place of the Torah."[1] Yet despite such an uncompromising stance, Jacobs added that it would be a mistake for Jews to conclude that God has not revealed himself to others or that other religions do not contain any truth. On the contrary, he asserted, the position one should adopt is that there is more truth in Judaism than in other religions.

Another contribution on this topic is by the Israeli Jewish theologian David Hartman. In "On the Possibilities of Religious Pluralism from a Jewish Point of View," he maintained that the Bible contains two covenants—that of Creation and that of Sinai. The Creation covenant is with all humanity; it is universal and for all generations. The Sinai covenant, on the other hand, is

---

[1] Louis Jacobs, *A Jewish Theology* (New York: Behrman House, 1973), 289.

119

with Israel. It is a parallel covenant and embraces other communities. On the basis of this scheme, Hartman argued that God's self-revelation has been to different peoples at various times in history.[2] In a later work, *Conflicting Visions*, he stressed that revelation in history is always fragmentary and incomplete because divine-human encounters cannot exhaust God's plenitude:

> Revelation expresses God's willingness to meet human beings in their finitude, in their particular historical and social situation, and to speak to them in their own language. All of these constraints prevent one from universalizing the significance of the revelation. . . . Revelation . . . was not meant to be a source of absolute, eternal, transcendent truth. Rather, it is God's speaking to human beings within the limited framework of human language and history.[3]

More recently, Orthodox scholar Norman Solomon discussed the issue of religious pluralism in his *Judaism and World Religion*. In a chapter entitled "The Plurality of Faiths," he argued that Judaism is a religion with a mission to all people. In times of persecution, he stated, this universal goal has been overlooked—yet it has never disappeared. In bad times it focuses on the messianic task; in enlightened eras it is expressed in the Jewish quest to work for the improvement of humanity. In pursuing this goal, the "covenant of Noah" (as expressed in the seven Noachide laws) offers a pattern to propose to others without requiring their conversion to Judaism. What is demanded instead is faithfulness to the highest principles of justice and morality. In this context the dialogue of faiths becomes an imperative that emerges through our common mission with other religious traditions. "In this interfaith encounter," he wrote, "we cannot set the bounds of truth; we must listen and try to learn, grow in experience and forge language, remain open to the world around us with its myriad peoples and ways, and read and interpret the words of scripture and sage constantly, critically, in the context of our own age and society."[4]

The chief rabbi of Britain and the Commonwealth, Jonathan Sacks, has also discussed the issue of religious pluralism in his recent book, *The Dignity of Difference*. In this work he argues that today we must accept that God has manifested Godself to others outside the Jewish community:

> Religion is the translation of God into a particular language and thus into the life of a group, a nation, a community of faith. God has spoken to mankind in many languages: through Judaism to Jews, Christianity

---

[2] David Hartman, "On the Possibilities of Religious Pluralism from a Jewish Point of View," *Immanuel* 16 (Summer 1983).

[3] David Hartman, *Conflicting Visions: Spiritual Possibilities of Modern Israel* (New York: Schocken Books, 1990), 247–48.

[4] Norman Solomon, *Judaism and World Religion* (New York: St. Martin's Press, 1991), 244.

to Christians, Islam to Muslims. . . . Only such a narrative would lead us to see the presence of God in people of other faiths. Only such a worldview could reconcile the particularity of cultures with the universalism of the human condition.[5]

These varied responses by Orthodox and non-Orthodox writers point to the need for a more thoroughgoing examination of Judaism and the universe of faiths. The aim of this essay is to offer a basis for formulating a Jewish theology of religious pluralism.

JUDAISM AND OTHER RELIGIONS

Through the centuries Judaism has adopted a relatively tolerant attitude toward other religions. In the biblical period ancient Israelites were encouraged to view the Gods of other peoples as nonentities. In this respect ancient Israelite faith was exclusivist in orientation. Yet foreign peoples were not condemned for their pagan practices. Although the religion of the Jewish people was perceived as the one true faith, there was no harsh condemnation of idolatry. Furthermore, it was the conviction of the prophets that in the end of days all nations would recognize that the God of the Israelites was the Lord of the universe. Thus, there was no compulsion to missionize among nonbelievers. There was hope even for pagan peoples in the unfolding of God's plan of salvation.

In the rabbinic period this tradition of tolerance continued to animate Jewish life. According to the rabbis, all non-Jews who follow the Noachide laws are viewed as acceptable to God. In this context even those who engage in polytheistic practices are admissible as long as the Gods they worship are conceived as symbolically pointing to the one God. Here in these rabbinic sources is the beginning of a form of inclusivism in which foreign peoples—despite their seeming polytheism—were seen as "anonymous monotheists." In the medieval period such writers as Rabbenu Tam applied this rabbinic conception of symbolic intermediacy to Christian believers. In his opinion Christianity is not idolatry since Christians are monotheists despite their belief in the Trinity. Other writers, such as Judah Halevi, formulated an even more tolerant form of Jewish inclusivism: for these thinkers Christians as well as Muslims play an important role in God's plan for humanity by spreading the message of monotheism.[6]

Such a positive stance toward other faiths continued into the early modern period due to the impact of the Enlightenment. In the eighteenth century the Jewish philosopher Moses Mendelssohn argued that the Jewish people were the recipients of a divine revelation consisting of ritual and moral law. Nevertheless, Mendelssohn was convinced that God's reality can be discerned

---

[5] Jonathan Sacks, *The Dignity of Difference* (London: Continuum, 2002), 55.

[6] Judah Halevi, *Book of the Kuzari* (New York: Schocken Books, 1964).

through human reason. Thus all human beings—regardless of their religious persuasion—are capable of discerning God's nature. So Mendelssohn could appreciate Christianity while at the same time adhering to the belief that Judaism is the superior religion.[7] The French scholar Joseph Salvador, for example, believed that in the future Christians would help to bring about a new philosophical religion resembling Judaism; in this respect his positive evaluation of Christianity provided a form of Jewish inclusivism tempered by the scientific spirit of the age.[8] Similarly, German reform rabbi Abraham Geiger argued that Christianity embraces God's revelation to his chosen people, yet Judaism constitutes the ideal faith for the modern age.[9]

During the Age of Emancipation, Jewish thinkers grappled with the currents of Western philosophical thought and in their different ways offered a positive evaluation of both Christianity and Islam. Preeminent among nineteenth-century Jewish writers German theologian Samuel Hirsch maintained that throughout history Judaism struggled to overcome the threat of paganism. According to Hirsch, in this quest Christianity has an important role; however, the Jewish faith as the purest form of monotheism is humanity's ultimate hope for the future.[10] A similar form of Jewish inclusivism was espoused by German reform rabbi Solomon Formstecher, who argued that even though Judaism is the ultimate form of religious life, Christianity and Islam play an important part in the unfolding of God's plan.[11] Such a view was also advanced by another German thinker of this age, Solomon Ludwig Steinheim, who viewed Christianity as furthering God's eschatological scheme.[12] An even more positive assessment of Christianity was fostered by British Jewish writer Claude Montefiore, who stressed that God reveals in different ways throughout history. For Montefiore, the Christian faith is one such disclosure, and Jews can be enlightened by a knowledge of the New Testament. In Montefiore's work there is thus a full endorsement of Judaism with tentative steps toward the formulation of a more pluralistic stance.[13]

The quest to explore the origins of Christianity, its subsequent development, and the relationship between the Jewish and Christian faiths was a major concern of a number of modern Jewish thinkers. Czech writer Max Brod, for example, admired Jesus as a Jewish preacher. Yet he was critical of

---

[7] Moses Mendelssohn, *Judaism and Other Writings* (New York: Cambridge Univ. Press, 1969), 61, 68–69.

[8] Joseph Salvador, *Das Leben Jesu und seine Lehre* (Dresden: Walther's Buchhandlung, 1841), 5ff.

[9] Abraham Geiger, *Judaism and Its History* (Lanham, MD: Univ. Press of America, 1985 [original 1911]), 392.

[10] Samuel Hirsch, *Die Humanität als Religion* (Leipzig, 1854), 243.

[11] Solomon Formstecher, *Die Religion des Geistes* (Frankfurt: Joh. Chr. Hermann'sche Buchhandlung, 1841), 411.

[12] Solomon Ludwig Steinheim, *Die Offenbarung nach dem Begriff der Synagogue* (Leipzig, 1863), 76ff.

[13] Claude Montefiore, *The Synoptic Gospels* (London: Macmillan, 1927), xliii.

Paul's transformation of the Christian faith. According to Brod, Christianity was corrupted through the centuries by the infusion of pagan elements. In his opinion Judaism is the only hope for the future.[14] Such an inclusivist stance was further elaborated by German Jewish theologian Franz Rosenzweig, who regarded Christianity as fulfilling a crucial role in spreading the message of monotheism to all peoples.[15] A similar endorsement of the Christian faith was affirmed by German Jewish leader Leo Baeck, who, like other Jewish writers before him, attempted to reclaim Jesus as an authentic Jewish figure despite his criticism of Pauline Christianity and its negative impact on the growth of Christian theology.[16] Likewise, German Jewish theologian Martin Buber admired Jesus as a typical Jewish figure of the first century who should evoke esteem from the Jewish community.[17] In Jacob Kalusner's opinion, Judaism will eventually become the religion for all people; nevertheless, Jews should acknowledge their debt to Christianity for paving the way for this outcome.[18]

Such reflections about the relationship between Judaism and Christianity were eclipsed by the Holocaust. With rare exceptions—such as the writings of Hans Joachim Schoeps[19]—it was no longer possible for Jews to foster such a positive assessment of Christian origins and the role of Christianity in the unfolding of God's plan for humanity. Instead, many Jews wished to distance themselves from the Christian faith, which they held accountable for the destruction of six million Jews. For Jewry, the death camps came to symbolize the last link in the chain of twenty centuries of anti-Semitism. Despite this rift, several Jewish theologians were influenced by various aspects of Christian thought in attempting to make religious sense of the events of the Nazi period. American Jewish theologian Richard Rubenstein, for example, was profoundly affected by an encounter he had in the 1960s with the dean of the Evangelical Church in East and West Berlin. Provoked to reformulate his understanding of God, he advanced a mystical theology akin to the religious systems of the East.[20] A very different approach has been undertaken by American theologian Emil Fackenheim, who argued that in Auschwitz God issued the 614th commandment. The divine imperative to resist the forces of modern secularism, he believed, was issued to both Jews and Christians. In his writing he cited the example of a Polish Catholic whose reaction

---

[14] Max Brod, *Der Meister* (Gutersloh: C. Bertelsmann, 1952), 88ff.

[15] Franz Rosenzweig, *Der Stern der Erlösung*, vol. 2 (Heidelberg: Verlag L. Schneider, 1930), 200–201.

[16] Leo Baeck, *Judaism and Christianity* (Philadelphia: Jewish Publication Society of America, 1958), 100ff.

[17] Martin Buber, *Two Types of Faith* (New York: Harper, 1961), 65–68.

[18] Joseph Klausner, *Jesus of Nazareth: His Life, Times, and Teaching* (New York: Macmillan, 1964), 406.

[19] Hans Joachim Schoeps, *Paul: The Theology of the Apostle in the Light of Jewish Religious History* (Philadelphia: Westminster Press, 1961).

[20] Richard L. Rubenstein, *After Auschwitz* (Indianapolis, IN: Bobbs-Merrill, 1966).

to the Nazis symbolized such resistance.[21] Two other theologians of the contemporary period—Ignaz Maybaum and Arthur A. Cohen—also struggled to make religious sense of the Nazi onslaught by appealing to Christian theological motifs. In his explanation of God's role in the slaughter of the Jewish people, Maybaum appealed to the themes of Calvary, Golgotha, the suffering servant, and vicarious sacrificial atonement, arguing that God utilized Hitler and the Nazis as instruments to bring about the modernization of Jewish life.[22] Cohen, on the other hand, transformed the concept of *Mysterium Tremendum* (as found in the work of the Protestant scholar Rudolf Otto) in his discussion of the significance of the Holocaust; for Cohen, the Holocaust is the *Tremendum* of the modern age.[23]

So, for nearly four millennia Judaism has in various ways espoused a generally indulgent attitude toward other religions. Unlike the Christian faith with its long tradition of exclusivism, Jews have been encouraged to grant other religions a role in the unfolding of God's purposes. Although such Jewish inclusivism presupposes the superiority of the Jewish faith, it recognizes that God's purposes have been served by other nations and that God has had an authentic encounter with other peoples. Such ideas have been largely confined to a consideration of Christianity, and in some cases Islam. Only occasionally are there references to other religions. Yet there is no denying the inclusivist thrust of centuries of Jewish teaching; religious tolerance has been the hallmark of Judaism through the ages.

A PLURALISTIC MODEL

Given the largely tolerant attitude of Judaism to other faiths, should Jews move beyond such inclusivism? Arguably, the inclusivist position suffers from serious theological defects: inclusivists appear to affirm two incompatible convictions—the belief in God's universal concern and the conviction that divine revelation was given definitively only to a particular group. Such a position appears internally incoherent; if God is truly concerned with the fate of all humanity, God would not have disclosed Godself fully and finally to a particular people, allowing the rest of humanity to wallow in darkness and ignorance. Rather, what is required today is an even more open approach to the world's religions. To use a model of the universe of faiths formulated by John Hick, a Copernican revolution is now required in our understanding of religion. In the past even the most liberal Jewish thinkers

---

[21] Emil Fackenheim, "God's Presence in History: Jewish Affirmations and Philosophical Reflections," in *Holocaust Theology,* ed. Dan Cohn-Sherbok (London: Lamp Press, 1989), 46.

[22] Ignaz Maybaum, *The Face of God after Auschwitz* (Amsterdam: Jpolak and Van Gennep, 1965), 80.

[23] Arthur A. Cohen, *Tremendum: A Theological Interpretation of the Holocaust* (New York: Crossroad, 1981), 18–19.

retained the conviction that Judaism contains the fullest divine disclosure. While recognizing the inherent value of other religions—particularly Christianity—they were convinced that Judaism is humanity's future hope. These Jewish thinkers were like scientists who previously endorsed a Ptolemaic view of the universe in which the earth is at the center.

In the modern world, however, where Jews continually come into contact with adherents of other religious traditions, it is difficult to sustain such a narrow vision. Instead, a Copernican revolution is currently required in our understanding of the universe of faiths. Instead of placing Judaism at the center of the world's religions, the Divine will hold this central place. Such a transformation demands a paradigm shift from a Judeo-centric to a divine-centric conception of religious history. On this basis the world's religions should be understood as different human responses to the one Divine Reality. In previous ages religions conceived of this one Reality either theistically (as a personal deity) or non-theistically (as non-personal), but such differences were in essence the result of historical, cultural, or psychological influences.

On this view there is one ultimate Reality behind all religious expressions. To use kabbalistic terminology, the Godhead is the *Ayn Sof*—the Infinite beyond human comprehension. The Godhead is the eternal Reality that provides the inspiration for all religions, including Judaism. This ultimate Reality is interpreted in a variety of different modes, and these different explanations of the one Reality have inevitably given rise to a variety of differing and competing conceptions. Such a view of the Divine in relation to the world's religions can be represented by the image of alternative paths ascending a single mountain—each route symbolizes a particular religion with Divine Reality floating like a cloud above the mountaintop. The routes of these faith communities are all different, yet at various points they intersect. These intersections should be understood as those areas where religious conceptions within the differing traditions complement one another. Thus, as pilgrims of different faiths ascend to the summit, they will encounter parallels with their own traditions. But the Divine Reality they all pursue is in the end unattainable by these finite quests. As the Infinite, it is unknowable and incomprehensible. It is the cloud of unknowing.

Such a pluralistic model implies that conceptions of the Divine in the world's religions are ultimately human images—they represent the myriad ways of approaching the one indescribably Divine Reality. Doctrinal differences reflect differences in the historical, social, and cultural factors lying behind these convictions. Not only does this pluralistic framework offer a more comprehensible theoretical basis for understanding differences among religious systems, but it also provides a wider forum for interfaith encounter. Instead of assuming, as Jewish inclusivists have in the past, that Judaism embodies God's all-embracing truth, of which other religions possess only a share, Jewish pluralism encourages Jews to engage in fruitful and enriching dialogue with members of other traditions. This new pluralistic model further reflects our current understanding of the world in which no truth is viewed as unchanging. Rather, truth-claims by their very nature must be open to other insights. They prove themselves not by triumphing over their belief systems, but by testing their compatibility with other truths. Such a conception of relational truth affords a new orientation to our understanding of truth in religion; on this view religious truth is not static but instead undergoes continual interaction and development.

This model of truth-through-relationship allows each religion to be unique. The truth it contains is uniquely important for its religious adherents. But it is not true in a universal sense. Religious truth is relevant only for those who subscribe to it. Judaism thus should not be conceived as the one, true faith for all human beings, as a number of previous Jewish inclusivists have argued. Rather, Judaism is true only for the Jewish people. A pluralist confessional stance is thus both certain and open-ended. It enables Jews to affirm the uniqueness of their faith while urging them to recognize the validity of other traditions. Jewish inclusivism—with its insistence on completeness and finality—simply does not fit what is being experienced in the arena of religious diversity. In place of a Judeo-centric conception of God's activity, Divine Reality must be placed at the center of the universe of faiths. Within such a context, Judaism can be seen as an authentic and true religious expression. Here, then, is a new framework for positive encounter and religious harmony. If Jews can free themselves from an absolutist standpoint in which claims are viewed as possessing ultimate and universal truth, the way is open for a radically new vision of Jewish dialogue with the world's faiths.

RESOURCES FOR NEW JEWISH THEOLOGY

Throughout the history of the Jewish faith there has been a conscious awareness of the distinction between God-as-he-is-in-himself and human conceptions of the Divine. Scripture, for example, frequently cautions against describing God anthropomorphically. Thus Deuteronomy states: "Therefore take good heed to yourselves. Since you saw no form on the day that the Lord spoke to you at Horeb out of the midst of the fire" (Dt 4:15). Again, Exodus 33:20 declares:

> And he said, "You cannot see my face; for no one shall see me and live." And the Lord said, "Behold there is a place by me where you shalt stand upon the rock; and while my glory passes I will put you in a cleft of the rock, and I will cover you with my hand until I have passed by; then I will take away my hand, and you shall see my back; but my face shall not be seen."

In rabbinic literature there are comparable passages that suggest that human beings should refrain from attempting to describe God. Thus the Palestinian teacher Abin said: "When Jacob of the village of Neboria was in Tyre, he interpreted the verse, 'For thee, silence is praise, O God' to mean that silence is the ultimate praise of God. It can be compared to a jewel without price: however high you appraise it, you will undervalue it." In another talmudic passage a story is told of the prayer reader who was rebuked by the scholar Hanina. This individual praised God by listing as many of his attributes as he could. When he finished, Hanina asked if he had exhausted the praises of God. Hanina then said that even the three attributes "The Great," "The Valiant," and "The Tremendous" could not legitimately be used to describe God were it not for the fact that Moses used them and they subsequently became part of the Jewish liturgy. This text concludes with a parable: if a king who possesses millions of gold pieces is praised for having millions of sliver pieces, such praise disparages his wealth rather than glorifies it.

The later development of such a view was continued by both Jewish philosophers and mystics. In his treatise *Duties of the Heart*, for example, the eleventh-century philosopher Bahya Ibn Pakudah argued that the concept of God's unity involves the negation from God of all human and finite limitations. According to Bahya, if we wish to ascertain the nature of anything, we must ask two fundamental questions: (1) if it is; and (2) what it is. Of God, however, it is possible to ask only if he is. And once having established his existence, it is not possible to go on to enquire about his nature, since it is beyond human understanding. Given this standpoint, how is one to make sense of the descriptions of God in scripture and the Jewish liturgy? For Bahya, there are three main attributes that should be understood in a negative sense: God's existence, unity, and eternity. Even when these three attributes are expressed positively, they are in fact understood negatively. Hence, to say that God exists implies that he is not nonexistent. When one asserts that he is one, this means that there is no multiplicity in him. And, finally, when he is depicted as eternal, this signifies that he is not bound by time. God's nature is thus inscrutable; nonetheless, we do have knowledge about him. Concerning other positive attributes (such as his goodness), these can be understood in a positive sense, because unlike the other three attributes, they deal with God's acts rather than his essence.[24]

In *Guide for the Perplexed*, the twelfth-century Jewish philosopher Moses Maimonides also focused on the concept of negative attributes. For Maimonides, the ascription to God of positive attributes is a form of idolatry because it suggests that his attributes are coexistent with him. To say that God is one, Maimonides contended, is simply a way of negating all plurality from his being. Even when one asserts that God exists, one is simply affirming that his nonexistence is impossible. Positive attributes are only admissible if they are understood as referring to God's acts. Attributes that refer to his nature, however, are only permissible if they are applied negatively. Moreover, the attributes that refer to God's actions imply only the acts themselves—they do not refer to the emotions from which these actions are generated when performed by human beings.

---

[24] Bahya ben Joseph ibn Pakuda, *The Book of Direction to the Duties of the Heart* (London: Routledge and Kegan Paul, 1973).

Following Maimonides, the fifteenth-century philosopher Joseph Albo in Ikkarim maintained that God's attributes, referring to God's nature, can only be employed in a negative sense. On the other hand, attributes that refer to God's acts can be used positively as long as they do not imply change in God:

> But even the attributes in this class, those taken from God's acts, must be taken in the sense involving perfection, not in the sense involving defect. Thus, although these attributes cause emotion in us and make us change from one of the contraries to the other, they do not necessitate any change or emotions in God, for his ways are not our ways, nor are his thoughts our thoughts.

Like these Jewish philosophers, Jewish mystics advocated a theory of negation in describing God. For these kabbalists, the Divine is revealed through the powers that emanate from him. Yet God as he is in God's self is the *Ayn Sof* (Infinite). Thus, the *Zohar (Book of Splendor)* asserts that the *Ayn Sof* is incomprehensible. It is only through the *sefirot*—the emanations of the *Ayn Sof*—that the Divine is manifest in the world. Yet Jewish mystics were anxious to stress that the Divine is a unity. According to the *Zohar,* even the higher realms of the Divine—the stages represented by God's will, wisdom, and understanding *(Keter, Hokhmah,* and *Binah)*—should be understood negatively. Thus God's will, which is represented by the *sefirah Keter,* is referred to as *Ayin* (Nothingness)—it is so elevated beyond human understanding that it can only be represented by negation. Concerning divine wisdom, represented by *Hokhmah*, the *Zohar* declares that one can ask what it is but should expect no answer.

Here then is a new theological framework—deeply rooted in the Jewish tradition—that can serve as a basis for a new vision of Jewish theology. Acknowledging the limitation of human comprehension, such a way of unknowing reveals that there is no means by which to ascertain the true nature of Divine Reality as-it-is-in-itself. In the end, the doctrines of Judaism must be regarded as human images constructed from within particular social and cultural contexts. Thus, the absolute claims about God as found in biblical and rabbinic literature should be understood as human conceptions arising from the religious experience of the Jewish nation.

THEOLOGICAL IMPLICATIONS
OF JEWISH PLURALISM

For over two thousand years Jews have daily recited the Shema: "Hear, O Israel, the LORD our God, the LORD is One" (Dt 6:4). Jewish children are taught this verse as soon as they can speak, and it is recited at their deathbed. Jewish martyrs proclaimed these words as they gave up their lives.

Throughout the ages it has been the most important declaration of the Jewish faith. In making this statement, Jews, whether exclusivist or inclusivist in orientation, attest to their belief that there is only one God, who is indivisible. God is an absolute unity who cannot be syncretistically linked with other gods. In addition, since the word *one* in Hebrew also means unique, Jews imply that God is different from anything else that is worshiped; only God possesses divinity. Nothing can be compared to this one Divine. Thus Jewish monotheism denies the existence of any other divine being; there is only one Supreme Being who is Lord of all.

Within a pluralistic framework, however, such absolute claims about God should be understood as human conceptions stemming from the religious experience of the ancient Israelites as well as later generations of Jewish sages. Jewish monotheism—embracing a myriad of formulations from biblical through medieval and modern times—is rooted in the life of the people. In all cases pious believers and thinkers have expressed their understanding of God's activity on the basis of their own personal as well as communal encounter with the Divine. Yet, given that the Real *an sich* is beyond human comprehension, this Jewish understanding of the Godhead cannot be viewed as definitive and final. Rather, it must be seen as only one among many ways in which human beings have attempted to make sense of the Ultimate. In this light it makes no sense for Jews to believe that they possess the unique truth about God and about the divine action in the world; on the contrary, universalistic truth-claims about Divine Reality must give way to a recognition of the inevitable subjectivity of beliefs about the Real.

The same conclusion applies to the Jewish belief about God's revelation. According to tradition, the Hebrew scriptures were communicated by God to the Jewish people. In Maimonides' formulation of the thirteen principles of the Jewish faith, this belief is a central tenet: "The Torah was revealed from heaven. This implies our belief that the whole of the Torah found in our hands this day is the Torah that was handed down by Moses and that it is all of divine origin."[25] Further, the rabbis maintained that the expositions and elaborations of the Written Law contained in the Torah were also revealed by God to Moses on Mount Sinai; subsequently they were passed on from generation to generation, and through this process additional legislation was incorporated. Thus, traditional Judaism affirms that God's revelation is two-fold and binding for all time.

A theory of Jewish pluralism, however, calls such convictions into question. Instead of affirming that God uniquely disclosed the divine word to the Jewish people in scripture and through the teachings of the sages, Jews should acknowledge that their Holy Writ is only one record of divine communication among many. Both the Written and the Oral Torahs have special significance for the Jewish people, but this does not imply that these writings contain a uniquely true and superior divine communication. Instead the Tanakh

---

[25] Moses Maimonides, *Commentary on the Mishnam, Sanhedrin*, 10:1.

and rabbinic literature should be perceived as a record of the spiritual life of the people and a testimony of their religious quest; as such, they should be viewed in much the same light as the New Testament, the Qur'an, the Bagahavad Gita, the Vedas, and so forth. For the Jewish people this sacred literature has particular meaning—yet it should not be regarded as possessing ultimate truth.

Likewise the doctrine of the chosen people must be revised from a pluralistic viewpoint. Throughout history the belief that Israel is God's chosen people has been a central feature of the tradition. Through its election, Jewry believed it had been given a historic mission to bear divine truth to humanity. God's choice of Israel thus carries with it numerous responsibilities: Israel is obligated to keep God's statutes and observe divine laws, and in doing so, the nation will be able to persuade others that there is only one universal God. By carrying out this task, Israel is to be a light to the nations.

Here again Jewish pluralism must draw attention to the inevitable subjectivity of these claims about Israel's relationship with God and its universal role in a divine providential plan. Although Jews have derived great strength from such convictions, they are based on a misapprehension of Judaism in the context of the universe of faiths. Given that the Real *an sich* transcends human understanding, the conviction that God has selected a particular people as God's agent is nothing more than an expression of the Jewish people's sense of superiority and impulse to spread its religious message. In fact, however, there is simply no way of knowing if a specific people stands in a special relationship with the Divine.

Again, a pluralistic approach challenges the traditional Jewish conviction that God has a providential plan for the Jewish people and for all humankind. The Bible asserts that God controls and guides the universe—such a view implies that the manifestation of a wise and benevolent providence is found everywhere. Subsequently, the doctrine of divine providence was developed in rabbinic literature, and the belief that God is concerned with each individual as well as the world in general became a central feature of Jewish theology.

From a pluralistic perspective, however, such a religious conviction must be seen as simply one way of interpreting Reality. The belief that God's guiding hand is manifest in all things is ultimately a human response to the universe; it is not, as Jews have believed through the ages, certain knowledge. This is illustrated by the fact that other traditions have postulated a similar view of providence, yet maintain that God's action in history (as, for example, in the case of Jesus' passion or the growth and development of Islam) has taken an entirely different form. In other cases non-theistic religions have formulated conceptions of human destiny divorced from the activity of God or the gods. Such differences in interpretation highlight the subjectivity of all these beliefs.

The Jewish doctrine of the Messiah must also be seen in a similar light. Throughout history the Jewish people longed for a messianic figure who would redeem the nation from exile and inaugurate a period of peace and harmony. According to tradition the messianic age will last for a millennium and will be followed by a final judgment in which the righteous will be rewarded and the wicked punished. For more than two millennia Jews have waited patiently for the coming of the Messiah and daily prayed for his arrival.

Within a pluralistic framework such longing must be perceived as a pious hope based on personal and communal expectation. Although this belief has served as a bedrock of the Jewish faith through the centuries, it is inevitably shaped by human conceptualization. Like other doctrines in the Jewish tradition, it has been grounded in the experience of the Jewish people and has undergone a range of changes in the history of the nation. Because the Real *an sich* is beyond comprehension, there is simply no way of ascertaining whether this belief in a personal Messiah accurately mirrors the nature of ultimate Reality.

Finally, Jewish pluralism demands a similar stance regarding the doctrine of the afterlife. Although the Bible does not contain an elaborate doctrine of the hereafter, the rabbis developed a complex eschatological picture of human history. According to tradition, the world-to-come is divided into several stages: first, there is the time of messianic redemption. Peace will reign throughout nature; Jerusalem will be rebuilt and at the close of this era, the dead will be resurrected and rejoined with their souls. Final judgment will then come upon all. Those who are judged righteous will enter into heaven, and the wicked will be punished in hell.

While this set of beliefs regarding the eschatological unfolding of history has been a central feature of the Jewish faith from rabbinic times to the present, it is simply impossible to ascertain whether these events will unfold in the future. In our finite world—limited by space and time—certain knowledge about life after death is unobtainable. Belief in the hereafter in which the righteous of Israel will receive their just reward has sustained the nation through suffering and tragedy, yet from a pluralistic outlook these doctrines are no more certain that any other features of the Jewish religious heritage.

The implications of such a Copernican shift from inclusivist to a pluralist model for understanding religious diversity are radical and far-reaching. Judaism, like all other religions, advances absolute, universal truth-claims about the nature of Reality—but given the separation between our finite understanding and the Real *an sich*, there is no way of attaining complete certitude about the veracity of these beliefs. As many voices in Jewish tradition attest, the Real transcends human comprehension, and hence it must be admitted that Jewish religious convictions are no different in principle from those found in other religious traditions; all are lenses through which Divine Reality is conceptualized. Judaism, like all other major world religions, is built around its own distinctive way of thinking and experiencing the Divine, yet in the end Jewish pluralists must remain agnostic about the correctness of their own religious convictions.

CONCLUSION

On the threshold of the third millennium Judaism stands on the verge of a new awakening. Drawing on centuries of tolerance, the way is now open for Jews to formulate a complete reorientation of the Jewish faith in relation to other religious traditions. With a shift from inclusivism to pluralism, there is no longer any need to interpret other religions from a Judeo-centric standpoint; rather, with the Divine at the center of the universe of faiths, Jewry can acknowledge the inevitable subjectivity of all religious beliefs, including those contained in the Jewish heritage. Jewish pluralism thus demands the recognition that all religions constitute separate paths to Divine Reality—yet the summit of this ascent, the Real *an sich*, remains beyond comprehension; it is the cloud of unknowing beyond human grasp. As the *Shekhinah* led the children of Israel for forty years through the wilderness—always present, always ahead, and always unreachable—so the Divine hovers just beyond the range of human apprehension.

PART V

Christian Perspectives

11

The Spirit
and Religious Pluralism

PETER C. HODGSON

In his last published writing Paul Tillich suggested that the whole of systematic theology will have to be rethought in light of the history of religions, and his own rethinking pointed toward a "Religion of the Concrete Spirit."[1] Similarly, Karl Rahner in one of his late essays remarked that the time may have come to reverse the perspective that has given Christology its priority over pneumatology in Western theology. In light of "the universal salvific will of God and in legitimate respect for all the major world religions outside of Christianity," he predicted that pneumatology in the sense of "a teaching of the inmost divinizing gift of grace for all human beings" will become the fundamental point of departure for a new Eastern theology. Scriptural passages that prioritize Christ over the Spirit will be less suitable than those that "let the Spirit speak through all the prophets and know that the Spirit has been poured out on all flesh."[2]

I shall return to Tillich and Rahner, but these briefly quoted remarks are sufficient to commend the topic of this essay. My thesis in part is that it may prove fruitful for a theology of the Spirit to start with the widest scope of the Spirit's communication to and transformative presence in the religions of the world, and to work inwardly from there to the more determinate and strictly

---

A slightly different version of this essay was published in *Horizons* 31, no. 1 (2004), 22–39.

[1] Paul Tillich, "The Significance of the History of Religions for the Systematic Theologian," in *The Future of Religions,* ed. Jerald C. Brauer (New York: Harper and Row, 1966), 90–91.

[2] Karl Rahner, "Aspects of European Theology," in *Theological Investigations,* vol. 21, trans. Hugh M. Riley (New York: Crossroad, 1988), 97–98.

configured presence of the Spirit in the church and in Christ. From this perspective everything will appear in a new light, a light that may also illumine the reverse journey—from the Spirit of Christ and the church to the Spirit of the world.

PNEUMATIC TRINITARIANISM AND PLURAL ULTIMACY

I start with some proposals about the doctrine of the Trinity, which I call pneumatic Trinitarianism. I do so because I take seriously the injunction of Rowan Williams and others that if Christians are to embrace religious pluralism, such pluralism needs to be grounded in the very reality of God and not imposed simply out of philosophical, anthropological, or comparative-religious considerations.[3] God has something to do with the fact that a diversity of independent ways of salvation appears in the history of the world. This diversity reflects the diversity or plurality within the divine life itself, of which the Christian doctrine of the Trinity provides an account. The mystery of the Trinity is for Christians the ultimate foundation for pluralism.[4]

Here is a brief summary of my construal of this doctrine.[5] First, God is God in and for Godself as the perfect yet still abstract being. Then the distinction or relatedness that is already implicit within God is made explicit, and God lets be what is not God—the world. Yet what is not God, the world, remains a dimension within the divine life, for God is not a static supreme being but a process that encompasses both identity and difference, oneness and manyness, ideality and reality. The distinction between God and the world generates three, not two, relational figures or gestalts: God's self-identity apart from the world (God as God, "the One"), the creative-redemptive act by which the world is established as the cherished other of God (the figure of "Christ"), and the consummation of the world in God by which a more inclusive whole is generated (the figure of the "Spirit"). This insight, I believe, lies at the core of the doctrine of the Trinity.

In respect to the second moment, I want to stress that the world as a whole is to be understood as God's other, as the "body" in which God becomes

---

[3] Rowan Williams, "Trinity and Pluralism," in *Christian Uniqueness Reconsidered: The Myth of a Pluralistic Theology of Religions,* ed. Gavin D'Costa (Maryknoll, NY: Orbis Books, 1990), 6, 13.

[4] See Raimundo Panikkar, "The Jordan, the Tiber, and the Ganges: Three Kairological Moments of Christic Self-Consciousness," in *The Myth of Christian Uniqueness: Toward a Pluralistic Theology of Religions,* ed. John Hick and Paul F. Knitter (Maryknoll, NY: Orbis Books, 1987), 107–11.

[5] For elaboration, see Peter C. Hodgson, *Christian Faith: A Brief Introduction* (Louisville, KY: Westminster John Knox, 2001), 60–73; Hodgson, *Winds of the Spirit: A Constructive Christian Theology* (Louisville, KY: Westminster John Knox, 1994), chap. 11.

incarnate in a diversity of concrete figures and practices. God needs the otherness of the world to extend and complete God's own logical otherness, for without the world God would remain an abstract universal, an isolated potency, a beautiful ideal, but not a concrete, living, suffering, connected reality. Christ for Christians symbolizes this connectedness of God with the world. But, in truth, the connectedness is rich and diverse. One of the features of the world, which serves to keep it distinguished from the One, is its inexhaustible diversity, its manyness, its plurality of physical structures, life forms, peoples, cultures, and religions. Under the conditions of finitude, this diversity is a blessing, for it constrains the tendency of any one form to monopolize the others, to overreach itself, and to become an idol. This tendency is the source of the demonic in world history. Christ is a determinate, limited, self-critical manifestation of divine creative-redemptive power. For Christians, he is the definitive clue to the whole process but not the whole itself. Of necessity he points beyond himself to other creative-redemptive figures and practices and demands of us openness toward them. As Paul Knitter suggests, "The Logos, in becoming enfleshed in history, will have to be the *logoi spermatikoi*—the multiple word-seeds cast upon the field of history."[6]

If Christ is the figure (in the Christian Trinity) of God in the world as creative-redemptive love, then Spirit is the figure of God and the world together in consummate freedom. If love is the power of difference, by cherishing the other in its otherness, freedom is the power of mediation and communion, by giving the one and the other a liberating wholeness, a space of togetherness-in-difference. But love and freedom, differentiation and reunification, are inseparable, and their attributes are reversible. Love is also the power of communion and freedom of difference. Difference occurs for the sake of a richer unity, and mediation preserves and cherishes differences as its own precondition. God is free love and loving freedom—or as Karl Barth says in a well-known formulation, "the One who loves in freedom."[7] This is the most compact trinitarian formula. In the formula each figure encompasses and transcends the preceding one in a spiraling eschatological process by which God becomes God and the world is redeemed. In history the process remains fragmentary, ambiguous, incomplete, but nonetheless oriented to a goal, the consummation of all things in God.

The theological tradition never found a proper place for the Spirit. There are important exceptions, but for the most part the logic of the tradition was binary rather than triadic (as Cyril Richardson points out), and it viewed the Holy Spirit as an appendage to the Father and the Son, a subordinate instrument in the economy of salvation. Three persons were required on the basis of

---

[6] Paul F. Knitter, *Jesus and the Other Names: Christian Mission and Global Responsibility* (Maryknoll, NY: Orbis Books, 1996), 80.

[7] Karl Barth, *Church Dogmatics*, ed. G. W. Bromiley and T. F. Torrance, vol. 2/1 (Edinburgh: T. and T. Clark, 1957), §28.

scriptural authority, but the Spirit only grudgingly received technical equality within the Trinity. By contrast, I agree with Tillich that Spirit is the richest, most encompassing, and least restricted of the trinitarian symbols.[8] Similarly, in his last lectures on the philosophy of religion, Hegel said: "The abstractness of the Father is given up in the Son—this then is death. But the negation of this negation is the unity of Father and Son—love, or the Spirit."[9] In other words, the abstract God, the Supreme Being, the Father, dies in the death of the Son, a particular male human being; and both Father and Son are reborn as concrete, world-encompassing Spirit—a rebirth in which the negation of death is not forgotten. The abstract oneness of God and the specific incarnation of God are not lost but preserved in a richer, more inclusive unity. This logic is not binary and linear but triadic and spiraling, moving interactively through God and the world into Spirit.

It is no surprise that Spirit is a more universally available religious symbol than Christ, found in one form or another in most of the great religions of the world. It helps to open Christian theology to a genuine religious pluralism, and, in the framework of the doctrine of the Trinity, it provides a Christian way of construing this pluralism. The pneumatic Trinitarianism that I am proposing contrasts therefore with the christocentric Trinitarianism recommended by advocates of an inclusivist theology of religions. The latter view allows for the Holy Spirit to be active in other religions, but this is a Spirit strictly defined by and subordinated to Christ.[10]

Pneumatic Trinitarianism provides a way of construing and connecting the diverse features of ultimate reality to which John Cobb attends in an intriguing formulation. Cobb argues that ultimacy is irreducibly plural, having multiple aspects, which he calls theistic, acosmic, and cosmic. The theistic element is God as a personal being, the One. The acosmic (or uncreated) element is the power of being, which appears in religions as Logos/Wisdom, Brahman/Atman, or World Soul. On my reading the most adequate name for it is Spirit, which serves to connect God with the world. The cosmic (or created) element is the whole of nature and humanity, including paradigmatic revelatory figures such as Moses, Jesus, Buddha, Muhammad. Cobb himself observes that these diverse features of the totality cannot be unrelated to one another, and he remarks that each is necessary for the other. But he doubts that they can be synthesized in a trinitarian proposal such as the one I am offering. Rather the ultimate in its multiplicity and mystery exceeds

---

[8] Paul Tillich, *Systematic Theology,* 3 vols. (Chicago: Univ. of Chicago Press, 1951, 1957, 1963), 1:249–52.

[9] Hegel, *Lectures on the Philosophy of Religion*, vol. 3, ed. and trans. Peter C. Hodgson et al. (Berkeley and Los Angeles: Univ. of California Press, 1985), 370, cf. 323n-24n.

[10] Gavin D'Costa is the most consistent representative of this view. See his essay "Christ, the Trinity, and Religious Plurality," in D'Costa, *Christian Uniqueness Reconsidered;* and D'Costa, *The Meeting of Religions and the Trinity* (Maryknoll, NY: Orbis Books, 2000).

all that we can ever know or think.[11] By connecting the elements in a Trinity, I do not reduce the mystery but seek to render it intelligible. This is one of the tasks of theology: to *comprehend* God as precisely a *mystery*, and thus to hold positive (kataphatic) and negative (apophatic) elements in balance. God is a rational mystery. Without such an effort, the ultimate mystery remains unknown and unknowable, a noumenal reality that resides beyond its apprehension as personal in some religions and as impersonal in others—the view of John Hick, which has been widely criticized.[12] The doctrine of the Trinity attempts to show how and why God can be experienced as both a personal presence and an impersonal power.

SPIRIT AS ENERGY, KNOWLEDGE, LOVE, FREEDOM

What is Spirit?[13] From its etymological and metaphorical associations in the Hebrew and Greek Bibles, we can answer that Spirit is what is alive, active, energetic, moving, fluid *(Ruach/Pneuma)*, but also rational and conscious *(Hochmah/Sophia, Dabar/Logos)*. It is both primal energy and liberating knowledge. This conjunction of *natural* power (associated with breath, wind, fire, light) and *rational* power (associated with mind, consciousness, wisdom, language) is characteristic of the concept of Spirit in Hebraic religion. Spirit is simply the creative and redemptive power of God at work in the world. It is the power by which God calls into being and dwells within all that is. It is the power of being by which beings are. Without this power, beings would collapse into non-being, the abyss of nothingness from which they are fashioned and preserved. God is the supreme or perfect being who has this power of being absolutely and who is thus supremely spiritual— Holy Spirit or Absolute Spirit. Human beings, created in the image of God, are also spiritual, but in the mode of finitude and fallenness. Other created beings share in the spirituality of the creative act in different but equally potent ways that we can but dimly understand. Spirit has the form not only of Holy Spirit and human spirit but also of world spirit and natural spirits.

---

[11] See John B. Cobb, Jr., *Transforming Christianity and the World: A Way Beyond Absolutism and Relativism,* ed. Paul Knitter (Maryknoll, NY: Orbis Books, 1999), 114, 120–24, 136–37, 184–86.

[12] See John Hick, *A Christian Theology of Religions: The Rainbow of Faiths* (Louisville, KY: Westminster John Knox, 1995), 29–30. Cobb criticizes the idea of the Real as noumenal or as a common essence behind religious manifestations. His position is that God is known only in particular manifestations and that we cannot resolve the contradictions between them. See Cobb, *Transforming Christianity and the World,* 147–48.

[13] In the following paragraphs I summarize an analysis that I have developed at length in Hodgson, *Winds of the Spirit,* chap. 17, and more briefly in Hodgson, *Christian Faith,* 135–45.

The Holy Spirit is not, in my view, something that exists in advance as a person or hypostasis of the Godhead. There are no such preexisting persons in God but rather potentials for relationship (or modes of coming to be, *tropoi hyparxeos*) that become actual when God creates the world. God does have a primordial self-relatedness, an inner dynamic of identity-difference-mediation, but this relatedness should not be thought of mythologically as subsistent persons. The Spirit is an *emergent* person, proceeding from the interaction of God and the world, in the process of which the world is liberated and God is perfected. The Spirit "proceeds" or "spirates" through the "outpouring" of God in the world. The metaphors of "pouring" (Jl 2:28; Acts 2:17), "proceeding" (Jn 15:26; patristic theology), and "spirating" (Thomas Aquinas) accord nicely with the idea of God as *becoming* in relation to the world. The Spirit spirates from the love between God and the world, and the Spirit becomes the power of reconciling freedom in this love. It may be perplexing to think of the Spirit as both the power of being that *precedes* the world and as an emergent power that *proceeds* from the world. Yet we must attempt to think this paradox. The power of being comes *into being* only in relation to what it lets be; it is an activity, a *dynamis,* not a static substance.

God's Spirit is creative energy—but wise, intelligent energy. As such, it is directed toward an end, the engendering of knowledge, love, and freedom. Powerful images can be assembled from Pauline and Johannine texts to develop a theology of the Spirit as the one who pours God's love into our hearts, brings about a new birth of freedom, reveals the truth, and establishes God's wisdom over against the folly and falsehood of the world. I hope to show how these qualities of energy, knowledge, love, and freedom are fruitful for discerning the presence and work of the Spirit in a religiously plural world. They can perhaps be summed up in a single word: grace. For they are experienced as gifts, as empowering powers.

Karl Rahner describes the experience of the Holy Spirit as the presence of the self-communicating God in the form of sanctifying grace in the depth of human existence.[14] In this depth, which is a depth of knowledge and freedom, human being is the being of transcendence, of openness to the boundless horizon, the unencompassable infinity. A movement toward the nameless mystery is intrinsic to human being, but the movement is weak, faltering, diffuse. Thus God must be the condition of possibility of this movement: the Spirit comes to us, pours new life into our languid love, strengthens our vacillating resolve.[15] We describe as grace, as Holy Spirit, says Rahner, the self-communication of God as goal and strength of the movement toward

---

[14] Karl Rahner, "Experience of the Holy Spirit," in *Theological Investigations,* vol. 18, trans. Edward Quinn (New York: Crossroad, 1983), 189–210, esp. 192–93, 195–99.

[15] This is the language of George Eliot. See Peter C. Hodgson, *The Mystery beneath the Real: Theology in the Fiction of George Eliot* (Minneapolis: Fortress Press, 2001), esp. 23.

God. This transcendental experience of God in the Holy Spirit is present in ordinary life unthematically, anonymously. It becomes thematic through concrete mediating figures and practices.

THE SPIRIT AND CHRIST

Jesus Christ is certainly the central mediating figure for Christians through whom the redemptive grace of the Holy Spirit becomes thematic and recognized.[16] The relationship between Christ and the Spirit is complex. The Spirit both precedes Christ and follows Christ. Spirit, in the shape of Logos or Wisdom, is the power that indwells or "inspirits" Jesus of Nazareth, making him the Christ, the anointed one of Israel, who does not triumph but is crucified, thereby becoming a different kind of savior figure. The specific configuration of compassionate, liberating, revelatory power in Jesus Christ defines the Spirit and provides a basis for distinguishing between divine and demonic forms of spiritual power. The concrete incarnation of God in Christ is not reduced in significance but placed in a larger context. According to the Gospels, Christ sends the Spirit into the church and the world for the purpose of taking up and completing his mission. Yet the Spirit transcends Christ and appears in a diversity of religious figures and traditions, which also contribute to the delineation and enrichment of spirituality. Thus we cannot say exhaustively what Spirit is; Spirit is both concretely configured and open to new possibilities. The difference between Christ and the Spirit is not, in my view, the difference between two distinct hypostases in the Godhead, but the difference between God's concrete historical presence and universal indwelling power, between fixity and fluidity, history and mysticism, incarnation and communion. Both are necessary to any religion of the "Concrete Spirit," as I will suggest later.

In arguing for the emergence of the Spirit from the interaction of God and the world, I have advocated a double procession. The Spirit proceeds not simply from the Father and the Son but from God and the world. Thus there can be no question of a subordination of the Spirit to Christ. But does not such a proposal face the reverse danger of an uncritical spiritualism? I respond in two ways.

First, the world from which the Holy Spirit proceeds is a world, so Christians believe, in process of being shaped and configured by Christ. The world does not outgrow Christ but grows into Christ, and it does so through the Spirit, which precedes and follows the historical figure around whom the shape of Christ coalesced. The Spirit emerges neither independently of Christ nor in sole dependence on him. The relationship is one of thoroughgoing reciprocity.

---

[16] For this section, see my discussion in Hodgson, *Christian Faith*, 71, 143–45, and in Hodgson, *Winds of the Spirit*, 287–91.

Second, the theological tradition thought only in terms of the opposition between Christ and Antichrist. There surely are Antichrists, but there are also those who are *other* than Christ, different from Christ, without being antagonistic toward Christ. Today we must recognize a plurality of saving shapes of divine presence, and we should be able to affirm that the Spirit proceeds from this plurality, not from Christ alone. Judgments as to what is truly *anti-* (antidivine, antihuman, antichristic, antinatural) are not thereby eviscerated but arise from a communicative consensus rather than from a single authoritative revelation.

In my view it is naive to think that Christ provides an absolute criterion by which to judge history, for Christ is known and interpreted only through the witness of the Spirit in concrete situations. It is the complex interplay of Christ and Spirit that enables Christians to make always ambiguous and relative judgments in history. There is no absolute guarantee against illusions and demonic distortions, no absolute authority to which to appeal, but rather a constant struggle of interpretation. In this interpretative struggle we are helped by concretions of the Spirit in other religions, but we must use these and all spiritual manifestations critically rather than in a state of uncritical enthusiasm, whether for Christ or for another savior figure or for a people or nation. The critical principle is the true spiritual principle.

THE SPIRIT
AND A THEOLOGY OF RELIGIONS

Antecedents of a broadened understanding of the Spirit are found already in Hellenistic Judaism and the Wisdom tradition, which stressed the universal creative role of *Pneuma/Sophia;* in Irenaeus, who conceived of the Spirit as one of the "two hands of God" that work in relative independence; in the Cappadocians, who argued for the distinct individuality of the three hypostases and viewed the Spirit as having its own complementary role alongside and cooperating with the Son; and in Augustine, who thought of the Spirit as the mutual love of Father and Son, the consubstantial bond that unites them, and who thus was on the way toward a view of the Spirit as the final and most inclusive of the divine figures, indeed as the communion between God and the world.[17] Of course, Augustine did not actually arrive at this position, and the possibility of affirming a truly global economy of the Spirit has arrived only in our own time. George Khodr, metropolitan of the Greek Orthodox Church in Lebanon, was among the first to glimpse this possibility. "The Spirit," he wrote, "fills everything in an economy distinct from that of the Son. . . . We must . . . affirm their hypostatic independence and visualize

---

[17] See Alasdair I. C. Heron, *The Holy Spirit* (Philadelphia: Westminster Press, 1983), 36, 65–66, 80–85; and J. N. D. Kelly, *Early Christian Doctrines* (London: Adam and Charles Black, 1958), 262–63, 273–78.

in religions an all-comprehensive phenomenon of grace."[18] Another striking formulation comes from the Christian-Hindu-Buddhist theologian Raimon Panikkar. Using the image of rivers that meet not on earth but in the skies when their waters are vaporized in the form of clouds, he suggests that the religions of the world do not coalesce as organized religions. Rather, they meet when they are "metamorphosized into Spirit, which then is poured down in innumerable tongues."[19]

The Spirit is moving through the great religious traditions. It has always been so, but today communication, travel, and research bring these traditions together as never before. We now have a far richer and more accurate sense of the diversity of religious manifestations from which the Spirit proceeds—for it proceeds from the interaction of God and the whole world. God does not tightly control the particulars of this interaction, which depend on the contingencies of the world, but we have reason to believe that God creates the world and sends the Spirit toward an end—an end that can never be fully grasped but includes such goals as an enhancement of life and diversity, a harmonious dwelling together of the whole cosmos, a struggle to heal tragic conflicts, a growth in love and freedom, enlightenment and wisdom, goodness and beauty. The reason for believing this is that such goals and values are affirmed, often in strikingly different ways, by the great religions and cultures of the world. A few deep and enduring values have emerged from the refinery of history, despite the recalcitrance and self-centeredness of human beings, and we can take this as proof that God's Spirit has been at work in the great cultural trajectories. These values are often distorted by the interests that produced them, and in every culture outright contradictions and ambiguities occur. The special challenge today is to keep the refining process going by encouraging religions, through dialogue and interaction, to identify one another's blind spots and to contribute reciprocally to the spiritual growth of all. The outcome will not be a melding of religions but a deepened insight into each tradition and a sharing of resources toward the end of mutual enrichment and transformation.

The Holy Spirit provides a window for Christians onto the diversity and plurality of world religions. A theology of the Spirit is a Christian way of construing this diversity and plurality, relating it to the purposes, activity, and being of God. It is only one such construal, and it must accept that other religions interpret the diversity differently. It has no monopoly on the truth. If faith in the Spirit of Jesus Christ means openness to truth wherever it manifests itself, Christians should have no fear of entering into the dialogical

---

[18] George Khodr, "An Orthodox Perspective of Inter-Religious Dialogue," *Current Dialogue* 19 (1991): 27. Quoted in and commented on by Knitter in *Jesus and the Other Names*, 113. See also Amos Yong, *Discerning the Spirit(s): A Pentecostal-Charismatic Contribution to Christian Theology of Religions* (Sheffield: Sheffield Academic Press, 2000), 60–65.

[19] Panikkar, "The Jordan, the Tiber, and the Ganges," 92.

process, offering their own deep insights and eager to learn from others. Not everything in a religious tradition is true or helpful—indeed, much is harmful—and critical judgments are unavoidable. Such judgments are possible in an open network of interpretation.[20]

A theology of religions seems to have a twofold task, one critical and the other constructive: exposing idolatries and drawing out convergent truths. The Spirit is at work in both of these tasks as a "refining fire" that burns away the evil present in all religions and as an "attracting wind" that draws the religions into mutually enriching dialogue and practices. An example of the former is the feminist critique of patriarchal structures that oppress and marginalize women in all the major world faiths.[21] An example of the latter is David Krieger's attempt to articulate a global theology based on Ludwig Wittgenstein's vision of a universal community of discourse combined with a pragmatics of nonviolence inspired by Mohandas Gandhi.[22] Where the Spirit is leading on this adventure no one knows. I do not believe it is toward a monolithic world religion but rather toward the discovery of a liberative and compassionate core of spiritual wisdom present in the great religious traditions. I believe there can and will be a heightened appreciation of both plurality and solidarity among the religions. Solidarity arises through a mutually correcting coalescence of diverse interests and insights rather than by the imposition of totalitarian claims. The plurality will frequently remain recalcitrant, resistant to easy unification; and when solidarity is achieved under such conditions it is a spiritual gift.[23]

Elements of a pneumatological theology of religions are anticipated by Paul Tillich and Karl Rahner, who continue to instruct us in profound ways. In his essay, "The Significance of the History of Religions for the Systematic Theologian,"[24] Tillich sets forth several propositions: revelatory religious experiences are universally human; these experiences are always limited and distorted under the conditions in which they are received; thus a critical revelatory process is needed that will have mystical, prophetic, and secular elements; there *may* be a central event in the history of religions that gathers up the positive insights of diverse traditions; and finally, the sacred does not lie beside the secular but is its depth. Rather than a progressive-developmental theology of religions, Tillich offers a "dynamic-typological" approach. There must be a sacramental basis to all religions (the concrete presence of the Holy in figures such as Christ and Buddha and in rituals and liturgies),

---

[20] See Hodgson, *Christian Faith*, 149–50; Knitter, *Jesus and the Other Names*, 106; and Hick, *A Christian Theology of Religions*, 139–47.

[21] See the essays by Delores Williams, Lina Gupta, Riffat Hassan, Rita Gross, and Judith Plaskow in *After Patriarchy: Feminist Transformations of the World Religions*, ed. Paula M. Cooey, William R. Eakin, and Jay B. McDaniel (Maryknoll, NY: Orbis Books, 1991).

[22] See David Krieger, *The New Universalism: Foundations of a Global Theology* (Maryknoll, NY: Orbis Books, 1991).

[23] An elaboration of these ideas is found in Hodgson, *Winds of the Spirit*, 304–15.

[24] In Brauer, *The Future of Religions*, 80–94.

but there must also be a critical-mystical movement against the demonization of the sacramental and a prophetic element that articulates a vision of justice against its denial in the name of holiness. Tillich imagines that these three elements come together to form "the Religion of the Concrete Spirit"—concrete because of sacramental presence but spiritual in the mystical-prophetic transcendence of presence. The Concrete Spirit is concrescent Spirit, coalescing into material, perceptible forms but always standing out from them. The inner aim of the history of religions is to become a Religion of the Concrete Spirit, but the latter cannot be identified with any actual religion, not even Christianity as a religion. It appears only fragmentarily in many moments in the history of religions. Tillich believes that one such moment is found in Paul's doctrine of the Spirit, where two fundamental elements, the ecstatic and the rational, are united. Ecstasy is present, but its highest creations are *agape* and *gnosis,* love and knowledge. It is also present in the cross of Christ as a negation of every idolatrous claim and as the negation of negation, the victory of life over death. The spiritual marks of ecstasy, love, knowledge, suffering, and negation are present not just in Christianity but in all the major faiths.

I have already mentioned Rahner's essay "The Experience of the Holy Spirit," which is one of many he wrote on the Spirit, a fact that gives credence to the claim that his late theology is principally a theology of the Spirit.[25] Of particular relevance to a pneumatological theology of religions is Rahner's suggestion that the presence of the Spirit may be discerned through many pointers in everyday life, most clearly so "where the definable limits of our everyday realities break down and are dissolved." Of the numerous examples he provides, here is an excerpt:

> When, over and above all individual hopes, there is the one and entire hope that gently embraces all upsurges and also all downfalls in silent promise,
> when responsibility is undertaken and sustained, even though no evidence of success or advantage can be produced,
> when someone experiences and accepts his ultimate freedom, of which no earthly constraints can deprive him,
> when the fall into the darkness of death is accepted with resignation as the dawn of incomprehensible promise,
> when the sum total of all life's accounts, which we cannot work out ourselves, is seen as good by an incomprehensible "other," although this cannot be "proved,"
> when the fragmentary experience of love, beauty, and joy is felt and accepted as promise of love, beauty, and joy purely and simply, and not regarded with deep cynicism and scepticism as facile consolation in face of ultimate bleakness, . . .

---

[25] Yong, *Discerning the Spirit(s),* 71–77 (citing studies by Joseph Wong and Gary Badcock).

when . . . (it would be possible to go on for a long time),
then God is present with his liberating grace. Then we experience what
we Christians describe as the Holy Spirit; then an experience occurs
that is inescapable in life . . . and is offered to our freedom. . . . The
mysticism of everyday life is there, God is found in all things; here is
that sober intoxication of the Spirit of which the Church Fathers and
the early liturgy spoke.[26]

It is evident that these examples are not limited to Christian experiences
of the Spirit. They are present in all religious experience, and they are
thematized in diverse yet recognizable ways by the great religious traditions.
These are the criteria for discerning or testing the presence of the Spirit.
Earlier I suggested that they cluster around the motifs of energy (or empowerment), knowledge (or wisdom, truth), love (or compassion, communion)
and freedom (or justice). These qualities belong to the mysticism of everyday
life, and religions can enrich each other in the process of articulating them.

THE SPIRIT IN HINDUISM AND BUDDHISM

Hinduism and Buddhism are religions of the Spirit, contributing
fragmentarily to what Tillich calls the Religion of the Concrete Spirit. Christians can learn from and reflect on their contribution. The same is true of
Judaism and Islam, indeed of all historically enduring faiths. For a test case,
I focus on the two great India-born religions. Here I am entering on territory
with no pretense of expertise, and I ask the reader's indulgence of a thought
experiment.[27] The experiment employs a Jewish-Christian category, that of
Spirit, in an attempt to interpret these religions.

Brahman/Atman, the ultimate reality for Hinduism, is understood philosophically to be a universal spiritual matrix. "Through a process that is inex-
plicable, this universal ultimate reality became subdivided into myriad individual *atmans* [spirits]. They are the truly real entities in the world. . . . All
beings, then, are spiritual beings, sharing with one another and the forces

---

[26] Rahner, "Experience of the Holy Spirit," 199–203.

[27] I have been guided by the treatment of Hinduism and Buddhism in John L.
Esposito, Darell J. Fasching, and Todd Lewis, *World Religions Today* (New York:
Oxford Univ. Press, 2002), chaps. 5–6; by a few books that focus on Hindu-Chris-
tian and Buddhist-Christian dialogue: Francis X. Clooney, SJ, *Hindu Wisdom for All
God's Children* (Maryknoll, NY: Orbis Books, 1998); Rita M. Gross and Terry C.
Muck, eds., *Buddhists Talk about Jesus, Christians Talk about the Buddha* (New
York: Continuum, 2000); John B. Cobb, Jr., *Beyond Dialogue: Toward a Mutual
Transformation of Christianity and Buddhism* (Philadelphia: Fortress Press, 1982);
John B. Cobb, Jr., and Christopher Ives, eds., *The Emptying God: A Buddhist-Jew-
ish-Christian Conversation* (Maryknoll, NY: Orbis Books, 1990); Aloysius Pieris,
Love Meets Wisdom: A Christian Experience of Buddhism (Maryknoll, NY: Orbis
Books, 1988); and Cooey, Eakin, and McDaniel, *After Patriarchy*.

that move the universe a common spiritual essence."[28] Brahman appears to be both impersonal and personal. As the underlying substance of things it is impersonal, but as the original and true self it goes out from itself, creates gods, other selves, a world that keeps evolving, becoming more complex. Everything interacts in the spiritual nexus. As an individual self I am implicitly identical with the universal self, and my spiritual journey is to find my way back to the original interconnectedness of things, reversing the process of creation whereby the original self becomes many. The one is many and the many are one; Advaita Vedanta (one of the Hindu schools) grasps the non-identity and non-duality of things more subtly than most Western philosophy does. It reflects the Hegelian vision of Spirit as the unity of substance and subject. It holds together the two central attributes of divinity, impersonal power and personal presence, without dissolving the tension between them or the mystery of their connection.

The personal aspect of Spirit appears in a multitude of Hindu divinities. Brahma, though a relatively minor figure in ritual practice, is the creator of gods and mortals, and a wise counselor. In Vishnu, God comes down to earth and is present in many incarnations, of which Krishna is the most complex and multifaceted, appearing in diverse human forms from infant to guru. Shiva, by contrast, represents the transcendent, unpredictable, creative-destructive aspect of divinity, symbolized as sexual yet spiritual. The function of these divinities is to manifest the inexhaustible complexity of Brahman-Spirit in forms that humans can grasp and with which they can interact. Intellectual knowledge is not enough; the truth must be realized through ascetic practices (yoga), which achieve a progressive sensing of the spirit within and a reversing of ignorance and egoistic desire.

The goddess figure, Mahadevi, combines and unifies the several functions of the male divinities more completely than they themselves do. In this respect she is closer to Brahman, the unmanifested Spirit. She represents the materialization of spiritual energy—a materialization that is necessary if Spirit is to proceed from the interaction of God and the world, the immaterial and the material, the ideal and the real. The goddess appears as Kali, the Great Mother, the consort of Shiva, combining violent power and gentle protection; she is the source of death and destruction, on the one hand, and of strength and justice, on the other. As such, she reflects the role played by women in primitive matriarchies as well as the respect and fear of female power. What is the significance of having a goddess figure at the heart of a religion that is deeply patriarchal in tradition and practice? Does she point to an egalitarian and liberating core, to the fact that, if all things have their being within Brahman, then all distinctions and hierarchies, including spirit and nature, male and female, brahmin and outcast, are opposed to the Advaitic Spirit?

Hinduism portrays the unity and diversity of what we call Spirit more dramatically and colorfully than anything known in the West. Compressed

---

[28] Esposito, Fasching, and Lewis, *World Religions Today,* 282.

into Brahman, Spirit then explodes into a pandemonium of divinities. Contrasts and paradoxes are heightened, but they prove ultimately not to be paradoxes because they lie beyond dualistic logic. Hinduism is overwhelming in its wild and sensuous variety, its celebration of raw spiritual power. Because of its internal pluralism, it is tolerant of other religions and is capable of subsuming them within its own mythic structures. Sharp tensions are evident between its core philosophical insights and its social practices insofar as they legitimate class hierarchies, encourage extreme forms of asceticism, and perpetuate the subordination of women. From a Western Christian post-Enlightenment perspective, legitimate concerns can be raised about Hinduism as it struggles with the challenges of modernity and post-modernity. But we also have much to learn from its ancient wisdom. The Spirit that comes together in the gods, goddesses, myths, philosophies, rituals, and practices of Hinduism is like a whirlwind that shakes and disturbs the settled spiritualities of our own religion, reminding us that the Spirit blows where and how it will.

Buddhism represents a reform and simplification of the old Vedic religion from which both Hinduism and Buddhism emerged. It is often said to be a non-theistic religion, and if this is true, how can it be called a religion of the Spirit? Brahman disappears as a thematized concept and is replaced by Nirvana as its negative counterpart. Nirvana refers to the "cooling" of feverish desires that create karma and bind individuals into *samsara,* the world of rebirth and suffering. It means "freedom and existence in an eternal state beyond all material description." Human beings can realize Nirvana by the cultivation of insight or wisdom *(prajna)*, by appropriate moral practices, and by proper meditation. The way to Nirvana is established by the Four Noble Truths and the Eightfold Path attributed to the Buddha (Gautama Siddhartha). Accompanying the concept of Nirvana is that of the non-self, which rejects the idea of "an essential, unchanging interior entity at the center of a person"—the soul or *atman* of Hinduism. Human beings are subject to the law of impermanence and are simply a continuously changing, interdependent relationship among five aggregates: the physical body, feelings, perceptions, mental dispositions, and consciousness.[29] Despite the rejection of the substantial soul, Buddhism does not reject, as far as I can tell, the Hindu conviction of a universal spiritual matrix in which everything subsists. Nirvana is the purest form of this matrix.

Westerners have found deep spiritual wisdom in the teaching and practices of Buddhism. Gautama, John Cobb points out,[30] taught that we suffer because we are attached to things, and that when we relinquish this attachment we become free. The result is a freedom for all things because it is a complete freedom from all things. This detachment is more radical than anything known in the West: it is both a total emptiness and a total fullness. Christian spirituality approximates this sense of total detachment, but it is hindered by a cultural heritage of possession, ownership, self-activity, and

---

[29] Ibid., 361–64, 371–73.
[30] Cobb, *Beyond Dialogue,* chaps. 4–5.

individual fulfillment. What Buddhists call detachment, Christians call grace, a term that refers to the empowering power of the Holy Spirit, the sanctifying gift of wisdom, compassion, and freedom. Living by grace entails a complete letting go, not a holding fast, an openness to what presents itself in experience, a gaining of life by losing it. Such grace is the basic condition and constitutive reality of the church as a spiritual community, which is a community of compassion, freedom, communion with and for the other. Such a community is a utopian ideal in our consumer-oriented, materialist, individualist culture. Buddhism can help the Christian church to be a community of grace in a graceless culture by showing more clearly what it means to have faith without attachment, to find fulfillment in emptiness, to become a communal self by giving up private selfhood. Conversely, questions can be raised from a Christian perspective about the relative failure of Buddhism to develop an ethic of social transformation that corresponds to its vision of compassion and freedom, although Buddhist scholars such as Masao Abe[31] have argued for a dynamic interpretation of Nirvana *(Sunyata)* that might yield such an ethic. In any event, dialogue with Christians can help Buddhists move in this direction.

Perhaps the central issue between Christians and Buddhists is whether humans need a source of strength outside themselves to break the power of ego. Is it a question of other-power or of self-power? Christian trust in grace and the Holy Spirit clearly indicates that the source comes from outside ourselves, although the empowering power of the Spirit works within the self as well as in history and culture. If Buddhism is a non-theistic religion, it might seem that enlightenment comes solely from our own disciplined efforts,[32] although it is somewhat ironic to speak of self-power in the context of a doctrine of the non-self. Rather, for Buddhism, it may be more a matter of connecting oneself with the universal *dharma*, the path of truthful teaching and enlightenment that functions rather like grace and has a numinous, sacred aspect. Taitetsu Unno quotes William James to the effect that what is involved in Buddhism is "not a deity *in concreto,* not a superhuman person, but the immanent divinity in things, the essentially spiritual structure of the universe." He goes on to say that the embodiment of *dharma* (*dhamma* in the Pali spelling) in the Buddha "is central to the radical self-sufficiency found in the [Buddha's] injunction, 'Be ye lamps unto yourselves.' The self here is not the unenlightened ego self, but the enlightened non-ego self imbued with *dhamma*, as clearly understood in the subsequent passage, 'Hold fast to the *dhamma* as a lamp. Seek salvation alone in the *dhamma.*'"[33]

---

[31] In Cobb and Ives, *The Emptying God*, 3–65.

[32] This is clearly the position of José Ignacio Cabezón and Rita M. Gross in *Buddhists Talk about Jesus, Christians Talk about the Buddha*. See also the essay in the same volume by Bonnie Thurston, who is critical of this position from a Christian perspective.

[33] Taitetsu Unno, "Contrasting Images of the Buddha," in Cabezón and Gross, *Buddhists Talk about Jesus, Christians Talk about the Buddha*, 140–42.

This lamp, for Jews and Christians, is the light of the Holy Spirit.

> Your word [O Lord] is a lamp to my feet
> and a light to my path. (Ps 119:105)

Here Buddhism, Judaism, and Christianity share deep spiritual insight. For Judaism the *dharma* is the Torah, while for Christianity it is the teaching not just of Jesus but of the cumulative wisdom of Judaism and the saints and theologians of the church. Can we Christians share with Buddhists the injunction to "rely on the teaching and not the teacher"?[34] But if the teaching is completely realized in a teacher, as is believed to be the case with both the Buddha and Jesus, then the teacher and the teaching, while distinguishable, are inseparable. The teacher is the concrete proclaimer and performer of the teaching. The teaching itself is the gift of the Spirit, or more directly, the teaching *is* the Spirit. The concrescence of the teaching in the teacher signals that Buddhism and Christianity are manifestations of the Religion of the Concrete Spirit.

Dare we say that in today's complex, interconnected, and conflicted world we need not only the Torah and the gospel but also the *dharma*; not only Christ but also Buddha; not only the one personal Spirit of Christianity but also the impersonality of Brahman and the multiple Spirits of Hinduism?

---

[34] Ibid., 142.

12

Pluralist Christology as Orthodox

ROGER HAIGHT

Many Christians today, even those whose sympathies may lie with a pluralist conception of Jesus Christ, do not understand how a pluralist Christology can be considered orthodox. This essay primarily addresses these Christians and aims at explaining, at least in the form of an extended outline or map, the reasons why a pluralist Christology is orthodox. It is possible that the logic that is deployed here may find analogies within other religious traditions.

I begin by simply defining the terms as they are used in this discussion. By Christology I mean a Christian theological understanding of Jesus of Nazareth with special attention to his status relative to God and to other human beings. A pluralist Christology affirms Jesus as the Christ in a way that does not construe Christianity as the one and only true faith and way of salvation uniquely superior to all others. An orthodox Christology meets the criteria of being faithful to the normative teaching of the New Testament and the classical christological councils of Nicea and Chalcedon. It thus conforms to traditional doctrine and respects an intrinsically conservative impulse of Christians.

With these definitions in place I develop the thesis in four parts. The first offers some premises gathered from the domain of the philosophy of religion. The second outlines schematically key elements of the logical structure of Christology. The third then argues within that structure to conclusions about the way Christians can and should regard other religions. This sets up the fourth part regarding the orthodoxy of this understanding of a pluralist Christology. This essay is not meant to break new ground in Christian theology. Everything that is said here is well known, and this allows me to state things succinctly, as though merely pointing to ideas, rather than developing them. My intent is to bring together many of the insights that have been generated in this discussion in a clear unified statement of how a pluralist Christology, understood along the lines that are drawn here, is orthodox.

BASIC CONSIDERATIONS IN THE MODE
OF A PHILOSOPHY OF RELIGION

Often the positions theologians take on fundamental questions in theology depend on premises that are tacit in their understanding and arguments. In this first part of the discussion I want to lay out a number of theses or propositions that are well known to Christian theologians and that set the context of the argument that follows. The Christian theologians who do not accept the conclusions arrived at in this essay quite possibly disregard or dissent from the context defined by these principles.

Globalization. We have entered a new phase of interdependence and commerce among peoples that is having a major influence upon the existence of the human species. Globalization is opening up new ways of thinking that are relevant to all religions. Some of the features of this new world context that have a bearing on religious consciousness are these: a new vision of the universe and story of the planet; interdependence of all peoples so that each is affected by the others in a new way; new perception of the degree of differences among us and the bonds that unite us, the possible values of pluralism understood as unity in difference; new awareness of the fragility of human life on the planet and of corporate human responsibility for massive social oppression and suffering; and a new humility in religious claims.

The unity of reality. The vision behind this essay depicts reality as unified or held together in an integrated way: being is one. It proposes that the human species today is single and unified, although it was formed through various evolutionary biological trajectories and is shaped differently by cultural forms. In Christianity, monotheism and the doctrine of creation correlate with a belief of the unity of the human race and a moral conviction about the equality and absolute value of human beings. Whether or not the unity of ultimate reality can be proved, it operates as a premise in these reflections. (I believe this is a premise that followers of most, if not all, religious traditions can endorse.)

Qualities of religious knowledge. Knowledge of ultimate reality is mysterious, mediated, and dialectical. First, religious knowledge has as its object transcendent reality, which, insofar as it is transcendent, is not available for immediate perception and thus not able to be identified with our conceptions of it. This ultimate reality is often characterized as infinite or without any limits. It thus presents itself to us as unfathomable and incomprehensible mystery. Second, because ultimate reality is transcendent, human beings can only perceive and appreciate it through finite this-worldly symbols. Religious symbols are media by which transcendent reality is represented, embodied, made available to human consciousness. Religious symbols are mystagogical; they draw the human spirit through the capacity of the imagination into the realm of absolute and infinite transcendence. Third, the perception and knowledge mediated by religious symbols end up as inherently dialectical in the sense that they both represent and do not represent that which they mediate. The content of Christian affirmations about God are simultaneously denied in their very affirmation in the light of the transcendence of that to which they point and which they mediate.

Soteriological character of religion. Religious conviction responds to a religious question whose answer intrinsically engages the self and becomes soteriological. The "salvation" at the basis of all religious knowledge is understood here broadly and generically, so that it may take different forms in different religions. But salvation always correlates with the fact that religious knowledge responds to those human issues that affect individuals and cultures at a level that has a direct bearing on their ultimate destiny.

These four themes do not exhaust the tacit background of this essay, but they help define the field on which it is played out.

THE LOGIC OF CHRISTOLOGY

The significance of the title of this section—"The Logic of Christology"—lies in its abstractness. One can only represent the structure and dynamics of the study of Jesus Christ in Christian theology in the most general of terms. Christological discussion within Christian theology is so extensive and complicated that it constitutes a subdiscipline. Although the particular option in Christology represented here should be defended at greater length, it is stated here in the schematic form of five theses in order to further define the context for the discussion that follows.

1. *Jesus is the historical medium of Christian encounter with God, so that Christology is interpretation of Jesus of Nazareth.* On one level this thesis consists in a straightforward descriptive statement of what goes on in Christology. But at another theological level it implicitly contains the premises of a Christology "from below" that some Christian theologians would contest. For example, some Christian theologians take the Christian scriptures as a self-contained or closed system of revelation and understanding that draws consideration of Jesus' historical life up into itself. This form of Christian theology and Christology frequently takes an absolutist form. By contrast, Christology "from below" is taken here to mean that, as in the case of any other historical set of convictions, to understand Christology one must trace its historical genesis. That historical genesis began with the appearance of Jesus of Nazareth, although one should not forget that Jesus was born into a Jewish tradition.

2. *The New Testament of the Christian Bible contains a pluralism of Christologies all of which share a soteriological structure.* The New Testament as a whole consists in a collection of interpretations of Jesus as the Christ and of his impact on the Christian community. That the New Testament does not contain one common Christology but a variety of different

Christologies has been demonstrated by the exegetes of scripture and is commonly accepted. But some Christian theologians hold that some Christologies have more authority than others, and they interpret these "higher" Christologies that accent the divinity of Jesus Christ as normative relative to others which, in their turn, are viewed as stages in the development of a fully authoritative view. Still, many other theologians would support the proposition offered here that all of the Christologies of the New Testament should be considered as having a certain validity and that none should rule out the others, even when they cannot be made to coincide logically.

The thesis also finds the unity of the various Christologies of the New Testament to lie in their common soteriological structure. All have Jesus of Nazareth as their implicit referent or object of interpretation. Because Jesus is the event or historical medium through which Christians encounter salvation from God, all implicitly give expression in various different ways to that experience of salvation. This soteriological principle will play a large role in the interpretation of pluralist Christology that is offered here.

3. *The person of Jesus embodies a divine quality or character.* All of the Christologies of the New Testament portray Jesus mediating salvation from God. The Christologies of the New Testament, in various and diverse ways according to the different metaphors that make up particular Christologies and the distinct historical traditions that lie behind each one, point to the presence, power, and quality of the divine in Jesus or at work through him. One way of explaining this is to appeal to a more general principle that the historical symbol which mediates salvation from God (Jesus) tends to share in the quality (divinity) of that which is mediated (salvation by divine power) because the symbol renders it present and effective. According to this principle one would expect Jesus to share in some way in the divine saving power and reality of God. This became a forceful argument in the development of Jesus' divinity in the course of the formation of the doctrinal tradition.

4. *The point of the metaphor of incarnation and the doctrine of Nicea is that Jesus makes true God, and nothing less than God, present and effective in history for human salvation.* This thesis makes more explicit the principles and reasoning found in the last thesis. But it can also be verified or at least corroborated by historical-exegetical analysis of the metaphor of incarnation as that is found in the Prologue of John's Gospel, its most explicit instance in the New Testament. It also correlates with an analytical account of the development of Christology from the second century through the early fourth century that came to term in the doctrine of Nicea. That doctrine says that the Logos or Word that was incarnate in Jesus is of the same nature as God. This was officially declared as a response directly contradicting the teaching of Arius, who affirmed that what was present and active in Jesus was a Logos who was less than God in being. This response has turned out to be a classical Christian doctrine. The theological principle that confirmed it was soteriological: if what was present and active in Jesus was less than God, Jesus could not in the end be a bearer of God's salvation.

5. *The point of the doctrine of Chalcedon is to confirm the human crea-*
turely status of Jesus and to underline the intrinsic dialectical character of
orthodox Christology. The doctrine of Chalcedon is also a Christian classic.
It says that the one individual, Jesus Christ, possessed or possesses within
himself two distinct and different kinds of being: a human nature and a
divine nature. These two natures are at the same time both inseparable and
unmixed, distinct but joined to form one "person," a technical term roughly
meaning a distinct, subsisting individual. This doctrine too has a history
apart from which it cannot be adequately understood. Part of that history
included a christological pattern of thinking that undermined what today is
usually taken for granted by theologians, namely, that Jesus was a human
being equal to other human beings in all things essentially human. To re-
trieve the figure of Jesus from an exaggerated emphasis on his divinity,
Chalcedon proposed the formula of one person with two natures. The most
adequate way to understand this classic doctrine is to construe it as intrinsically dialectical, that is, by not attempting to resolve the tension between
these two natures, but to affirm both, as Chalcedon says, unmixed and inseparable. This corresponds to the historical function of the doctrine that
was to compromise between two competing theologies, the one emphasizing
the divinity of Jesus and the other his humanity, without sacrificing either.

This dense summary of the development of Christology provides a platform to support further reflection on how Christology may affect views of
other religions.

OTHER RELIGIONS FROM A CHRISTIAN STANDPOINT

The next discussion unfolds within the context of the classical doctrine of
Jesus being a genuine human being but also embodying no less than God for
our salvation. While remaining in that context, what can a Christian say
about other religions that both remains faithful to the classical doctrine and
accommodates the new sensitivity to the value and vitality of other religious
traditions? The extensive argument that follows is controversial within Christian theology, but it remains within the boundaries of accepted doctrine. I
shall not present the reasoning in the form of theses, because such a strong
assertion would betray its tentative nature with respect to general Christian
sensibility, but I will advance the argument through distinct steps.

1. In Jesus the Christian encounters a God who as creator is immanent
and active in all of creation. The idea of creation developed after the period
of the New Testament into the doctrine of creation out of nothing. That
formula implies a direct or immediate presence and activity of God to all
finite reality. No form of presence and activity can be closer, for the being
itself of the creature depends on God sustaining it in being. Christian belief
in God entails a God who is so absolutely immanent in and present to all
reality that all things, even though they are other than God, may be said to
exist in God because God exists within them. This God is not distant.

2. Jesus reveals the very nature of this creating God to be loving and bent on the salvation of all. This has already been affirmed as part of the logic of Christology. The usual way this teaching from the New Testament is stated is that God wills the salvation of all human beings. But I also want to underline that, when Christians affirm the revelation of God's universal will and character as benevolent and saving, this is applicable to all human beings. In the measure that such a proposition on the very character of God is true, it is relevant for all.[1] In other words, the subject matter aimed at here transcends the sphere of the socially and culturally relative. This is rather a matter that has bearing on the human as such. One can see the significance of the conception of the unity of the human race at this point. A true characterization of the nature and character of ultimate reality is valuable for all human beings. In short, truth and what is often referred to as normativity in substantive religious matters are synonymous.

3. To be effective in history, God's active saving presence to all requires mediation through historical symbols and religious institutions. *Historical effectiveness* in this statement really refers to the revelation of God's saving presence and *action* to human consciousness. One can, of course, creatively imagine God at work within human beings apart from all human consciousness of it. But this would come very close to sheer projection. The issue in this discussion precisely revolves around human religious consciousness of the effectiveness of transcendent power immanent to the human condition. The discussion itself rests on the implicit premise that religious consciousness responds to and correlates with God's presence and power in history. Nothing less than this can explain the longevity and power of antique religious traditions.

4. From a Christian standpoint, therefore, a pluralism of religions is to be expected. That is to say, if one is convinced that God wills the salvation of all people, and that that salvation is not a sheerly eschatological reality but a presence and power in human life that is accompanied by some form of human consciousness of it, then it follows that the same consciousness would take the social form of a religion. This means that the multiplicity of religions from a Christian standpoint is not surprising but entirely coherent with the Christian conception of God as transcendent but immanently present and operative in the lives of all human beings. Not to affirm an expectation of religious pluralism, or to be embarrassed by it, runs counter to the basic Christian conception of God. It would entail a view of God's saving will as not being universally effective in history. Positively, precisely because God creator and savior relates to all of history, the articulation and experience of God's presence takes on multiple different forms.

5. The other side of the historicity of the experience of God's engagement with human beings is the limitation of any particular experience and

---

[1] Often the term *normative* is used for the word *relevant*. But normativity has become an ambiguous and perhaps dysfunctional category at this point, and I use it sparingly.

expression of it. Given the limitation of all historical mediation, and given the transcendent character of ultimate reality, no single salvific mediation can encompass God's reality or human understanding of it. This represents the standard Christian view that God as transcendent can be characterized as infinite and incomprehensible. Ultimate reality, which in the Christian view is God, so transcends every and all finite mediations of it, that no single mediation of God can be said adequately to encompass or be equal to the infinite reality itself of God.

6. From the transcendence of ultimate reality, or God, it follows that no religion in the sense of a set of religious truths can adequately portray its object. From a Christian standpoint, therefore, the plurality of religions mediates more revelation of God than any single religion, including Christianity itself. To view one religion as the fullness of revelation in any historical or categorical sense does not cohere with the object revealed; there can be no such thing as a historical representation of infinite reality that is adequate or comprehensive. The frequently cited Christian idea that Jesus Christ is the fullness of God's revelation has a bearing on the ontological reality of God that is truly revealed because present and at work in him, but this cannot be understood in concrete quantitative or qualitative terms.

7. In the measure in which other religions are historically distinct from Christianity, autonomous in their mediation of revelation of ultimate reality, and true, they are normative for all human beings. This idea applies the same principle considered earlier (no. 2) that advanced the universal relevance of Christian truth insofar as it is really true to all religions. Likewise, if the beliefs of other religions are true in matters concerning the stance of humanity itself before reality and the character of ultimate reality in relation to the human, they are in that measure universally relevant. This correlation of fundamental religious truth and the universally human provides the very ground for interreligious dialogue. To subvert this universal relevance or "normativity" directly undermines the deep anthropological conviction that supports interreligious dialogue itself and the common interest in it.

8. But this means that Christianity should not be understood as absolute in the sense that it relates to no other religion while other religions are dependent upon it or relate to it as their fulfillment. The revelation of God found in the religions possesses a historical autonomy that enters into a dialogical relationship with Christianity and other religions, and not one of dependence. In the measure that the conceptions about ultimate reality are true, they are relevant to all and bear a normativity that makes a universal claim. This does not mean that all religions are equally revelatory of transcendent reality or the human; some may be more adequate and thus more universally applicable than others. But this is something that must become apparent within a dialogical situation.

9. Thus the conviction that Christianity is not absolute, but that other religions contain salvific truth not formally contained in Christianity, can through inference be regarded as entailed in the teaching of Jesus. This formulation expresses the point of the argument that has been schematically

outlined here thus far. That point places the source and quality of the positive conviction about religious pluralism within the core of Christian faith and revelation. The positive view of other religions possesses its value in being drawn out of Christian revelation itself. That core consists in the nature of God revealed in Jesus as a savior God who wills the salvation of all whom God created, and the historical efficacy of that divine and salvific initiative. The conclusion, therefore, does not consist in a proposal that comes from outside Christian faith and threatens it but lies implicit in the revealing message of Jesus himself. Surely the depths of Christian revelation are inexhaustible and always yield new convictions in new situations. Our globalized situation and the current press of religions up against one another have yielded new awareness of what has been revealed in Jesus Christ.

AN ORTHODOX PLURALIST CHRISTOLOGY

In this concluding section I outline theological reasons that explain why a pluralist Christology such as has been described thus far is orthodox. In this question we get closer to the narrow christological issue and the place it holds within Christian theology. The issue deals with the estimate Christians have of Jesus Christ in relation to God and how this relationship of identity with God is explained. This is a complex discussion within a tradition that I hope will not be compromised by the following brief treatment in nontechnical terms. I will again resort to theses to ensure clarity and to measure the elements of the argument.

A Christology is orthodox when it meets the three criteria of intelligibility, faithfulness to tradition, and empowerment of the Christian life. An orthodox statement must first of all be intelligible within the context of the contemporary world. It would make little sense to proclaim a doctrine that people generally could not understand because it was alien to the world view of a people. Transcendent mystery should not be confused with what is unintelligible. One must be more careful in stating this than the brief space allows, for Christianity stands against the sin of the world (in which it also participates) and contains what is in many respects a prophetic and countercultural message. But even prophecy has to be understood to be effective. Unintelligible orthodoxy can give no glory to God.

Second, orthodox doctrine and theology conform to the data of Christian tradition. Here tradition is taken broadly to include Christian scriptures and classical doctrines. *Conforming* in the context of historical interpretation does not mean literal repetition in new contexts, which inevitably betrays the very message that is repeated, but consists in an essential fidelity of interpretation in the present to the object of interpretation as that is given in and through the traditional witness. I have to assume here a sensitivity to the dialectical character of Christian theological interpretation: the community always lives in a tension, which often breaks out in dispute, between fidelity to the past and a contemporary possibility of relevance and meaning. All movement into the future along this line of loyalty to the past entails contention, because orthodoxy demands interpretation, and all interpretation is contextual.

The third vital criterion for the adequacy of orthodox interpretation consists in the preservation of the soteriological character and empowerment of the traditional teachings. The soteriological structure of religious faith becomes practically real in the spiritual life it simultaneously reflects and generates. An orthodoxy irrelevant to the spiritual life becomes empty and therefore nonexistent.

Let me now apply each of these criteria to pluralist Christology:

A pluralist Christology is surely intelligible in today's globalized world. It is precisely the current world that has raised the question to which pluralist Christology is the answer. The more common problem for Christian consciousness consists not in the applicability of pluralist Christology to our current situation but in whether such an understanding conforms with scripture and classical doctrine and the manner in which it empowers.

A pluralist Christology conforms to the data of Christian tradition insofar as it "explains" how no less than true God is present and active in the life of Jesus. Often the idea of orthodoxy has been reduced to whether or not a Christology adequately portrays the agency of God at work in Jesus. Although orthodoxy entails more than that, the divinity of Jesus is a central issue. In the New Testament this agency of God is primarily expressed through the symbol of God's Spirit. Less frequently, but dramatically, it is also represented as an incarnation of the Word of God in the human individual Jesus. Other Christologies imply or connote the presence and agency of God in less forceful metaphors. None of these images confuses Jesus with Yahweh or identifies him with the one Jesus addressed as Father.[2]

Christology today also employs the symbols of God's Word and God's Spirit to formulate or express God's agency in Jesus. A pluralist Christology can be formulated in a language that privileges either one of these symbols. A particular pluralist Christology would have to be worked out in considerably more detail before a judgment could be made on its orthodoxy. The goal of such a Christology is to preserve the idea of God acting in Jesus in a language of today's culture that is proportionate to the way the Christologies of the tradition represented God acting in Jesus in the language of the cultures in which they were proposed. It is worth noting in passing that no Christology is ever without critics within Christian theology.

Relative to the construction of an orthodox Christology it is crucial that Christians understand that the issue of a pluralist Christology does not depend on how "high" or how "distinctly divine" it portrays Jesus. It depends rather on whether what is predicated of him is so unique to him that it cannot

---

[2] It is often said today that Jesus did not preach his own person but was theocentric in focusing his message on the reign of God. This contextual reflection is important and significant. This whole discussion aims at negotiating a shift from christocentrism to theocentrism.

be shared by others. If God's being present and active in him bears no parallel with our own relationship to God, then the whole topic of his relevance for us and our salvation is undermined. The point of incarnation language is that Jesus is one of us, that what occurred in Jesus is the destiny of human existence itself: *et homo factus est* (and was made human). The projecting upon Jesus of a divinity that radically sets him apart from other human beings does not correspond to the New Testament and undermines the very logic of Christian faith. Analogously, if God's being present and active in Jesus has no parallel manifestation in other religions that mediate consciousness of God at work for human salvation, then once again the content of the revelation of Jesus about God is undermined.

A pluralist Christology empowers the Christian life insofar as it proposes Jesus as representing a meaning and direction of human existence that leads to final salvation in the reality of God. The New Testament contains a pluralism of understandings of how Jesus Christ is savior. There is no single answer to the question, What did Jesus do for human salvation? The many soteriological formulas all reach out to the mystery of God's saving approach to human beings in Jesus. That salvation appeared in his public ministry. It is read in a crucial way in a life dedicated to the reign of God that led through death to God's raising of Jesus into divine glory. Many other images and symbols across the New Testament characterize the way God acted in Jesus for human salvation. But all of these metaphors and conceptions are not equal; many depend upon the particular culture and tradition in which they were constructed. For example, a pluralist soteriology rules out conceptions of the salvation mediated by Jesus as limited and confined in principle to Christians. The teaching of the New Testament that God wills the salvation of all human beings has been brought into new focus in today's context as an essential element of the meaning of Jesus. This renewed emphasis has so relativized the exclusivist themes that are also found in the New Testament that, when they stand alone, they seem like cultural myopia.

Orthodoxy is not measured by any one of its three criteria but in the balance of all three. There are multiple ways of expressing a response to the narrow christological question of the status of Jesus Christ in relation to God and other human beings. This is true especially of the New Testament, before christological discussion became narrowed down to the terms of an incarnation of the Word of God. But that which binds all the Christologies of the New Testament together is the soteriological conviction that God has worked human salvation through the mediation of Jesus of Nazareth. That mediation of salvation is the point of Christology in this sense: the experience of salvation is that out of which christological reasoning is generated, and that which it attempts to explain and express. In the New Testament and patristic periods that experience took the form of the culture, language, and problems that were raised at that time. The tradition was intelligible to those who formulated it in the terms of the historical moment.

That logic is not different today. A pluralist Christology conforms to the data of the past in the measure that it preserves the existential point of the many Christologies of the New Testament and the classical doctrines, namely, that it is truly God who is operative in Jesus Christ for human salvation. In other words, the measurement of orthodoxy cannot be reduced to the comparison of words today with words of the past as though the words had no historical basis and communitarian life. A pluralist Christology conforms to tradition when it preserves the existential, soteriological, and spiritual point of past teachings. Therefore a Christology is meaningful and orthodox in the measure in which it intelligibly expresses and "explains" the salvation from God that Christians experience in and through Jesus of Nazareth. But to be intelligible today, that explanation must include within God's reign the possibility of the effective salvation of all in history. And the concrete efficacy of that entails in its turn recognition and functional validation of the religions that make the religious question and the experience of ultimate reality available to people.

The new and distinctive character of pluralist Christology lies in its non-competitive premise and context. I conclude this schematic map of a Christology that is pluralist and orthodox with a statement of where its specific difference from earlier Christologies lies. This does not consist in lowering a Christian estimate of Jesus but in expanding its relevance. The difference lies in recognizing that what God has done in Jesus, God does generally. Pluralist Christology does not differ from Christologies of the past in what it affirms about Jesus Christ but rather in the context in which christological doctrine is formulated and in the noncompetitive way in which Jesus Christ is understood. Pluralist Christology recognizes that other religions and other religious symbols mediate the "same" transcendent source and power of salvation. Put simply, pluralist Christology is orthodox in affirming the basic experience and conviction of Christians regarding the true divinity of Jesus, but it does so in a noncompetitive way.

13

Pluralism Calls for Pluralistic Inclusivism

An Indian Christian Experience

K. P. ALEAZ

In this essay I understand *pluralism* as the view that holds other religions to be equally salvific paths in terms of how they view reality or realities, even though such views differ from one's own. The thesis of this essay is that pluralism calls for "pluralistic inclusivism"; it calls each religious faith to be pluralistically inclusive, that is, to include and relate to other faiths in such a way that the theological and spiritual contents of one's own faith are fulfilled in and through the contributions of other living faiths. I would like to show how Indian Christian experience bears out this thesis; Indian Christians have experienced religious plurality not as a problem but as a given and positive reality (that is, pluralism) that calls them to what I am terming pluralistic inclusivism.

The first section of this essay describes pluralism among Indian Christians, focusing particularly on the theology of religions of the Thomas Christians in the pre-sixteenth century, as well as on the thought of Indian theologians S. K. George and Manilal C. Parekh. Since it was the Indian religio-cultural ethos of openness to the other that encouraged Indian Christians, the second section offers an overview of this ethos of openness. We will especially consider Syadvada of Jainism and the approach of Sri Ramakrishna. The third and final section concretely demonstrates how, encouraged by pluralism, the approach of pluralistic inclusivism can be put into practice in the construction of an Indian Christian theology.

THOMAS CHRISTIANS' THEOLOGY OF RELIGIONS

From an analysis of the Acts and Decrees of the Synod of Diamper of 1599 imposed by the Portuguese Roman Catholic intruders, we are able today to infer the theology of religions of the Thomas Christians who were living in India since the first century CE.[1] In their theology they held pluralism and in their social life they followed the perspectives of pluralistic inclusivism. In Kerala there existed the spirit of mutual acceptance among the communities of Hindus and Christians; the prohibitions and restrictions imposed by the Synod of Diamper witness to this communal harmony. Act III, Decree 4 of the synod states: "That everyone may be saved in his own law; all which are good, and lead men to heaven. Now this is a manifest heresy, there being no other law upon earth in which salvation is to be found, besides that of our Saviour Christ." We can infer from this that the Thomas Christians upheld pluralism in their theology of religions. They took it for granted that a Hindu can be saved in his or her own *dharma*.

What upset the synod was that in social life there were no external signs to distinguish Christians from the *nayaras* (the chivalry class of Kerala); in dress, hairstyle, in everything, Christians and *nayaras* looked alike. Thus we can understand that the synod demanded that Christians stop boring ear lobes (IX.17). Other prohibitions of the synod included the use of "non-Christian names" (IV.16, 17); Hindu musicians singing in Christian churches (V.14); sending children to schools run by Hindu *panicars* (teachers), and Christian *panicars* keeping Hindu idols in their schools for the sake of the Hindu children attending lessons (III.12, 13); and the clergy eating with Hindus (VII.11). The synod urged Christians to live together far from the "danger" of communication with non-Christians (IX.23).

All such warnings and prohibitions are a negative reflection of the social harmony that existed between Hindus and Christians of Kerala. In their social lives Thomas Christians practiced what we are calling pluralistic inclusivism. The local churches functioned in tune with the social and religious customs of Kerala. The governance of the Hindu temples and their properties was in the hands of the *Yogam,* or assembly of local people. The Thomas Christians adopted this same democratic system of government in their parishes. The local church councils *(palliyogam)* looked after the temporal matters and the ecclesiastical discipline of the community, while the bishops had no temporal or administrative authority over the local churches. The present system of bishops having temporal power over the church came into being only after the arrival of the Portuguese. Previously the bishops had only limited ecclesiastical powers such as consecrating the church, administering baptism, and ordaining *Cathenars (priests),* and they did this only on the request of the local congregation and not independently of the *palliyogam.* Obligatory clerical celibacy, as well episcopal control of clerical

---

[1] Scaria Zacharia, ed., *The Acts and Decrees of the Synod of Diamper 1599* (Edamattam: Indian Institute of Christian Studies, 1994); Mathias Mundadan, *Emergence of the Catholic Theological Consciousness,* Documentation No. 7 (Alwaye: St. Thomas Academy for Research [STAR], July 1985), 5–6; K. P. Aleaz, *Dimensions of Indian Religion. Study, Experience, and Interaction* (Calcutta: Punthi Pustak, 1995), 219–22.

assignments and salaries, was introduced by the Portuguese rulers. Thus, the reality of religious pluralism inspired the early Thomas Christians to evolve their own democratic and decentralized ecclesiology—something that can well inspire and guide present-day Thomas Christians, as well as Christians in general.[2]

THE THEOLOGIES OF S. K. GEORGE
AND MANILAL C. PAREKH

Back in the 1920s and 1930s, S. K. George (1900–1960) and Manilal C. Parekh (1885–1967) advocated a pluralistic theology of religions; S. J. Samartha joined them in the 1990s.[3] For S. K. George, the redemptive suffering love manifested in the cross of Christ is the central principle of Christianity, but the power of this principle becomes real in practice, not in the preaching of dogma. Thus, for George, Mahatma Gandhi's *satyagraha* movement was the cross in action; so, resigning a secure teaching job at Bishop's College in Calcutta, he joined Gandhi wholeheartedly in 1932.[4] Even prior to this, as a bachelor of divinity student of Bishop's College (1924–27), he had his doubts about the exclusive divinity of Christ. As early as 1937, S. K. George helped in organizing the All Kerala Inter-religious Students Fellowship, which tried to bring together students of various religions for mutual understanding and cooperation. The first conference of the fellowship was held at Alwaye in May 1937 and adopted the following statement as its "Aim and Basis":

Amidst the conflicting claims made on behalf of different religions . . . we believe there is an urgent need for a full and free exchange of our differing religious experiences, in a spirit of mutual respect, appreciation and sympathy. We consider that for such mutual respect and sympathy to be real it is absolutely necessary that no member of the Fellowship should claim for his religion any exclusive and final possession of truth. We believe that such an interchange of experience will lead to: (a) An enrichment of one another's religious life; (b) Mutual respect, understanding and tolerance; and (c) Cooperation in purifying and strengthening the religious attitude of mind . . . from which our . . . problems have to be tackled.[5]

---

[2] See *The Indian Journal of Theology* 34, nos. 1–3 (1985). The whole issue is devoted to Kerala ecclesiology (see 17–18, 89–98, 99).

[3] S. J. Samartha, *One Christ Many Religions* (Bangalore: Sathri, 1992).

[4] See K. P. Aleaz, "S. K. George: A Pioneer Pluralist and Dalit Theologian," *Bangalore Theological Forum* 32, no. 1 (2000): 91–111; S. K. George, *Gandhi's Challenge to Christianity*, 2nd ed. (Ahmedabad: Navajivan Publishing House, 1947).

[5] George, *Gandhi's Challenge to Christianity*, 80.

The fellowship intended to explore fully the value of all the different religious traditions and disciplines and present them for the benefit of all. But at the same time, nobody in the fellowship was to be persuaded to take on another's religious belief and practice. To weaken the hold of the truth of any religion upon humankind was considered a weakening of religion itself. The central intent of the fellowship was to help one another to understand and to live up to the best in all religions.[6]

S. K. George was convinced that the hope of world unity and human fellowship had to be based on interreligious cooperation. Therefore, the first goal of the interreligious movement was to eliminate religious conflicts and intolerance. The spirit of cooperation that he found among Christians he wanted to extend to the different religions as well.[7] He was well aware that the interreligious movement faced many misunderstandings. One of the most common criticisms was that of syncretism: interreligious dialogue will only lead to the addition of new, exotic religions to the already crowded world of religions. To this, George replied:

> The inter-religious movement does not aim at evolving a single universal religion for all mankind. That . . . is the dream of the militant missionary faiths, which would blot out all other religions. What interreligionism stands for is the acceptance of the need and the fact of variety in religious experience, of diversity in man's approach toward and realization of the One Eternal Reality, which is the common object of religious quest throughout the ages. It admits the limitations of all human understandings of the Divine—even unique revelations are mediated through human channels—and is, therefore, humble and willing to accept light from various sources. It accepts the revelations through the spiritual geniuses of all mankind and while it does not aim at, or believe in, evolving a uniformity of creed and conduct, it looks forwards to a time when the spiritually-minded of all religions will unite in the appreciation of all known truth and in welcoming fresh revelations from the unspent deep resources of God.[8]

Founded in 1951 under the inspiration of S. K. George (he was its secretary for the first seven years), the Fellowship of the Friends of Truth sought to embody such ideals for the interreligious movement.

According to George the place of Jesus Christ in the Hindu religious heritage of India is as one of the *Ishta Devatas*—that is, chosen or favorite deities. Hinduism readily grants such a place to Jesus Christ. In response to this Hindu view, the followers of Jesus should not deny that there are other mediators between God and humans, other experiences of God's presence in the

---

[6] Ibid., 80–91.

[7] Ibid., 52.

[8] Ibid., 53–54.

human heart; therefore, they can affirm the validity of other *Ishta Devatas.* Any denial of such validity simply lies outside the positive experience of the Christians and therefore lacks any foundation in Christian experience.[9]

Manilal C. Parekh was born in a Jain home in Rajkot, Gujarat. He was introduced to Hindu Vaishnava Bhakti by his father. A serious illness became the occasion for him to experience and affirm theism. He was also influenced by the writings of Keshub Chunder Sen, the leader of the Hindu Reform Movement, Brahmo Samaj, and he served for some years as a *pracaraka* (propagator) of the Church of the New Dispensation (the name of the Sen's movement in later days) in Sindh and Bombay. In the next stage of his pilgrimage, because of the influence of Keshub, he grew increasingly interested in Christ. A serious bout with tuberculosis gave him opportunity to study and reflect on the Bible and the *Vacanamrit* of Swami Narayana, the famous Gujarati Vaishnava religious and social reformer of the early nineteenth century. The study of Vaishnava Bhakti led him beyond the rationalism of the Brahmo Samaj to the conviction that God becomes incarnate, and this belief pointed him to the Christ of whom he had read in the New Testament.[10]

Baptized in the Anglican Church in Bombay in 1918, Parekh considered baptism as only a spiritual matter. His disillusion with the Westernization of the Indian Christian community grew. He wanted a Hindu Church of Christ, free from Western influence. Because he strongly felt that new disciples of Christ should remain within their own community, witnessing from there, he drew a clear distinction between evangelism—the proclamation of the gospel to individuals—and proselytism—seeking mass-conversion by dubious means. Like the Bengali Brahmabandhav Upadhyaya (1861–1907), Parekh made a distinction between *samaja dharma* (social aspect of religion) and *moksha dharma* (spiritual aspect of religion). Christianity should be *moksha dharma* only.[11]

By the end of 1930s, Parekh came to the final stage of his spiritual pilgrimage—what he called *Bhagavata Dharma.* He conceived *Bhagavata Dharma* as a universal personal religion of devotion in which Christian devotion is one element among others, perhaps the central and organizing element. He used this term to describe a religion of personal *bhakti,* which is realized at its clearest in Christianity and Vaishnavism but is also experienced in all other theistic faiths. He included in it Christanity, Judaism, Islam, Zoroastrianism, and all the religions that believe in God. His bitter experiences in both Brahmo Samaj and the Christian church had eventually brought him to the conclusion that change of religion is undesirable, since it tends to lead to exclusiveness and communalism. For the new harmony that

---

[9] Ibid., 48; S. K. George, "Christianity in Independent India," in *S. K. George Souvenir, The FFT Quarterly* 7, nos. 1–2 (1959–60): 37.

[10] See R. H. S. Boyd, ed., *Manilal C. Parekh 1885–1967 Dhanjibhai Fakirbhai 1895–1967 A Selection* (Madras: CLS, 1974).

[11] K. P. Aleaz, *Religions in Christian Theology* (Kolkata: Punthi Pustak, 2001), 95–96.

he was envisioning, he wanted a name that would not imply that one particular tradition had a monopoly of the truth; he found the name in *Bhagavata Dharma*.[12]

THE PLURALISTIC RELIGIO-CULTURAL ETHOS OF INDIA

In the Hindu religious tradition, religious pluralism is theologically affirmed in many ways. In the announcement of the Rig-Veda (1.164.46) that *Sat* (Truth, Being) is one but sages call it by different names, Brahmanism tried to solve the conflict between one religion and another. Orthodox Hindus argue for religious pluralism, saying that plurality is rooted in the diversity of human nature itself, in the principle of *adhikarabheda* (difference in aptitude or competence); therefore, the question of the superiority or uniqueness of any one *dharma* over others does not arise.[13] This general assessment of religious pluralism is affirmed and advanced in the *Syadvada* of Jainism as well as in the life and thought of Sri Ramakrishna.

SYADVADA: AN INDIAN CONTRIBUTION TO PLURALISM

For Jainism, all objects of the world are multiform *(anekanta)*, and each of these substances has innumerable characters *(dharma)*, both positive and negative, essential and accidental. This contention is called relative pluralism. Further, Jaina thought holds that reality can be considered from different points of view *(nayas)*. No judgment is absolute; all are relative. Perhaps the most important feature of Jaina philosophy is its respect for all opinions implied in this conception. Every object has infinite aspects judged from different points of view. Every judgment is true only in relation to a particular aspect of the thing seen from a particular point of view and hence is not the whole truth. This is *Syadvada*. There are seven ways of predication, and this is called *saptabhangi*.[14]

Every judgment that we pass in daily life about an object is true only in reference to the standpoint occupied and the aspect of the object considered. We quarrel and disagree because we forget this, as in the parable of the blind men arguing what an elephant is, each from the particular part of the elephant

---

[12] Ibid., 97. See Manilal C. Parekh, *A Hindu Portrait of Jesus Christ* (Rajkot: Sri Bhagavata Dharma Mission, 1953); Parekh, *Christian Proselytism in India—A Great and Growing Menace* (Rajkot: Sri Bhagavata Dharma Mission, 1947).

[13] K. P. Aleaz, "Hindu-Muslim and Hindu-Christian Relations in the Context of the Rise of Hindutva in India," *Missonalia* 30, no. 3 (2002): 376–88. For a different perspective on Hindu theology of religions, see G. Gispert-Sauch, "Soundings into the Hindu Tradition for a Theology of Religions," in *Religious Pluralism: An Indian Christian Perspective*, ed. Kuncheria Pathil, 111–31 (Delhi: ISPCK, 1991).

[14] K. P. Aleaz, "Syadvada: An Indian Contribution to Pluralism," *Bangalore Theological Forum* 33, no. 1 (2001): 133–44.

he was touching. The different systems of philosophy, according to Jainas, represent different and partial aspects of reality. Accordingly, they insist that every judgment should be qualified by a word like *syat* (in some respect), so that the limitation of this judgment and the possibility of other alternative judgments from other points of view may be clearly recognized. Thus, instead of a judgment such as "the elephant is like a pillar," it should be said, to remove the chance of confusion, "in some respect, the elephant is like a pillar." This theory of the Jainas is called *Syadvada*. The principle underlying *Syadvada* makes Jaina thinkers truly catholic in their outlook; they go beyond the limitations of narrow dogmatism *(ekanta-vada)* and affirm its opposite, *anekantavada,* which is the metaphysical claim that reality has innumerable characteristics. This leads logically to the epistemological claim that we can know only partial aspects of reality and therefore all our judgments are necessarily relative.[15] Such an epistemological perspective is called *Syadvada*.

Vardhamana Mahavira (599–527 BCE), the twenty-fourth Tirthankar (Teacher of Jainism) and a contemporary of Buddha (from whom Buddha may have drawn some of his own teachings) is said to have established *Syadvada* as a means of opposing the Agnosticism *(Ajnanavada)* of Sanjaya:

> For as the *Ajnanavada* declares that of a thing beyond our experience the existence, or non-existence or simultaneously existence and non-existence can neither be affirmed nor denied, so in a similar way, but one leading to contrary results, the *syadvada* declares that "you can affirm the existence of a thing from one point of view *(syad asti)*, deny it from another *(syad nasti)*; and affirm both existence and non-existence with reference to it at different times *(syad asti nasti)*. If you should think of affirming existence and non-existence at the same time from the same point of view, you must say that the thing cannot be spoken *(syat avaktavyah)*. Similarly, under certain circumstances, the affirmation of existence is not possible *(syad asti avaktavyah)*; of non-existence *(syad nasti avaktavyah)*; and also of both *(syad asti nasti avaktavyah)*.[16]

Regarding the history of *Syadvada*[17] we should note that references to *Syadvada* occur in the writings of Bhadrabahu, who is believed to have described it as *syat* (maybe) and *vada* (assertion)—thus, "the assertion of possibilities."

---

[15] Satischandra Chatterjee and Dhirendramohan Datta, *An Introduction to Indian Philosophy*, 7th ed. (Calcutta: Univ. of Calcutta, 1968), 82; Surendranath Dasgupta, *A History of Indian Philosophy*, vol. 1 (Cambridge: Cambridge Univ. Press, 1922), 181.

[16] Hermann Jacobi, trans., *Jaina Sutras, Part II, The Uttaradhyayana Sutra: The Sutrakritanga Sutra* (Delhi: AVF Books Distributors; reprinted 1987, S.B.E. Series, vol. 45), Introduction, xxvii–xxviii.

[17] See Satis Chandra Vidyabhusana, *A History of Indian Logic* (Calcutta: Univ. of Calcutta, 1921), 167–84. For an English translation of Syadvadamanjari, see Sarvepalli Radhakrishnan and Charles A. Moore, eds., *A Source Book in Indian Philosophy* (Princeton, NJ: Princeton Univ. Press, 1973), 260–68.

(There are two Bhadrabahus, a senior [433–357 BCE] and a junior [ca. 375 CE], and although this description is generally attributed to the senior, we cannot be certain.) There is clear mention of *Syadvada* in the *Nyayavatara* of Siddhasena Divakara (ca. 480–550 CE). Samantabhadra (ca. 600 CE) has given a full exposition of the seven parts of *Syadvada* or *saptabhanginaya* in his *Aptamimamsa*. So it is clear that *Syadvada* was well developed by the sixth century CE. In the medieval period of Indian logic this theory received a great deal of attention. For example, in the thirteenth century we have a separate treatise entitled *Syadvadamanjari* by Mallisena. There are many other later works on the *Syadvada,* such as Vimala Dasa's *Saptabhangit-arangini.*

INSPIRATION FROM SRI RAMAKRISHNA

Sri Ramakrishna (1836–86) of Bengal was a pluralist through and through, and still today he serves as an example of and inspiration for openness within Bengali culture. Besides having a deep Goddess-experience, he was initiated by different teachers in different paths toward realization of the Divine: in Tantrism by Bhairavi, in Vaishnavism by Jatadhari, and in Advaita by Tota Puri. He also practiced Islam in 1866 and had a Christ experience in 1874.[18]

Sri Ramakrishna compares God to a chameleon that changes color, and he held that those who quarrel about the doctrine of God are like those who quarrel about the color of a chameleon. God reveals Godself to seekers in various forms and aspects. All paths lead to God. People worship God according to their tastes and temperaments, and this is like different children eating different dishes cooked by a mother who knows the taste of each child. "Don't you know what difference in taste is? Some enjoy fish curry; some, fried fish; some, pickled fish; and again, some, the rich dish of fish pilau."[19]

According to Sri Ramakrishna, different religions address the same reality in different ways, like children addressing the same father differently; the elder ones' may call him distinctly as Baba or Papa, but the babies can at best call him Ba or Pa. Surely the father will not mind. He knows that they too are calling him, only they cannot pronounce his name well.[20]

Sri Ramakrishna was of the following firm conviction: "God can be realised through all paths. All religions are true."[21] He explained this through the

---

[18] K. P. Aleaz, *Harmony of Religions: The Relevance of Swami Vivekananda* (Calcutta: Punthi Pustak, 1993), 33–44.

[19] *The Gospel of Sri Ramakrishna (G.R.)*, original in Bengali by Mahendranath Gupta (M), a direct disciple of Sri Ramakrishna, and translated by Swami Nikhilananda, vol. 2, 8th ed. (Madras: Sri Ramakrishna Math, 1985), 910–11; see *G.R.*, 1:149; 2:559, 859.

[20] *G.R.*, 1:112.

[21] *G.R.*, 1:111.

analogy of reaching the roof through different ways, either by stone stairs or wooden stairs or by bamboo steps or by a rope or a bamboo pole.[22] Or, in another analogy:

> It is like your coming to Dakshineswar by carriage, by boat, by steamer, or on foot. You have chosen the way according to your convenience and tastes; but the destination is the same. Some of you have arrived earlier than others, but all have arrived.[23]

For Sri Ramakrishna, dogmatists are those who see only one aspect of God and limit God to that aspect; they are like the blind men who examined the elephant and came to different conclusions and quarreled about their partial or limited standpoints.[24] Further, "He is indeed a real man who has harmonized everything. Most people are one sided. But I find that all opinions point to the One. All views . . . have that One for their center. He who is formless, again, is endowed with form. The attributeless Brahman is my Father. God with attributes is my Mother."[25]

THE WAY FORWARD:
PLURALISTIC INCLUSIVISM

Pluralistic inclusivism is a perspective in which the religious resources of the world are understood to be the common property of humanity. It envisages a relational convergence of religions that will make possible the enrichment of religious experiences through mutual sharing. Thus, this approach can enrich not only Christian theology but also the theologies of other faiths.[26]

The age of considering different religions as isolated, self-contained compartments is over, together with the age of considering other faiths as inferior to one's own. Mutual interaction and enrichment on an equal footing are the inevitable reality for today and for the future. Different religions will help each other to arrive at the content of the faith-experience of each. The different "paths" are no longer entirely different, isolated paths. Each path becomes a path by receiving insights from other paths. Hence, the thorny question about the uniqueness or superiority of one path over others does not arise any more. Rather, what we are interested in is the unique blending of two or more paths in order to realize their inbuilt creativity. This is dynamic

---

[22] *G.R.*, 1:514.

[23] *G.R.*, 2:1010.

[24] *G.R.*, 1:191.

[25] *G.R.*, 1:490.

[26] See K. P. Aleaz, "Religious Pluralism and Christian Witness—A Biblical-Theological Analysis," *Bangalore Theological Forum* 21, no. 4, and 22, no. 1 (1990): 48–67; Aleaz, *Theology of Religions: Birmingham Papers and Other Essays* (Calcutta: Moumita, 1998), 168–99.

interaction. Furthermore, in this perspective, conflict among different paths no longer has the last word, for there is always the possibility for natural growth from relational divergence to relational distinctiveness to relational convergence of religions.[27]

Pluralistic inclusivism gives significance to the process of hermeneutics or understanding and interpretation. It is the hermeneutical context or the contextual socio-politico-religio-cultural realities that decide the content of our knowledge and experience of the gospel. Knowledge is formulated in the very knowing process, and our understanding of the gospel of God in Jesus is a continuous, integrated, non-dual, divine-human process. Nothing is pre-given or pre-formulated. We cannot accept a timeless interpretation from somewhere else and make it applicable to our context. Understanding and interpretation belong exclusively to us and to our context, and there is therefore always the possibility for the emergence of new meanings of the gospel.[28]

Within the Asian context of religious pluralism, the Christian pilgrimage is a progressive integration of the truth revealed to others into the Christian experience of the story of Jesus. We Christians therefore have the duty to identify the glorious ways in which God has revealed Godself in the lives of other believers and to allow these revelations to help us discover new dimensions of meanings in the gospel of God in Jesus.[29] Rather than evaluating other religious experiences in terms of pre-formulated criteria, we have to allow ourselves and our understanding of the gospel to be evaluated by them. Rather than our dictating the truth to them, they, in the power of the Holy Spirit, will offer us the possibility of discovering new meanings of the person and function of Jesus. This will enable us to understand the particular Jesus in light of the universal Jesus.[30] The universal Jesus belongs to the whole of humanity in the Holy Spirit.

The approach of pluralistic inclusivism will help us deal with the complex and pivotal questions of how to arrive at an authentic, meaningful understanding of Christ and the gospel, and who is responsible for this process. The meaning of Christ and the Christian gospel has to emerge in the process of interreligious communication. Neither theologians nor religious hierarchs by themselves have the authority, or the capacity, to determine the "authentic gospel." Rather, people from diverse religio-cultural backgrounds

---

[27] K. P. Aleaz, *Dimensions of Indian Religion: Study, Experience, and Interaction* (Calcutta: Punthi Pustak, 1995), 262–63; Felix Wilfred, "Some Tentative Reflections on the Language of Christian Uniqueness: An Indian Perspective," *Vidyajyoti* 57, no. 11 (1993): 652–72; K. P. Aleaz, "Dialogical Theologies: A Search for an Indian Perspective," *Asia Journal of Theology* 6, no. 2 (1992): 274–91.

[28] K. P. Aleaz, *The Gospel of Indian Culture* (Calcutta: Punthi Pustak, 1994), 177–282.

[29] See K. P. Aleaz, *An Indian Jesus from Sankara's Thought* (Calcutta: Punthi Pustak, 1997).

[30] K. P. Aleaz, *The Role of Pramanas in Hindu-Christian Epistemology* (Calcutta: Punthi Pustak, 1991), 99–100.

will, in terms of their contexts, decide the content of the gospel. And this will lead to new and different interpretations and theologies.

Asia provides us with examples of this newness and variety. Hindus, for example, despite the missionary aggression toward their religion, have experienced the gospel of God in Jesus in terms of Neo-Vedantic thought.[31] Neo-Vedanta finds in the gospel a Jesus who had a non-dual relation with God and who now inspires all humans to achieve the same relation with God through the renunciation of the lower self. Neo-Vedantic Christology is, of course, just one among many developments in Indian Christian theology. Similar developments in the understanding of Jesus and the gospel can be found in other parts of Asia, in the context of differing religious experiences; these new understandings are being explored by people both within and outside the official Christian churches. We therefore have to question the common notion that Christians are the sole custodians of the gospel of God in Jesus. Jesus transcends Christianity. We need, urgently and broadly, the help of diverse religious faiths to arrive at the meaning and message of Jesus. This is a task for both Christians and non-Christians, as they listen to and learn from each other.[32]

Pluralistic inclusivism wholeheartedly supports the views of Aloysius Pieris and Raimon Panikkar, who both affirm that in Asia cultural incursions have religious consequences. Asia calls for *en-religionization*—religion and culture must be joined in an intimate union, analogous to that of body and soul. This, for the most part, has not taken place. The prevalent theology of religions in the Roman Catholic Church and the World Council of Churches[33]— which informs approaches called "inculturation," or "indigenization," or "contextualization"—remains defectively *inclusivistic* without being sufficiently *pluralistic*. Such a theology labors under the following typical misconceptions: the gospel is external and alien to Asians; since the gospel is unchanging all we need to do is revise its language; the primary task is to translate the gospel; we can understand our own religion from the inside, and that of others from the outside; what is not indigenous to a culture can, by external means, be made so; God the creator is a foreigner to all cultures.[34] It is necessary and urgent that Christian theologians finally understand and recognize that in the Asian context, religion and culture are integrally related. There is no way of formally removing one religion from a culture and then inserting another, in this case the Western cultural gospel that is claimed to be *sui generis*.[35]

---

[31] See Aleaz, *Jesus in Neo-Vedanta—A Meeting of Hinduism and Christianity.*

[32] See M. M. Thomas, *The Acknowledged Christ of Indian Renaissance* (Madras: CLS, 1970; Bangalore: CISRS, 1970).

[33] Aleaz, *The Gospel of Indian Culture,* 99–176.

[34] Ibid., 129–33.

[35] K. P. Aleaz, "Hope for the Gospel in Divers Religious Cultures: A Response to the Salvador Conference on World Mission and Evangelism," *Asia Journal of Theology* 11, no. 2 (1997): 263–81.

EXAMPLES OF PLURALISTIC INCLUSIVISM
IN INDIAN CHRISTIAN THEOLOGIES

The dialogical theologies of Brahmabandhav Upadhyaya, P. Chenchiah, and K. Subba Rao are practical examples from the history of Indian Christianity of pluralistic inclusivism. Brahmabandhav Upadhyaya (1861–1907)[36] believed that the Vedantic understanding of God and that of Christian belief are fundamentally the same, and that *Maya* (the concept that explains the reality of creation as totally derived from Brahman) of Advaita Vedanta is the best available concept to explain the doctrine of creation. Though he sincerely believed that he was carrying out his basic assumption that Vedanta could supply a new garb for an already formulated Christian theology, Upadhyaya did not simply reinterpret the Vedantic concepts of *Saccidananda* (Being-Consciousness-Bliss) and *Maya* and conform them to contents of an already formulated and normative Christian theology. Rather, he showed that *Saccidananda is* Trinity and that *Maya* expresses the meaning of the doctrine of creation in a far better way than the Latin root *creare*.

P. Chenchiah (1886–1959)[37] discovered the supreme value of Christ not despite Hinduism but because Hinduism had taught him to discern spiritual greatness. For him, theology was based on direct experience of Jesus, and this experience varies according to the background and context of the believer. Hence, there are always possibilities for new interpretations of Jesus. His own experience was that Christianity is not primarily a doctrine of salvation but the announcement of the advent of a new creative order in Jesus, namely, the kingdom of God where the cosmic energy or *Shakti* is the Holy Spirit. We are incorporated into the new creation of Jesus today through the Yoga of the Holy Spirit, which is in line with the integral Yoga of Sri Aurobindo.

Kalagara Subba Rao (1912–81)[38] was of the view that in following Jesus the Guru, our foundation has to be Jesus Christ alone, beyond doctrines and rituals; he described his experience in confronting Jesus through Advaita Vedantic categories. Jesus died to the body and ego through self-sacrifice, and he calls us to follow his way through his grace. We are in reality Spirit. Ignorance *(ajnana)* of this fact makes us servants of the body; this ignorance is what constitutes the Fall, our "sinful" state. Jesus leads us from *ajnana* to *jnana* (knowledge), from the material realm to the spiritual realm, from sin to salvation.

In my own theological works I have tried to walk in the footsteps of such pluralistic inclusivistic Indian theologians and carry on the work of developing

---

[36] K. P. Aleaz, *Christian Thought through Advaita Vedanta* (Delhi: ISPCK, 1996), 9–38.

[37] See G. V. Job, et al., *Rethinking Christianity in India* (Madras: A. N. Sundarisanam, 1938).

[38] Aleaz, *Christian Thought through Advaita Vedanta*, 45–62.

a truly Indian Christianity. In this task Sankara's Advaitic Vedanta has been for me a particularly rich source for reinterpreting and reinvigorating the content of God's revelation in Jesus.[39] For instance, the person of Jesus can be seen and experienced anew as the extrinsic denominator *(upadhi)*, the name and form *(namarupa)*, and the effect *(karya)* of Brahman, or as the delimitation *(ghatakasa)* as well as the reflection *(abhasa)* of Brahman. Advaita can also provide a metaphysical basis for understanding and relating to the self-sacrifice of Jesus on the cross. In Jesus, Being itself *(Sat)* is perceived in a form other than Being; the entire purpose of Jesus' existence was to let Being take form and show Itself in and as him. Therefore, the total negation of Jesus on the cross is the total affirmation of Being. And in this, Jesus calls us to do likewise—to sacrifice ourselves as Jesus did in order to discover our own reality in Being and let Being be seen in us.

Furthermore, Advaita Vedanta provides us, I believe, with the conceptual and religious tools to understand the life and ministry of Jesus as the embodiment and representation of the all-pervasive *(sarva-gatatvam)*, illuminative *(jyotih)*, and unifying *(ekikritya)* power of the Supreme Atman. In Jesus we understand that the Supreme Brahman, as Pure Consciousness *(pragnanaghanam)*, is the Witness *(saksi)* and the Self of all that exists *(sarvatma)*; this means that human liberation is eternally present and possible *(nityasiddhasvabhavm)*. Many in both the East and West feel that Western Christian theology in the past has distorted the religion of Jesus that holds up renunciation as a means to realize one's own divinity and turned it into a secular, dogmatic religion that insists on the vileness of human nature and necessity of Jesus' death to atone an angry God. If there is truth in such accusations, an Indian Christology that understands Jesus' person and work from the perspective of Advaitic Vedanta can perhaps provide much needed help.

CONCLUSION

The idea that the diverse religious resources of the world are all our common property may be for many beyond the reach of their comprehension and commitments. But that is exactly the vision and the challenge of what I have described and proposed as pluralistic inclusivism. Pluralism (the diversity of religions) calls for pluralistic inclusivism (the mutual engagement and enrichment of all by all). The religious experiences and insights of others can provide me with deeper, broader understandings of my own experience. I have tried in this essay to describe not just how pluralistic inclusivism should work in theory but also how it has worked in the multi-religious context of India, particularly how it has worked for Indian Christians. The religious-theological acceptance of pluralism by Hindu thinkers in diverse dimensions

---

[39] See Aleaz, *An Indian Jesus from Sankara's Thought.*

provides the cultural context. The historical dealings of the Thomas Christians with their religious neighbors provide an early example. Syadvada and Sri Ramakrishna provide the atmosphere. The life and thought of Indian Christian theologians such as S. K. George and Manilal C. Parekh provide real possibilities.

Pluralism calls for pluralistic inclusivism. If the religious communities of our world can hear and respond to that call, ours will be a better world.

14

Power, Politics, and Plurality

The Struggles of the World Council of Churches to Deal with Religious Plurality

S. WESLEY ARIARAJAH

In an article entitled "Interreligious Dialogue as a Political Quest," well-known Indian theologian Felix Wilfred points to one of the missing dimensions in the practice and reflection on interreligious dialogue in India today. Dialogue is taking place mainly at two levels, says Wilfred. The first, which he calls "formal," is the one in which there is a "sharing and exchange in matters of doctrines, world-views, and ideals the various religious traditions propose, and the experience to which each religion leads its followers." The second, identified as "informal," happens in day-to-day life, where peoples of different religious traditions grow together in mutual understanding and foster goodwill in a dialogue of life. "While not denying the importance of the practice and theology of religions," says Wilfred, "I must point out that they do not deal with *religious* groups as units of power, nor do they take into account the *power relationships* in the wider society."[1]

Wilfred is, of course, concerned primarily with the current political situation in India, but he is well aware of many other places where political factions function also as religious entities and use religious identities as forces of mobilization. He is quite right in pointing out that in such situations any interreligious dialogue that ignores the "power dimension" would neglect one of the crucial elements that need to be addressed in seeking to foster interreligious relations.

---

[1] Felix Wilfred, "Interreligious Dialogue as a Political Quest," *Journal of Dharma* 28, no. 1 (2002).

What Wilfred says about the social dimension of interreligious dialogue is also true at the theological level. My own experience of dealing with the question of religious plurality within the ecumenical movement for over some three decades, especially in the setting of the World Council of Churches (WCC), has convinced me that the most difficult part in the discussions on religious plurality has been to admit, lift up, and deal with the power element, the political dimensions, and perceived threats that are part and parcel of theological discussions on plurality. This essay seeks to trace the discussions on religious plurality within the ecumenical movement in general, and the World Council of Churches in particular, in order to identify some of these issues and to explore ways in which they might be addressed.[2]

IMPERIAL LEGACY OF THE CHURCH

The story of how Christianity, a persecuted minority religious tradition, became the imperial religion of the Roman Empire is well known. Emperor Constantine not only reversed the historical fortune of Christian tradition at that time but also radically influenced the theological self-understanding of the church and its theology. His influence first affected the internal life of the church. Constantine was convinced that plurality of theological perspectives within the Christian tradition, and consequent divisions within the church, would bring about disunity within the empire with serious political consequences to Roman rule. He also thought that such divisions might offend the God of the Christian tradition, who, he believed, had been giving him his imperial victories.

It is not surprising, then, that the emperor himself got deeply embroiled in enforcing the theological unity of the church. Faced with the Arian controversy over the theological interpretation of the nature of the Trinity, Constantine called the Council of Nicea in May 325 and gave an opening address to the council. In an attempt to resolve the issue, he had written a letter in advance to the chief protagonist of the controversy, Arius of Alexandria, stating that the matter had to be settled at Nicea. When the question could not be resolved, Arius, who was sincere and astute in his theological struggle to deal with the trinitarian formula, was branded a heretic and condemned!

---

[2] The phrase *ecumenical movement* denotes all the movements within the church that seek to bring about its unity and renewal. The Roman Catholic Church, for instance, although not a member of the WCC, became an important player in the field after the Second Vatican Council. However, since the WCC includes most of the mainline Protestant churches, most of the Orthodox churches, and has membership that constitutes over 350 churches from over 100 countries, it is seen as the most comprehensive and significant instrument of the ecumenical movement. The WCC was inaugurated in 1948 in Amsterdam as the culmination of the Missionary, Faith and Order, and Life and Work movements that were inspired by the first ecumenical World Mission Conference held in 1910 at Edinburgh, Scotland.

Divisive theological issues had arisen within Christianity from its very beginnings, and theological compromises had to be found to keep the community together (Acts 10; Gal 2; 1 Cor 1). However, the excessive preoccupation with unity, preserving the "oneness" of the church and the "oneness" of its truth, the practice of arriving at and preserving that oneness of truth through exclusion, and consequent intolerance of theological plurality within the church were all now a part of Constantine's own interest in preserving unity in the political realm. The emperors who followed him kept up this pressure.

Following his logic, Constantine also outlawed, suppressed, or effectively marginalized all other religious traditions within the empire. An empire could not tolerate opposition, division, alternate powers, and questioning of authority. Its very life, legitimacy, and credibility depended on its "oneness." Constantine felt that this was also true in the religious realm. So he empowered the leadership of the church with authority and power to preserve and implement the "true religion" with the same rigor with which the provincial governors would enforce the laws of the empire among the people.

The church's practice, theology, and approach to internal and external religious plurality during the Middle Ages were, to a large extent, built on this legacy. No doubt, there was dissent, other expressions of the church, and alternate theological traditions. But the predominant approach of the church to plurality, both in attitude and in theology, was imperial. The church began to have powers on matters spiritual and theological similar to those of the empire on temporal matters. Often the temporal and spiritual powers were in the same hands.

It is this inability to cope with the "many" that lies behind the church's rejection of Judaism, along with the claim that it was now the "New Israel." And when Islam sprang up and began to expand, the church responded much the same way an empire would to the rise of a rival power. The instinctive response was to see Islam as an illegitimate rival religious tradition. This legacy still marks the Western churches' popular attitude to the Islamic reality in our day.

THE COLONIAL LEGACY OF THE THEOLOGY OF RELIGIONS

Unfortunately, the substantial expansion of the Christian tradition into Asia, sub-Saharan Africa, Latin America, and other parts of the world took place during Western colonial expansion into these regions. Colonizers were, of course, initially interested in creating trading outposts, which were eventually made into colonies. The church saw in this political expansion the opportunity to also spread the message of the gospel.

Columbus himself reflected on the religious motivation that went with his "discoveries." In the dedicatory opening of his diary of the first voyage (Friday, August 3, 1492) he wrote:

Your highnesses, as Catholics, Christians and Princes who love the Christian faith and long to see its increase, and as enemies of the sect of Mahomet and of all idolatries and heresies, have seen fit to send me, Christopher Columbus, to the said parts of the Indies to see . . . what way there may be to convert them to our holy faith.[3]

By the time the eighteenth- and nineteenth-century expansion began, the Enlightenment and Reformation had effectively undermined the imperial hold of the church on the populace; despite persecutions and outright wars to contain it, plurality had been established within the church. But both the Roman Catholic Church and the Protestant churches that broke off inherited the imperial and exclusivist attitude to plurality—both toward each other and toward other religious traditions. With the Enlightenment came the idea that the Western culture, now fortified by scientific thinking and technology, was superior to other cultures and ways of life. A genuine mission, therefore, had to both evangelize and Westernize; the preaching of the gospel also had to include the transmission of the "superior values" of the emerging Western culture. In other words, colonization, evangelization, and Westernization were seen as a continuum. They belonged together and were to enable one another.

Mission history is ambiguous. On the one hand, there are moving stories of profound compassion, humanization, and selfless service to the most depressed and marginalized communities in many parts of the world. On the other, the history of mission is closely associated with the domination, subjugation, genocide, cultural insensitivity, intolerance, and violence that accompanied colonization. At the heart of all this was the certainty of the assumed superiority of the Christian faith and of the Western culture over all other religious traditions and cultures.

Any attempt to understand the classical theology of religions of the church and its attitude to plurality without this political component would miss an important dimension of the question. Biblical and theological formulations were to serve and undergird this assumed superiority.

"EVANGELIZATION OF THE WORLD IN THIS GENERATION"

The modern ecumenical movement was born in this context. The superiority of the Christian religious tradition and of "Christian culture" over all other religious traditions and cultures was simply assumed. The conviction of superiority was not arrived at by comparison of the Christian tradition with other traditions or by assessing the merits and demerits of other cultures in relation to Western culture. Rather, it was believed to be self-evident.

---

[3] Quoted in Michael Prior, *The Bible and Colonialism—A Moral Critique* (Sheffield: Sheffield Academic Press, 1999), 53.

Hendrik Kraemer put it this way: "The Christian revelation as the record of God's self-disclosing revelation in Jesus Christ is absolutely *sui generis*. It is the story of God's sovereign redeeming acts having become decisively and finally manifest in Jesus Christ, the Son of the living God, in whom God became flesh and revealed His truth and grace."[4]

Claims to an encounter with God in Jesus Christ that was profound, life changing, and salvific would, of course, be quite legitimate. There would also be good reasons for those who have had such an encounter to want to share the experience with others; all who encounter profound religious experiences feel the need to share it with others. However, the conviction that what God has done in Christ is "self-evident" and that it is "decisive and final" and is therefore the "only way" in which humankind would have access to God are dimensions of Christian faith that cannot be justified on the basis of faith experience. Faith experience is of necessity positive about oneself and lies in the realm of inner certainty *(anubhava)*. It can lead one to the realization of the futility of what one had held to or believed in until that time. And yet, negative determinations about other experiences are not part of one's own faith experience. They are *theological constructs* that one builds on the basis of one's own experience.

Since human beings are rational beings, to use one's own experience as the basis for further reflection on wider issues, including the possibility of other religious experiences, is a natural and legitimate activity. Thus having a "theology" and a "theology of religions," explicit or implicit, is part of being a religious person or community. What is most important, therefore, is to seek to find the *factors* that influence a religious community when it builds theological constructs around its religious experience, both about itself and others.

It is unfortunate that the church's close association with political powers and the thinking that went with it of "conquering the world" informed the theological construct that was built around the message of the gospel during eighteenth- and nineteenth-century missionary activity. While the colonial powers were conquering the political entities for the kings in Portugal, Spain, Britain, and elsewhere, missionaries were to "conquer" the world for Christ on the spiritual plane.

It would be unfair to the history of Christian missions to attribute to it all the sentiments that drove political colonization. Much of the mission activities were based on the conviction about the gospel as a message of God's loving relationship to the world, of the power of the Christian message to liberate human beings from their "bondage to sin," and of Christ as a mediator of reconciliation between human beings and between human beings and God. These convictions were often accompanied by genuine service to those in need and by activities that liberated individuals and communities from

---

[4] Hendrik Kraemer, "Continuity or Discontinuity," *The Authority of the Faith: International Missionary Council Meeting at Tambaram, Madras, December 12–29, 1938* (London: Oxford Univ. Press, 1939), 1–2.

economic and social bondage. In fact, such noble goals were at the heart of the first World Missionary Conference of 1910, which saw the times in which it met as the "decisive hour of Christian mission"; and the leader of the conference, John R. Mott, called for the "evangelization of the world in this generation."

The "colonial" dimension of mission lies in its conclusion that its way was the *only* way that God could relate to humankind and humankind to God. And the power dimension is demonstrated in its unilateral conclusion that all other ways of relating to God are not valid, especially when that conclusion has been reached not on the basis of an informed understanding and experience of other ways but purely on the principle: since we are right, everyone else must necessarily be wrong.

This is the language of power.

In other words, the Christian theology of religions that informed the missionary movement was made up of a curious mix of positive theological affirmations of what Christians believed God to have done in Jesus Christ and a sense of power based on the necessary superiority of that message over all other messages. The "theological power" came from the actual political power that the "Christian" colonizing empires were having over the nations that they set out to conquer. It was Constantine again, but in a different garb.

POWER STRUGGLE WITHIN THE ECUMENICAL MOVEMENT

The story of the theology (or, theologies) of religions within the ecumenical movement is the story of the struggle to unravel this unholy mix. The power dimension of this story is evident, first of all, in the fact that those who were advocating changes in the churches' view of religious pluralism were those "in the field" with concrete experiences of relating to peoples of other religious traditions. Their challenge to rethink the theology of religions was experienced as a threat by those in ecclesial power who had the mandate to promote missions in order to enlarge the size, place, and influence of the church in the world.

What is of interest is that these "battles" between those who urged change in the churches' theology of religions and those opposed to it were not deemed to be personal conflicts or battles between two power groups within the church. Rather, many of the struggles about the theology of religions were considered theological battles. A number of positive and negative theological boundaries with clear "no go" areas had been built around the theology of religions that was developed during the colonial period. And these boundaries have, for a long time, been held up as the benchmarks for orthodoxy in Christian relationships to other religious traditions. These boundaries were based in theology, but their intent was to preserve power.

It is not the intention of this essay to examine in detail these positive and negative boundary markers of the classical theology of religions. However, it is important to note them in order to understand the theological controversies that have marked the ecumenical discussions of religious plurality and its significance for Christian theology and practice. In so doing, one should recognize that the Roman Catholic and Protestant traditions, although part of one ecumenical movement, have different emphases in dealing with plurality and different concerns in maintaining boundaries. The WCC is primarily a fellowship of Protestant and Orthodox traditions. The emphasis here is on the Protestant tradition.[5] The Orthodox tradition, much of which was under Communist rule during the period under discussion, had other preoccupations.

THEOLOGICAL BOUNDARIES

Three theological emphases fortified the Protestant/Ecumenical theology of mission that developed an exclusive attitude to other religious traditions. First was the concept of "salvation history," which looked at human history as God's arena of activity to bring humankind from its predicament to the state God intends for it. Here the church took over the self-understanding of the Jewish people as "chosen" to be "God's people" in God's plan of redemption of the world. Jewish people believed that God was still the "God of the nations" and that their own call to "live out God's righteousness among the nations" was part of the mystery of God's plan of establishing God's shalom in the world. In this thinking there was no need for a world mission to make everyone become Jewish.

Protestant theology of that time affirmed this Jewish understanding but only as a "preparation" for God's "decisive" act in history in Jesus Christ. It not only held that God has now created a new community, the church, but also believed that salvation of the whole humankind depended on it becoming part of this new historical community. In so doing the church had cornered itself, theologically, into rejecting the reality of other religious traditions, including the Jewish tradition, as possible avenues of God's self-revelation, and had assigned to itself the task of challenging all humankind to become part of its community.

Second, based on this first element, was the sharp distinction that was made by Karl Barth between the gospel, on the one hand, and religions and cultures, on the other. Barth's theology had an enormous impact on the ecu-

---

[5] The Roman Catholic Church, although active in the ecumenical movement, is not a member of the WCC. Its theological reflections on the issue put greater emphasis on ecclesiology, while Protestant thinking is centered in Christology. For historical reasons, the Orthodox branch of the church was not involved in the eighteenth- and nineteenth-century missionary movement and the kind of missionary expansion espoused by the Roman Catholic Church and the Protestant traditions. Therefore, even though there is much potential for a creative theology of religions in Orthodox theology, it has not been developed into major theological positions within Orthodox theology.

menical movement. In his view, the gospel, as God's unique act of self-revelation, was in discontinuity with all religious and cultural traditions of humankind (including Christianity as a religion), which were seen as part of human rebellion against God, or vain human attempts to grasp God, who was totally inaccessible to humans except through self-revelation. By locating all religions and cultures within humanity's rebellion against God, and by presenting the gospel as that which creates a "crisis" in the life of all humans, demanding repentance and faith, Barth had devalued all other religious traditions and the cultures that arose from them.[6]

Third, perhaps the most important emphasis within Protestant tradition, is a particular reading and interpretation of the Bible. The "missiological" reading of the Bible lifted up some of the strands of thought and some verses, taken out of their historical contexts, to "prove" that Jesus was the only way, the truth, and the life, and that no one can know God except through him. Given this reality, Christians were under "obligation" to go out into the world, to preach the gospel, to baptize other nations and peoples into the Christian faith.

In other words, salvation history gave the context, the gospel provided the rationale, and the Bible offered the authority to engage in world mission and, at the same time, to devalue other religious traditions.

THE "NO-GO" AREAS

The theological constructs above were broken down into three basic popular theological tenets that surface in almost all church and ecumenical debates on a Christian theology of religions:

- The *uniqueness and finality of Christ,* by which is meant that whatever merits may be found in other religious traditions, God's revelation in Christ and what God has done in the life, death, and resurrection of Jesus Christ are "decisive" for the salvation of humankind;
- *The mission imperative,* by which is meant that since Christians have become the recipients of the saving knowledge of what God has done in Christ for all humankind, it is an incontrovertible duty of the church to be in mission to the world; and
- *Biblical faith,* by which is meant that anything that moves away from the above convictions betrays the Bible, which as the revealed word of God witnesses to the truths above.

These three popular beliefs, which in reality function as the basic "creed" of the Protestant congregations, are further safeguarded by what I have elsewhere

---

[6] See Karl Barth, *Church Dogmatics* (Louisville, KY: Westminster John Knox Press, 1994), para. 16, "Knowledge of God" (IV, 2, 128); and paras. 21 and 22, "On the Question of Natural Theology" (I, 2, 301–2; I, 2, 299–300).

referred to as the "three classical fears" of the missionary movement: syncretism, relativism, and universalism. In most debates on Christian approaches to other religious traditions within the ecumenical movement one would run into these three terms. The outstanding example is the Nairobi debate at the Fifth Assembly of the WCC.

THE NAIROBI DEBATE

The WCC had begun a program entitled Dialogue with People of Living Faiths in 1971. At the Nairobi Assembly in 1975 a section report was offered under the title "Seeking Community"; it called for new ways of relating to people of other religious traditions in order to build community across religious barriers. The mission constituency from Europe within the assembly attacked the report for "compromising the uniqueness and finality of Christ," "promoting a universalistic view of salvation," "compromising the missionary mandate," and taking Christian theology in the directions of "syncretism" and "relativism." In other words, all the fears mentioned above were expressed in a single debate in a world Christian gathering of some three thousand persons from all the major branches of the church.

What is of greater interest was that most of those who defended a new relationship with peoples of other religious traditions came from the South, and those who opposed came from the powerful churches in the North, especially Europe. The opposition was vigorous, and it played to the Christian need for self-assertion as a religion that has been entrusted with "the truth." Christian faith was presented as in danger of dilution and compromise. There was no hope that the assembly would receive the report in the form it was presented.

The report was sent back to the drafting group with the request to accommodate the sentiments expressed in the debate. It would be accepted in a later session only with a "Preamble" that introduced all those theological sentiments that the traditionalists were looking for:

- We all agreed that the *skandalon* (stumbling block) of the Gospel will be always with us. . . .
- While we do seek wider community with people of other faiths, cultures and ideologies, we do not think that there will ever be a time in history when the tension will be resolved between the belief in Jesus Christ and unbelief.. . .
- We should make a proper distinction between divisions created by the judging Word of God and the division of sin. . . .
- We are all agreed that the great commission of Jesus Christ which asks us to go out into all the world and make disciples of all nations, and to baptize them in the Triune name, should not be abandoned or betrayed, disobeyed or compromised. . . .

f other religious traditions. The task of seeking clarity to these theological questions was seen as an important step in promoting the Christian theological task in a religiously plural world:

- What is the relationship between the universal creative/redemptive activity of God toward all humankind and the particular creative/redemptive activity of God in the history of Israel and in the person and work of Christ?
- Are Christians to speak of God's work in the lives of all men and women only in tentative terms of hope that they may experience something of him, or more positively in terms of God's self-disclosure to people of living faiths and ideologies and in the struggles of human life?
- How are Christians to find from the Bible criteria in their approach to people of living faiths and ideologies, recognizing, as they must, the authority accorded to the Bible by Christians of all centuries . . . and that partners in dialogue have other starting points and resources, both in holy books and traditions of teachings?
- What is the biblical view and Christian experience of the operation of the Holy Spirit, and is it right and helpful to understand the work of God outside the church in terms of the doctrine of the Holy Spirit?[9]

It is of interest that *Guidelines* raised all the crucial theological issues for good discussion of religious plurality within the ecumenical movement—the doctrine of God as creator, the significance of Christ, the authority of scripture, and the place and role of the Holy Spirit in the economy of salvation. A breakthrough in the Christian theology of religions required that these questions be faced with the seriousness they deserved. A closer look at the discussions that follow, however, shows that the problem has to do not so much with a lack of theological reflection but of political will.

DEVELOPMENTS IN ECUMENICAL THINKING

Over the decades since the World Mission Conference in Tambaram (1938), much has happened within Protestant and ecumenical theology. Most Christians have gradually moved away from the narrow concept of salvation history that marginalized Judaism as a preparation for Christianity and limited God's activity only to a narrow section of humankind. The missionary movement itself, in its World Mission Conference in Mexico City in 1968, developed the concept of the "mission of God," which affirmed that God was in

---

[9] *Guidelines for Dialogue with People of Living Faiths and Ideologies* (Geneva: WCC Publications, 1979), 13.

- We are all opposed to any form of syncretism, incipient scent or developed.
- We view the future of the Church's mission as full of hope is not upon human efforts that our hope is based, but or power and promise of God.[7]

As someone who had participated in the debate on the floor of bly, I was astounded by the "Preamble" that was added by the draf to make the report "receivable." It appeared to be catering to a dee logical need of some sections of the church. The "Preamble" did any additional theological light on the issue. Rather, it appeared the report from going into some of the "no-go" areas in Christian ship to other religious traditions. The North-South divide over the also significant.

David E. Jenkins (later to become the Bishop of Durham, UK) ticle on the assembly, said that the attempt of the churches livi giously plural societies to make claims at Nairobi for dialogue outcry about syncretism and betrayal of the Gospel," and that "the of the drafting committee to this outcry left many Asians and othe that their insights and convictions were being trampled on and be

Also of interest in the Nairobi debate was that many from Eu North America who came from churches that had foreign mission tacit agreement with the main content of the original report. Bu them, especially in leadership, maintained a studied silence when were pitched in terms of "compromising the uniqueness of Chris "betraying the missionary mandate." Many of the discussions on ogy of religions in official church gatherings suffer from this underl litical dimension." Many in leadership can ill afford to be accused promising Christ or of betraying the missionary mandate.

The Nairobi discussions cast a shadow over the possibility of co the dialogue program within the WCC. Fortunately, a special cons called in April 1977 at Chiang Mai, Thailand, to clarify the issues c tism, relativism, Christian understanding of mission, and so on, ena Dialogue Sub-Unit of the WCC to continue its mandate.

While clarifying interfaith dialogue and drawing up the *Guide Dialogue with People of Living Faiths and Ideologies*, the Chiang M ing identified some of the crucial theological questions that the needed to face in order to make theological sense of their life with n

---

[7] David M. Paton, ed., *Breaking Barriers, Nairobi 1975: The Official the Fifth Assembly of the World Council of Churches, Nairobi, 23 Nove December, 1975* (Grand Rapids, MI: Eerdmans; Geneva: WCC Publication 73–74.

[8] David E. Jenkins, "Nairobi and the Truly Ecumenical: Contribution cussion about the Subsequent Tasks of the WCC," *The Ecumenical Review* (1976): 281.

mission in the world in all aspects of its life. It interpreted Christian mission as participation in the mission of God.

The Barth-Kraemer concept of the gospel has come under challenge from many angles. There is a great variety of interpretations on the meaning and significance of the gospel in Asia, Latin America, Africa, as well as within the Western theological tradition. In fact, both Barth and Kraemer were uncomfortable with the way their interpretation of the gospel marginalized other religious traditions; they had begun to rethink their positions in their later writings. Certainly few are willing in our day to see all religions and cultures simply as part of human rebellion against God.

There have also been enormous changes in Christian approach to the Bible. The feminist/Womanist critique and the Latin American, Asian, African, and other "readings" of the Bible have resulted in radical changes in the way biblical authority is understood.

Christian approaches and relationships with people of other religious traditions have also undergone massive changes. Groups from even the most conservative sections of the church emphasize the need for respect and mutuality in interreligious relations. Interfaith dialogue has become an accepted form of Christian ministry. There has also been an enormous amount of rethinking in the area of the theology of religions.

What has all this meant to the discussions on religious plurality within the ecumenical movement? What has been the result of exploring the theological issues raised within the *Guidelines for Dialogue* at the Chiang Mai meeting?

Unfortunately attempts to go further in the theology of religions at the WCC's Sixth Assembly in Vancouver, Canada, in 1983 led to discussions not dissimilar to the Nairobi ones. Again the powerful mission agencies resisted attempts to recognize any statement that spoke of God's salvific presence among peoples of other traditions. The phrase that recognized God's creative presence "in the religious experience of people of other faiths" was contested, and the report was not accepted until it was revised to read, "we recognize God's creative work in the *seeking for religious truth* among the people of other faiths" (emphasis added). It became politically untenable to accord to people of other faiths the chance of *finding* God within their religious traditions. Again voices from sections of the powerful mission churches led the debate while those in leadership who disagreed with them from within those very churches maintained a studied silence.[10]

As interfaith relations grew rapidly in the 1980s and 1990s, more and more bold and creative thinking was coming out from many theologians on the issues of religious plurality, Christology, and the theology of religions. The WCC found itself increasingly lagging behind in its theology of mission, which, despite many attempts to move forward, appeared to be stuck in 1938. Therefore, a more concerted effort was made in the preparations for

---

[10] David Gill, ed., *Gathered for Life: Official Report, Sixth Assembly, World Council of Churches, Vancouver, Canada, 24 July–10 August 1983* (Grand Rapids, MI: Eerdmans; Geneva: WCC Publications, 1983), 31–42.

the 1989 World Mission Conference at San Antonio, Texas, to address the issue of the theology of religions. San Antonio was also the first World Mission Conference to which guests of other religious traditions were invited as observers.

It must be said that despite the deeply divisive debate over the same issues of syncretism and the "uniqueness of Christ," San Antonio could not ignore the revolution that has been taking place within Christian theology on religious plurality. For the first time there was willingness to move at least to a neutral position in relation to God's dealing with persons in other religious traditions: "We cannot point to any other way of salvation than Jesus Christ; at the same time we cannot set limits to the saving power of God" and "In dialogue we are invited to listen, in openness to the possibility that the God we know in Jesus Christ may encounter us also in the lives of our neighbors of other faiths."

The report recognized that it had not affirmed other faiths in a positive manner but had only succeeded in accommodating the growing pressure to move away from its negative views. It also recognized that it could not draw the necessary theological conclusions of some of its theological affirmations about God's activity outside the Christian experience. Speaking about its own convictions of the need of Christian missions, it said:

> We are well aware that these convictions and the ministry of witness [to Jesus Christ] stand in tension with what we have affirmed as God being present in and at work in people of other faiths; we appreciate this tension, we do not attempt to resolve it.[11]

TENTATIVE EXPLORATIONS

The Dialogue program of the WCC sought to explore the theological issues raised by religious plurality through a four-year study process in the churches. A study guide entitled "My Neighbour's Faith and Mine—Theological Discoveries through Interfaith Dialogue" was designed with nine sections that dealt with the theological issues raised by religious plurality. It was translated into eighteen languages and used widely to get feedback from the churches. These findings were then used to call a theological consultation of a group of Protestant, Orthodox, and Roman Catholic theologians who had struggled with the issue. This meeting, held in Baar, near Zurich, Switzerland, in 1990, made several affirmations that appeared to take the process forward. Here are some extracts of the Baar Statement:

> People at all times and in all places responded to the presence and activity of God among them, and have given their witness to their en-

---

[11] Frederick R. Wilson, ed., *The San Antonio Report: Your Will Be Done: Mission in Christ's Way* (Geneva: WCC Publications, 1990), 31–33.

counters with the living God. In this testimony they speak both of seeking and having found salvation, or wholeness, or enlightenment, or divine guidance, or rest, or liberation.

We therefore take this witness with the utmost seriousness and acknowledge that among all the nations and peoples there has always been the saving presence of God. . . .

We see plurality of religious traditions as both the result of the manifold ways in which God has related to peoples and nations as well as a manifestation of the richness and diversity of humankind. We affirm that God has been present in their seeking and finding.[12]

The Baar meeting was a consultation that had no official standing. When the next World Mission Conference was held in 1996 in Bahia, Brazil, every effort was made to feed the findings of the Baar meeting into its theological explorations. But Bahia would not go beyond San Antonio. The fears of syncretism, relativism, and universalism that would relativize the significance of Christ and the importance of mission still remained the main obstacle to responding meaningfully to the reality of religious plurality.

It appears that at the psychological level the church has not yet adjusted to the possibility of being one among the many. It has not learned the art of being deeply convinced about what it has experienced without having to deny the experience of others. It has not been able to contemplate the possibility that God may have many ways of bringing people to their intended destiny, the Christian way being one of them. Above all, it has fallen into the trap of thinking that if others are true, then it has to be wrong. In other words, a mentality has taken hold of the church that makes it impossible for it to accept plurality. This mentality has come from its long association with a kind of power that is intolerant of any challenge to its authority. Theological argumentation to conserve this power comes in the form of unexamined slogans like "uniqueness of Christ," "priority of mission," "obedience to the Truth," and so on. Politically, such hegemony over religious truth is maintained by accusing those who disagree of being universalists, relativists, or syncretists, and in some of the churches such people are still subjected to heresy trials.

In formal church gatherings, despite the great varieties of theological perceptions among the participants, no one dares to question or ask for explanation of such claims about the "uniqueness of Christ," the "urgency of mission," and the "truth" of the Christian assertions over all other truths. This situation can only be compared to the misguided understanding of patriotism advocated and practiced in much of the United States during the invasion of Iraq. To ask "Why are we at war?" "Is this war really necessary?" "Can this war really increase our security?" and other such questions

---

[12] "Baar Statement," in *Shared Learning in a Plural World—Ecumenical Approaches to Inter-Religious Education*, ed. Gert Ruppell and Peter Schreiner (Munster: Lit Verlag, 2003), 167–71.

was itself deemed unpatriotic. Those who controlled the mass media immediately branded anyone who asked such questions liberals or unpatriotic. Thus discussions end before they begin because those who consider themselves superior, right, and invincible set the parameters of the discussion. They are also on the side of those who wield the political power.

THE CHALLENGE TO THE ECUMENICAL MOVEMENT

Indian theologian A. P. Nirmal says that the Christian church has a way of putting the cart before the horse when it comes to discussions on interreligious dialogue:

> We ask for an "adequate" theological basis for dialogue rather than reexamining our theological traditions and formulations in the light of the specific dialogical experience. We are preoccupied with our concern to safeguard the uniqueness of Jesus Christ or the finality of Jesus Christ or our total commitment to Jesus Christ before entering into a dialogical situation, rather than examining the adequacy of the doctrine of the uniqueness of Jesus or the nature of our commitment to him in the light of our actual dialogue experience.[13]

What Nirmal says is also true of the discussions on the theology of religions within the ecumenical movement. Faced with religious plurality and the reality of the religious experience of others, the movement has not been able to ask, What does it say to us about the way we had conceived God, the significance of Christ, and the missionary mandate? Rather, the response has been to find ways of fitting the reality of religious plurality into existing theological convictions. Even though this very attempt has brought some shifts in theological perspectives (as in the move from exclusivism to inclusivism), it has *not* resulted in the radical rethinking necessary to meet the theological challenges of our day.

The ecumenical movement, therefore, needs to move toward a reconstruction of a theology of religion for our day that takes full account of the actual experience of knowing other spiritual paths and of living with peoples of other religious traditions. In other words, the ecumenical movement needs *a fresh starting point* for its theological reflections on the theology of religions. Such a reflection needs to move away from the "exclusive, inclusive, and pluralist" typologies and from "Christ-centered, God-centered, and Spirit-centered" universalisms. It needs to gain from many insights coming from many quarters over the past few decades; it needs to put on hold its "received theology" until it has adequately dealt with the theological imperatives that arise from concrete experience; only at a later stage should it seek

---

[13] Arvind P. Nirmal, "Redefining the Economy of Salvation," *Indian Journal of Theology* 30, no. 3–4 (1981): 214.

to see how the traditions of faith received through the ages can be understood and integrated in the light of its current convictions. This is the way a tradition remains a *living* tradition.

It is not the intent of this essay to spell out such a theology of religions. Noting, however, the many theological proposals that have been made in this field, I would like now to lift up the ingredients that would have to inform a fresh exploration of the theology of religions within the ecumenical movement.

1. *The nature of religious traditions*: Any viable theology of religions must begin with a realistic approach to the phenomenon called religion. Wilfred Cantwell Smith has done an enormous service to our discussions by challenging the concept of religion as such, and by isolating the components that make up the abstraction called religion. By making the distinction between "faith" as an attitude of dependence ("too profound, too personal, and too divine for public exposition") and "belief" as the intellectual articulation of that faith experience, he has helped to relativize all belief systems, theologies, doctrines, and claims to truth as "human constructs" that together constitute "cumulative traditions."[14] These cumulative traditions are very much limited by the historical, cultural, and philosophic context in which the faith experience is articulated. Therefore, while the cumulative tradition is necessary for any faith community, one needs to be aware that they are of necessity human constructs built up to give coherence to the faith community.

   Many of the discussions on the theology of religions in the ecumenical movement treat theological formulations and doctrines as if they were divine revelations. There is little open acknowledgment of the cultural and historical limitations that have played significant roles in the way the meaning and significance of the experience of Christ have been spelt out. In other words, theological discussions within the ecumenical movement should be more forthcoming in recognizing the limitations of doctrines, creeds, and theological traditions. No progress can be made without this acknowledgment.

2. *Acceptance of plurality*: John Hick has made a decisively significant contribution to the discussion by raising the philosophical, moral, and ethical issues involved in insisting that one religious tradition is "true," "valid," or "in possession of the truth" over against all other religious traditions. He has also been courageous in drawing out the implications of rejecting such an idea by introducing the much-needed "Copernican revolution" into the theology of religions. Even though many who write on theology of religions succumb to the temptation of what I have called "ritual Hick-bashing" (often, of necessity, by misrepresenting him),

---

[14] W. C. Smith, *The Meaning and End of Religion*, reprint (New York: Mentor, 1964), 70ff., 141ff.

Hick's fundamental thesis that all religious traditions must be treated seriously as responses to the "Real" (in whichever way humans have conceived it) should be the bedrock of a theology of religions within the ecumenical movement.

This is important because the movement, through its theological affirmations in its early World Mission Conferences (especially Tambaram 1938), is responsible for inculcating in the Protestant Christian minds the conviction that all other religious traditions, in one sense or another, are "false," "misguided," "devoid of God's revelation," and "inadequate as ways of salvation." The concern about "relativism" and "universalism" in ecumenical discussions stems from the misguided belief that all other religious traditions are in some sense "human attempts to grasp God," while Christianity is the only one based on God's own self-revelation. Therefore, Hick's insights on the relationship of religious traditions to the "Real" and to each other should inform the new theology of religion.

3. *Nature of religious language:* Almost all discussions on the theology of religions within the ecumenical movement eventually boil down to the question of the nature of religious language, especially as it is recorded in the Bible. Despite the advances made in biblical criticism and hermeneutics, much of the rhetoric against other religions at official church gatherings is based on one particular reading of the Bible. I have not been party to a discussion on other religious traditions in any church gathering where biblical verses like "I am the way, the truth and the life," "There is no other name by which we should be saved," "Go out into all the world and preach the gospel to all the nations," and so on have not been quoted. Again, even though many in the gathering would be well aware of the radical changes that have taken place in the understanding of the nature and authority of the Bible, few would venture to challenge the literal interpretation because a literal understanding of the Bible has also been unofficially "officialized" as the only possible reading of the Bible in Protestant church gatherings. Politically, who can be "against" what the Bible is supposed to be teaching?

The ecumenical discussions on the theology of religions, therefore, will make advances only when there is greater acceptance of the nature of religious language both in the Bible and in theology. It is important to recognize the importance and validity of "confessional" language, and yet to recognize it for what it is. George Lindbeck's insights on the nature of doctrine, its cultural linguistic idiom, and its "regulative function" within faith communities need to receive much more currency in ecumenical discussions.[15] Scripture needs to be recognized as central to the faith community and still as confessional material not appropriate to measure the truth or otherwise of the claims of other religions.

---

[15] Cf. George A. Lindbeck, *Nature of Doctrine: Religion and Theology in a Postliberal Age* (Philadelphia: Westminster Press, 1984).

4. *Resisting theological intimidation:* Many of the advances made in the Christian theology of religions have not found their way into the overall theological reflections, preaching, and teaching ministries of the church because of the fears of marginalization, rejection, and loss of members at the congregational level. Somehow it is believed that only a "superior," "powerful," "one and only," "clear-cut," and "decisive" faith, one that stands in opposition to all others, will win the hearts and minds of the congregations. This is indeed true of a section of the people who look for such a religious tradition for psychological and sociological reasons—and, given the world situation, they may even be on the increase. What we also see today are increasing numbers of people who, while rooted in a particular spiritual experience, are in search of a more authentic, open, dialogical, exploratory, and non-dogmatic religious tradition. In other words, the impact of religious plurality has begun to change the religious consciousness of people, and they are looking for a culture of openness and a spirituality of inclusion. This should give greater courage to those at the helm of exploring new ways of thinking about other religious traditions so they can resist the theological intimidation that is so much a part of the discussions on the theology of religions.

NEW FRONTIER

The ecumenical movement was conceived as a "frontier movement" to enable the churches to discern and respond to the new challenges they face as new situations arise. In fact, it has been a pioneer in the area of interfaith dialogue, calling the churches to a new relationship with people of other religious traditions. It also recognizes that such a relationship cannot be taken forward without some radical rethinking of the concepts and theological approaches that were shaped when Christianity was a religion of power and privilege. Even today, some sections of Christianity have aligned themselves with those who through the exercise of brutal power would build a new Christian empire. Resisting and overcoming the political forces that would use theology and the Bible to legitimize Christian superiority over others have become part of the attempt to build a truly pluralist theology of religions within the ecumenical movement. It is a struggle that is in process.

15

The *Real* and
the Trinitarian God

REINHOLD BERNHARDT

Both his supporters and his critics agree that John Hick has been one of the most creative and influential proponents of what over the past half century, and again in this book, has come to be known as a pluralistic theology of religions. For many, *pluralism* and *Hick* are almost synonyms. But Hick has been as controversial as he has been influential. For many Christians his "Copernican revolution," or his bold foray "across the Rubicon" from inclusivism to pluralism, has left them rather disconcerted, to say the least. Theologically, Christians wonder if Hick's understanding of pluralism does justice to the integrity of their own faith; philosophically, they ask whether Hick's revolution does justice to the integrity of other faiths.

So in this essay, which represents my own efforts to elaborate a Christian response to religious pluralism, I begin with John Hick. Pivotal in his pluralistic theology is his notion of the Absolute as "the Real." In what follows, I set forth how a trinitarian understanding of God can provide the framework for a theology of religions that is both genuinely open to other religions (and therefore pluralist) but also faithful to Christian tradition (and therefore inclusive).

JOHN HICK'S CONCEPT OF THE REAL

John Hick's work in the area of theology of religions shows a shift in the mid-1980s.[1] In the earlier phase of his efforts toward a new theology of

---

[1] This became clear in John Hick, *Problems of Religious Pluralism* (London: Macmillan, 1985; 7th ed. London: Macmillan, 1994) and was elaborated then in his main work, *An Interpretation of Religion: Human Responses to the Transcendent* (London: Macmillan, 1989).

religions—now termed the pluralistic approach[2]—he called for a "Coperni-can" turn in the Christian understanding of other religions. In the place of traditional ecclesiocentrism and christocentrism Hick proposed a theocentrism in which God is seen as the center within the cosmos of religions. As part of the shift in Hick's approach, his proposal was not only grounded in detailed analyses in the philosophy of religion (and the history of religions) but was expanded significantly in content and foundation. Hick introduced the "neu-tral" notion of "the Real," a nontraditional term with which he wanted to include theistic personal concepts of God as well as non-personal viewpoints. All personal connotations, he argued, could be attributed no longer to the "Real-in-itself" but only to a specific concept of the Real.

There was no mention of a communication with Ultimate Reality or of its self-communication (revelation), for this would assume a personal center within this reality, and it would contradict its trans-personal character. For Hick, under no circumstances can personal and non-personal concepts of the Ultimate Reality be understood as manifestations of its self-revelation. Such concepts are merely human-religious images and descriptions. Even the no-tion of personality is merely a human concept. Therefore, the question of whether in the inner being of "Ultimate Reality" we are dealing with a per-sonal or an impersonal entity is in the last analysis not only unanswerable but meaningless. At best, we can reach formal, analytically true sentences, independent of experience—such as Anselm's when he spoke of God as "id quo maius cogitari non potest" (God is that reality greater than which we cannot think). Hick does recognize that we must attribute to the Real-in-itself at least two characteristics: the affirmation of its existence (albeit in fundamental distinction from all human forms and concepts of existence), and "the property of 'being able to be referred to.'"[3] To this the notion of unity can be added.[4]

With these determinants—as in general in speaking of the Real-in-itself—one is dealing with theological-philosophical assumptions that arise from reflecting upon foundational experiences of the Transcendent—experiences that are constitutive of the great religious traditions of humankind. No "ob-jective" statements are possible about the Ultimate Reality in itself. It is inef-fable.

It is precisely here that we touch the problem in Hick's approach: all pos-sible statements about the Real–in-itself are, according to Hick, only qualifi-ers of a postulate. But the religions themselves, in making their statements and claims, do not consider these claims to be merely postulates, for they feel

---

[2] So termed since *God and the Universe of Faiths: Essays in the Philosophy of Religions* (London: Macmillan, 1973; 5th ed. Oxford: Oneworld Publications, 1993).

[3] Hick, *An Interpretation of Religion,* 239.

[4] See Hick, *An Interpretation of Religion,* 248–49: "The Real, then, is the Ulti-mate Reality, not one among others; and yet it cannot literally be numbered: it is the unique One without a second" (249); see also John Hick, *The Rainbow of Faiths: Critical Dialogues on Religious Pluralism* (London: SCM Press, 1995), 69ff.

they are saying something real about the Real. Evidently, what Hick is operating with is a way of seeing or knowing that is "above" the actual, existing religions.

Perhaps we can get at this problem with reference to epistemology and ontology.

Epistemologically: Because of the ineffability of Ultimate Reality—an ineffability that does not even allow analogous language—we cannot, according to Hick, ascribe attributes to Ultimate Reality—certainly not personal attributes such as love, grace, and righteousness, which are of central importance to a Christian understanding of God. Such talk would be an offense to the Infinite, whose distance from us does not permit any kind of descriptive language.

On the other hand, Hick postulates that the Real is *authentically* available to and through the various religions. This means that its essence and, what is more, its soteriological or transformative power, can be felt and understood with some clarity, although always in fragmentary and inadequate forms that are conditioned and so limited by cultural-historical forms of perception. All knowledge of the Infinite is perspectival, which means appropriate to the context but always limited.

Ontologically: The same problems that appear in the epistemological tension between ineffability and the limited perspectives that the religions have of the Real are present in the ontological polarity of immanence and transcendence: The heavy emphasis on the inalienable transcendence of the Real leads to a devaluing of its immanence in history and in the religions. The language and rituals of the religions cannot be considered to be real symbols of Ultimate Reality; they are only conceptual "signs."

And yet, Hick is not saying that the Transcendent is utterly absent in the immanent. Leading to what might look like pantheism, he affirms the ubiquity of Ultimate Reality, always adding, immediately, that this immanence can in no way be spoken of "objectively." The immanence of the Ultimate hovers numinously within, and yet out of reach of, all the phenomenal forms the religions give it with their differing cultural conditionings. Hick is speaking about a *mediated* immanence of a reality that in the final analysis lies beyond all mediations. What is most problematic in all this is whether it is really possible to claim authenticity for any religious concept or symbol. Since the Reality to which these forms point lies shrouded in indeterminacy, the only way left to claim any authenticity for religious forms is the pragmatic criterion of what Hick calls their soteriological potential: how much they promote the well-being of humanity and the earth.

The problems we have pointed out with Hick's notion of the Real can also be found, to lesser or greater extent, in all theological positions that try to logically think through affirmations of the infinity, incomprehensibility, and transcendence of God. How are we to avoid such problems and still hold to the utter mystery of the Divine?

I suggest that the doctrine of the Trinity can be an effective aid. In the contemporary discussion on a Christian theology of religions, the Trinity has recently been presented as an effective framework for working out a coherent theology of religions.[5] The doctrine of the Trinity, it is claimed, can balance and mediate the tension between the poles of divine transcendence and immanence, God's hiddenness and revelation.

But before I lay out my trinitarian proposal, another complex but important question must be taken up; that is, in making use of a specifically Christian doctrine as the framework for a universal theology of religions, don't we inescapably fall back into either an exclusivistic or an inclusivistic approach to other religious traditions?

GLOBAL THEOLOGY AND MUTUAL INCLUSIVISM

Any viable theology of religions must take place on two levels: on the *intra-religious* level, where one explores the relation between one's own religion and other religions, and on the *meta-religious* level, where one seeks to understand the variety of religions from the perspective of the philosophy of religion.

The Intra-Religious Level

On the intra-religious level one proceeds from one's own tradition and attempts to understand and interpret the world of other religions according to the beliefs and perspectives of that tradition. Such a procedure is clearly a self-conscious inclusivism, but it need not make any claims for the superiority of one's own religion. Instead, it can proceed as an "inclusivism

---

[5] See the works of Raimon Panikkar, beginning with *The Trinity and the Religious Experience of Man* (Maryknoll, NY: Orbis Books, 1973); the contributions of Rowan Williams, Gavin D'Costa, and Christoph Schwöbel in *Christian Uniqueness Reconsidered: The Myth of a Pluralistic Theology of Religions*, ed. Gavin D'Costa (Maryknoll, NY: Orbis Books, 1990), 3–15, 16–29, 30–46; Carl E. Braaten, "Christocentric Trinitarism vs. Unitarian Theocentrism," *Journal of Ecumenical Studies* 24 (1987): 17–21; Francis X. D'Sa, *Gott der Dreieine und der All-Ganze* (Düsseldorf: Patmos, 1987); M. D. Bryant, "Interfaith Encounter and Dialogue in the Trinitarian Perspective," in *Christianity and the Wider Ecumenism*, ed. Peter C. Phan (New York: Paragon House, 1990), 3–20; Anthony Kelly, *The Trinity of Love: A Theology of the Christian God* (Wilmington, DE: Michael Glazier, 1989), 228–48; Luco. J. van den Brom, "God, Gödel and Trinity," in *Christian Faith and Philosophical Theology: Essays in Honour of Vincent Brummer*, ed. Gijsbert van den Brink et al. (Kampen: Kok Pharos, 1992), 56–75; Ninian Smart and Steven Konstantine, *Christian Systematic Theology in a World Context* (Minneapolis: Augsburg Fortress, 1992), 149–99, 439–45; S. Mark Heim, *Salvations: Truth and Difference in Religion* (Maryknoll, NY: Orbis Books, 1995); Michael von Brück. *Einheit der Wirklichkeit: Gott, Gotteserfahrung und Meditation im hinduistisch-christlichen Dialog* (München: Kaiser, 1986).

of mutuality,"[6] a position that Hick recognizes as close to his own pluralistic model.[7]

The limitations of such a "mutually inclusivist" position are apparent: Despite its genuine openness to dialogue, it remains bound to the internal beliefs and perspectives of its own religious tradition. For this approach, there is no "higher" point of view. Ultimate Reality is understood as the God or as the Absolute that is experienced and conceptualized in the normative revelation of one's own religion. This is so despite the conscious recognition that such experience and concepts are socially constructed within one's own tradition. This approach can recognize that the Divine is truly grasped in other religions only as long as this does not negate the truth-claims of one's own tradition. Such a negation would occur if members of the religious tradition are told that all their truth-claims are only "postulates" that do not really disclose the reality of the Ultimate. Religious faith lives from the assurance that in the faith experience, no matter how much that experience is "socially conditioned," one is knowing and asserting something real and true about the Ultimate—not merely something that *appears* to be true. Religious experience, or faith, in all the religious traditions, operates out of these same presuppositions.

Religious experience, therefore, presupposes a very real and active point of reference or source for that experience; this source, in whatever manner, communicates itself (as distinct from an Aristotelian concept of God that Hick seems to suggest). For such communication to take place, it is not necessary to invoke the analogy of human self-communication; such communication can conceivably also take place from an impersonal, spiritual power that can radiate and make itself present without necessarily being experienced as a "self." For faith or religious experience, what is important is that there be an authentic disclosure of a *real* reality; religion cannot be based on the mere product of human religious consciousness. We can speak of authentic disclosure of the Divine Ground of Being only if it is clear that it owes its presence to itself. It seems to me that this is true not only for theistic God-experiences but also for enlightenment-experiences of Buddhism. For such non-theistic traditions as Buddhism, what matters most is not just the spiritual

---

[6] See Reinhold Bernhardt, *Der Absolutheitsanspruch des Christentums: Von der Aufklärung bis zur pluralistischen Religionstheologie*, 2nd ed. (Gütersloh: Gütersloher Verlag, 1993), 236–39; and Bernhardt, "Philosophische Pluralismuskonzepte und ihre religionstheologische Rezeption," in *Wege der Theologie ins dritte Jahrtausend,* ed. Günter Riße, Heino Sonnemans, Burkhard Theß (Paderborn: Bonifatius, 1996), 461–80. Michael von Brück describes that model as a "reciprocal inclusivism" (see his "Heil und Heilswege im Hinduismus und Pluralismus—eine Herausforderung für christliches Erlösungsverständnis," in *Der einzige Weg zum Heil? Die Herausforderung des christlichen Absolutheitsanspruches durch pluralistische Religionstheologien,* Qaestiones Disputatae 143, ed. Michael von Brück und Jürgen Werbick [Freiburg: Herder, 1993], 62–106, 88).

[7] Hick, *The Rainbow of Faiths*, 23.

achievement of the practitioner who meditates and to whom the breakthrough to the Nirvana is opened; rather, what is experienced is the self-presentation of Nirvana, which is a transcendental reality, not merely a state of consciousness.[8]

Such loyalty to one's own tradition and its basic convictions does not require one to hold up one's own religion as absolute or as having an exclusive claim to truth. If one continuously recognizes, as part of one's own tradition, that the Divine Ground of Being is universal and infinite, and if at the same time one is aware of the perspectival character of all one's religious perceptions, then it is impossible to make absolute claims for one's religion. Indeed, one will recognize that any religious community will come to deeper understandings of its own beliefs through interreligious dialogue and through wrestling with the issues of a theology of religions.

In the final analysis, the many religions and cultures of the world will always stand next to one another in their manyness; they will not be able to fashion or transform their plurality into a higher unity. There is no preestablished ground of unity existing before or outside of all of them. Therefore, in a certain sense, there can only be a "Ptolemaic" dialogue between the religions—that is, a struggle for the truth; they will never break through to a Copernican center that will overcome their diversity. The plurality of religious perspectives will not be dissolved into a higher monism; in this sense, the religions are incommensurable to each other.

Admittedly, such pluralism, without the postulate of a final unity, is in danger of sliding into relativism. This danger, however, need not become reality; there are ways to protect against this slide, for all the religious traditions offer universal norms for testing the authenticity of religious claims. Such universal norms proclaimed by particular religions can be brought into dialogue with each other.

THE META-RELIGIOUS LEVEL

An excessive focus on one's own religion is avoided with the help of a philosophy of religion that seeks an understanding of religions that goes beyond but embraces each individual religion. Such efforts move beyond the intra-religious perspective of "mutual inclusivism" and enter the meta-religious level. Here John Hick's "pluralistic theology of religion" finds voice.

Hick's project, which defines itself as "a second order philosophical theory or hypothesis" or as a "meta-theory about the relation between the historical religions," is not necessarily at odds with a "mutually inclusivistic" approach for which the point of departure is the central affirmation of the faith of one's tradition (which Hick calls "a first-order religious creed or gospel,"

---

[8] See Perry Schmidt-Leukel, "Buddha and Christ as Mediators of Salvific Transcendent Reality," in *Wandel zwischen den Welten* (Festschrift for Johannes Laube), ed. Hannelore Eisenhofer-Halim (Frankfurt: Peter Lang, 2003), 647–67, esp. 651ff.

or "a self-committing affirmation of faith"[9])—as long as the mutual inclusivists renounce any kind of exclusivism or superior inclusivism.

So, I would like to suggest:

- That we do not consider these two approaches to a theology of religions as opponents, but rather that we view them as a polarity, the poles of which are located on different levels.
- That in this polarity between philosophical meta-theories and theological interpretations of interreligious relations, we first seek to understand the presence of the Divine in the revelations of other religions from the viewpoint of our own truth-claims; then we can use the perspectives of each religion as bridgeheads to formulating philosophical meta-theories of religious pluralism.

In Christian efforts to do this, the doctrine of the Trinity can serve us well. But to show how that might be possible, we first have to clarify just what Christians can or should affirm when they speak about God as triune.

PAUL TILLICH'S TRINITARIAN THEOLOGY AND A THEOLOGY OF RELIGIONS

According to Paul Knitter, many of the current efforts to work out a theology of religions based on the Holy Spirit (pneumatology) and the Trinity end up in a form of christocentrism insofar as they subordinate the work of the Spirit to the Logos.[10] Knitter obviously is speaking of the Logos in terms of its particular incarnation in the historical figure of Jesus Christ.

In what follows I suggest that the trinitarian theology of Paul Tillich can help us avoid this subordinationist tendency in understanding the Trinity and especially in using trinitarian perspectives to formulate a theology of religions. I believe that Tillich's understanding of the Trinity lays the general foundation for a theology of religions and helps us build on it. As is well known, Tillich frequently reformulated his views of other religions; one of the main impulses to do so came through his dialogue with Shin'ichi Hisamatsu (1957) and his journey to Japan (1960).[11]

Tillich distinguished between the specific Christian doctrine of the Trinity and general trinitarian principles or perspectives.[12] The Christian doctrine of

[9] John Hick, "The Possibility of Religious Pluralism: A Reply to Gavin D'Costa," *Religious Studies* 33, no. 2 (1997): 161–66.

[10] Paul F. Knitter, "A New Pentecost? A Pneumatological Theology of Religions," *Current Dialogue* (January 1991), 32–41.

[11] See Dirk Chr. Siedler, *Paul Tillichs Beiträge zu einer Theologie der Religionen: Eine Untersuchung seines religionsphilosophischen, religionswissenschaftlichen und theologischen Beitrags*, Theologie Bd. 21 (Münster: LIT-Verlag, 1999), 178ff.

[12] Paul Tillich, *Systematic Theology*, vols. 1–3 (Chicago: Univ. of Chicago Press, 1951–63), 1:249–52, 2:143.

the Trinity is the product of a certain constellation of theological problems in the history of the early church. The relation between God and the Logos present in Jesus of Nazareth had to be clarified. This was achieved first by the elaboration of a binitarian, then of a trinitarian symbolism. Thereby Christians became aware of what we can call a trinitarian perspective that reached far beyond the doctrine of the Trinity itself; it became a perspective for understanding human existence, the relationship between God and humankind, and the God-experience itself. Tillich, therefore, could state that trinitarian symbols provide "insight into the 'depth of the Godhead.'"[13]

This insight, according to Tillich, grows out of three experiences, the first and the second of which clearly go beyond specific Christian experiences of God, and indeed, well beyond the problems that led the early church to formulate its trinitarian beliefs.[14]

1. For Tillich, every grasp of the Divine is characterized by a "tension between the absolute and the concrete elements in that which is of ultimate concern to us"—that is, between the unconditionality of the Unconditional and its manifestations in God-mediators (note the plural!), or between God as ground/abyss and God as form/self-manifestation. Here again we encounter the polarity between transcendence and immanence, between the Divine in its unfathomable mystery and the Divine in its revealed forms. These forms are essential, for only if the Divine is concretized in historical forms and figures can we encounter it. Yet each of these finite figures is only a *manifestation* of the Infinite. Therefore, Tillich reasoned, there must be a pole within the Godhead that can represent itself within the finite without losing itself in the finite.

2. Whenever the Divine Ground of Being is grasped as a living ground, it has to be understood according to the fundamental dynamics of life. The basic movement of life, however, consists of the dialectical process between identity, nonidentity (difference), and reintegration. The philosophy of German Idealism related this dynamic principle of all life (being-by-itself, proceeding-from-itself, and returning-to-itself) to the inner dynamics of the Divine Ground of Being.

3. Three different revelatory experiences require some kind of interrelatedness: God experienced as creative power, as manifest in Jesus the Christ (that is, as saving love), and as the ecstatic elevation of the human spirit to unambiguous life. These different God-experiences offer answers to fundamental existential questions: about the finiteness of life, about estrangement within life, and about the ambiguity of life. Such questions appear in all religions and cultures.

---

[13] Tillich, *Systematic Theology*, 3:283: "The trinitarian symbols are a religious discovery which had to be made, formulated, and defended."

[14] Ibid., 3:283ff.; see also 1:228.

In this way, Tillich sees the Christian doctrine of the Trinity as a mirror reflecting the broader existential-ontological aspects of human existence. This general-ontolological trinitarian structure finds its expression in the specific Christian conviction that the absolute universal Logos is represented in Jesus Christ. He manifests God's self-mediation in history.

For Tillich, a trinitarian perspective reaches far beyond Christianity and offers us a plausible understanding of "the unity in the manifoldness of divine self-manifestations,"[15] or it enables us "to express in embracing symbols the self-manifestation of the Divine life to man."[16] The *personae* of the Trinity are real-symbolic manifestations of the unconditioned One.

The christocentrism that is still present in this understanding of the Trinity is not a Jesus-centrism; rather, it gravitates around the universal Logos in whom the incomprehensible Divine Ground communicates itself. This self-communication has become concrete in Jesus as the Christ without being confined to just this concretization. Tillich clearly distinguishes between the Logos as the self-expression/self-alienation of God and its historical manifestation in Jesus of Nazareth.

Just as Christian trinitarian teaching is imbedded in broader trinitarian thought, christocentrism is surrounded by the universality of the Spirit of God. Pan-Chiu Lai rightly affirms: "While Christology as entry point of the doctrine of the Trinity is at the level of Christian doctrine, pneumatology as the foundation of the doctrine of the Trinity is at the level of the trinitarian principle. Perhaps we may say that Christ is the center of the Christian doctrine of the Trinity in an epistemological sense, whereas the Spirit is in an ontological sense the starting point or center of the trinitarian principle."[17]

In as much as God's self-manifestation in Jesus as the Christ requires a specifically Christian doctrine of the Trinity, it is God's self-communication in history in general (specifically in the history of religions) that calls for the general trinitarian symbolism. With such a trinitarian perspective, the Christian's vision is widened and better able to perceive God's revealing presence in other religions.[18] The manifestation of the universal Logos in Jesus as the Christ represents for Christian tradition the initial and normative context for detecting and relating to the trans-religious and trans-cultural working of God's Spirit.

If one wants to call Tillich's theology of religions inclusivistic, it can only be in a *hermeneutically* inclusive sense. A Christ-centered understanding of God can serve Christians as their normative epistemological starting point

---

[15] Ibid., 3:293.

[16] Ibid., 3:294.

[17] Pan-Chiu Lai, *Towards a Trinitarian Theology of Religions*, 153.

[18] What Tillich had to say about other "worlds" can be applied to non-Christian religions: "The God who is seen and adored in trinitarian symbolism has [by its self-communication in the Logos] not lost his freedom to manifest himself for other worlds in other ways" (*Systematic Theology*, 3:290).

and focus without any claims that this understanding exhaustively embraces all of God's—or Being itself's—revelation throughout the universe. The revelatory outreach of the Spirit is broader than the history of God's revelation in the incarnation of the Logos. The activity of the Spirit serves, as it were, as "the field of force" that from the beginning of time has been creatively at work in the cosmos. In this same field Jesus himself lived and found inspiration, but he certainly does not limit or exhaust this Spirit-field. The activity of the Spirit can thus have for Christians a normative representation in Christ that does not exclude but rather relationally includes other representations. If we understand God's incarnation in Jesus in this way, it does not lead to exclusivism.

Tillich did not fully develop his trinitarian framework for a theology of religions. Still, one can note how much the ingredients and concerns of this approach reflect John Hick's theology of religions. The emphasis on the infinity, universality, and ultimate incomprehensibility of the Divine Ground of Being that characterizes Hick's concept of the Real had already been advocated by Tillich. In Protestantism, according to Tillich, the unfathomable mystery of God had lost out to the Christian stress on the self-limitation of God in Jesus Christ.[19] John Hick's emphatic insistence on the incomprehensibility of the Divine Ground of Being can be seen as an effort to readjust this imbalance; it is certainly in line with Tillich's description of Being itself as unfathomable ground and abyss. But Tillich—more vigorously than Hick—counterbalances this emphasis on the ineffability of Ultimate Reality with a sound recognition of divine revelation, and he uses a trinitarian perspective to relate both poles. Therefore, he does not have to describe the relation between God-in-Godself and God-for-us in terms of a sequence. The God-for-us *is* the self-communication of the God-in-Godself, for it is the very essence or nature of God to communicate and reveal God's self.

Tillich's diagnosis of Protestantism stands in need of clarification and qualification. Different from Luther's emphasis on the self-communication of God in Jesus Christ, Zwingli stresses the universal working of God's Spirit and thereby offers a helpful and engaging avenue for a pneumatological theology of religions. Zwingli's "spiritualism" is theocentric, that is, oriented toward the Godhead in trinitarian terms. God's Spirit is not merely the mediator of the salvific truth opened up by Christ; rather, the Spirit serves as the active source of all truth, as well as of divine providence, in both its individual and historical agency.[20] It is not accurate, therefore, to present the whole of Protestantism as totally christocentric.

---

[19] Ibid., 3:291.

[20] Emil Egil et al., eds., *Huldreich Zwinglis sämtliche Werke* (Leipzig: Verlag von M. Heinsius), vol. 2 (1908), 172, 17ff.; vol. 3 (1914), 124, 15f.; vol. 9 (1925), 458, 25ff. Cf. Rudolf Pfister, *Die Seligkeit erwählter Heiden bei Zwingli: eine Untersuchung zu seiner Theologie* (Zollikon/Zürich: Evangelischer Verlag, 1952).

A TRINITARIAN THEOLOGY OF RELIGIONS

We can now draw some conclusions. A trinitarian framework for a Christian theology of religions can preserve the concerns of theocentric, christocentric, and spirit-centered theologies, as well as coordinate and modify those concerns.

THEOCENTRIC: THE GOD BEYOND GOD

A trinitarian approach to a theology of religions maintains the fundamental difference between the Divine Ground of Being and all finite beings. Ontologically, this difference preserves the categorical distinction between the Absolute-in-itself and all its historical manifestations. Epistemologically, this difference implies the ultimate unavailability of the Divine to all religious perceptions; that is, in all its genuine revelations, the Divine remains inexhaustible mystery. So, the vigor of the Second Commandment remains. So does the distinction between the economic and the immanent Trinity, or between God's relation to the world and God-in-Godself. Ultimate Mystery remains; God is not dissolved or captured in the divine self-communications, least of all in religious concepts of God. Therefore, the apparent theological alternatives between theistic und non-theistic conceptions are ultimately relative. This recognition of the ultimate mystery of the divine Being transcends any theistic theocentrism and calls us to embrace the apophatic dimension in all religions, especially in those religions of a mystical orientation or in the Buddhist experience of Nirvana and *shunyata*.

Such a recognition of the infinity and universality of the Divine Ground of Being, together with the perspectival character of all religious perceptions, is basic not only for a pluralistic theology of religions but for all God-talk that takes seriously the difference between theological language and the reality of the *Deus semper maior* (the ever-greater God, or Paul Tillich's "the God beyond God"[21]). Such a recognition is not simply the demand of a postmodern relativism; rather, it is the mark of any genuine spirituality open to transcendence and aware of being constituted in a reality beyond itself—that is, aware that its *Gestalten* are not identical with Ultimate Reality but directed toward it.

We must bear in mind, furthermore, that if such a "negative theology" is overemphasized, then any talk about Ultimate Reality becomes impossible. Impossible also would be any relationship with the Divine, or any access to it, for in a totally negative theology, the Ultimate is not an "end" that can be attained or a point from which one can be addressed. Rather, it is the numinous Ground/Abyss, in the face of which all one can do is keep silent. Such an

---

[21] Paul Tillich, *The Courage to Be* (New Haven, CT: Yale Univ. Press, 1952), final chapter.

understanding of the Divine dissolves into a realm of non-definition; it becomes what Luther called "the naked Absolute."

CHRISTOCENTRIC: THE SELF-REVEALING GOD

On the other hand, a trinitarian theology of religions allows a genuine self-differentiation and self-communication of God in historical concreteness (and rationality): God, the absolute Ground of Being, is manifest in creative, healing, illuminating, and fulfilling effects. In such a theistic perspective God becomes a partner in relationship with whom a specific form of communication is possible. For Christians, the universal and normative manifestation of God is found in the life and suffering of Jesus Christ as witnessed in the biblical tradition. Other religions will have other universal-normative manifestations valid for them.

Once again, if this aspect of the self-revealing character of the Divine is overemphasized, there is the danger of identifying the Absolute with its historical manifestations—the peril of idolatry.

SPIRIT-CENTERED: THE OMNIPRESENT GOD

A trinitarian theology of religions also affirms the omnipresent power of the Spirit of God, which penetrates the cosmic process as a whole and which inspires humans and enables them to recognize the reality and presence of the Divine. Such an inner experience of the Spirit can lead one into the depths of the Divine Ground of Being, even to the point of identification with it. And so we witness in various forms how religious traditions speak of the oneness of the human person with the universe, or the identity between Atman and Brahman.

If, however, this aspect of the omnipresent, all-penetrating, and enlightening immanence is overemphasized, there is the danger of an ahistorical pantheism: The Divine becomes identical with the innermost principle of existence and indistinguishable from it. It is experienced in the depths of human consciousness where the ego, the cosmos, and the Ultimate Reality coincide. Such a spirituality can easily lead to a withdrawal from earthly reality, considering it only an illusion. History is no longer a medium of specific revelations.

BALANCE

A trinitarian theology of religious pluralism, in trying to understand and articulate the relationship of immanence and transcendence within the Divine Ground of Being, achieves a balance among these three essential ingredients: it affirms (1) the radical otherness of God beyond all finite reality, (2) the authentic self-disclosure of the Divine, and (3) the active presence of the Divine in both natural and human history. This framework is designed from a Christian perspective and does *not* stand as some kind of meta-theory that is above all traditions and so to be adopted by all traditions. On the contrary, it is a perspective homegrown in Christian soil. And so it seeks to make room for this center of Christian identity and to allow this center to serve Christians as the means to understand the universal presence of the Divine within the plurality of religions, without, however, identifying monistically this universal presence with the very Ground of Being itself. But in no way does such a viewpoint wish to claim that because a trinitarian faith has the ability to integrate the diversity of religions, it is therefore the "true and absolute religion."[22]

From such a theological perspective the religious traditions of the world are seen as "platforms" for the active presence of God. And yet, it recognizes that not everything that presents itself in the dress of spirituality really is a manifestation of the Divine Ground of Being—neither in Christianity nor in other religions. How often in the history of religions have claims to "bring salvation" brought nothing more than misery and conflict? It is of critical importance to have criteria by which we can discern authentic from inauthentic religion. Each religion will bring to the table criteria from its own core beliefs and practices. For Christians, these criteria are found in seeking to conform to the Spirit that filled Jesus in his life and his suffering and that continues to act powerfully, beyond his death, in the life of the community.

On the basis of what we can call a revelatory or representative Christology, Christians can speak of a qualitative identity of the universal creative and innovative energy of God with the particular manifestation of this energy in Jesus the Christ. And Christians can do this without claiming that the universal Spirit of the eternal God is present exclusively or exhaustively in this Christ-representation, as if all of the Spirit's actions and revelations have to originate from Jesus the Christ.

The doctrine of the Trinity is the Christian answer to the question of the immanence of the transcendent. All religions of revelation have attempted to answer this question in their own ways. The different answers cannot possibly be harmonized. It seems to me, therefore, that the religions will never totally move beyond a "Ptolemaic" framework; they will have to engage each other in a never-ending dialogue of their "mutually inclusive" viewpoints, each worked out from the standpoint of one's own tradition. Each viewpoint includes others and stands ready to be included by others. Such a mutually inclusive model does justice to the requirements of a truly pluralistic

---

[22] See Gisbert Greshake, *Der dreieine Gott: Eine trinitarische Theologie*, 4th ed. (Freiburg: Herder, 2001). In Greshake, however, this statement is not to be understood in the sense of a religio-theological exclusivism but rather in the sense of an "appeased Christian inclusivism" connected with a reference to mutuality through which in interreligious dialogue the fullness of the dimensions of God can be discovered (516). But, in the last analysis, Greshake does want to make sure that the fullness of the ultimate word of revelation, spoken by God, has become reality in Christ. The final completion of the history of religions consists in the merging of the many ways of non-Chistian religions in *this* "Gestalt" of revelation.

theology of religions without falling into the problems inherent in John Hick's notion of the Real, especially the problem of losing a true immanence of the Transcendent. The particular contribution of a trinitarian theology of religions that would protect against this danger is its fundamental understanding of the Divine Ground of Being as a *relational* Ground; relationality is of the essence of the Divine. By the demands of its very being, the Divine must relate by representing itself in history, especially in the religious history of humanity.

I believe that what I have attempted to do in this essay—using my Christian trinitarian perspective—is what is needed within all the religious traditions: let each religious community make use of its own theological-philosophical resources to establish bridgeheads for recognizing and encountering other religions. Each bridgehead will be *inclusive* insofar as it starts on the side of one's own religion; but it will also be *mutual* since it will open one's own tradition to the challenging otherness of other religions. In this way, I believe, we can move forward toward a "second-order understanding" of religious pluralism that will be truly pluralistic.

—TRANSLATED FROM THE GERMAN
BY DIETRICH RITSCHL AND PAUL F. KNITTER

PART VI

Muslim Perspectives

16

Islam and Pluralism

ASHGAR ALI ENGINEER

Given the expanding processes of modernization, liberalization, and globalization, ours is a world that is becoming ever more pluralistic culturally, linguistically, and religiously. In societies long known to be resolutely traditional, feudal structures and attitudes about society, politics, and economics are shifting, or at least being persistently criticized. In such traditional societies, given an all-powerful state, there has been little chance for what we today call civil society to take root and grow. Loyal subjects were not granted, and felt they did not deserve, any rights, for their primary duty was service to the state. That has changed. In contemporary liberal democracies, citizens have (or are supposed to have) well-defined rights. Human rights make up the fiber of democracy and provide the fertile soil for civil society.

And where there is a vigorous civil society, there will be a vigorous plurality of political, religious, cultural viewpoints. Such perspectival pluralism will often be in tension with, but will also be a stimulus for, the policies of the state or of the majority community. Without free and multiple expressions of ideas, debated in the arena of civil society, democracy cannot be nourished and grow.

Herein lies a problem and challenge for much of the Islamic world. In many, if not most, of the Islamic nations of the world, a functioning democracy does not exist because the affirmation of human rights necessary for civil society to grow does not exist. The right and the possibility for a diversity of ideas to be expressed and debated in civil society have not been clearly, or actually, put into practice in many Islamic societies. In fact, most Islamic rulers either outwardly or actually condemn human rights as a Western—some would even say an "un-Islamic"—notion. Islam, they would say, means unity. As there is one God, there is one society. As the oneness of God excludes polytheism, so the unity of society excludes pluralism. Thus, the "human right" to follow whatever religious or political path one wishes cannot, they claim, be affirmed by Islam.

So it is essential for Muslims—and non-Muslims as well—to examine, from a theological perspective, the attitude of Islam toward pluralism. Does Islam affirm pluralism, or does it promote a monolithic society? This is the question this essay will try to answer. The focus will be on religious and cultural pluralism, which are different from, though vitally related to, political pluralism.

THE PLURALISTIC VISION OF THE QUR'AN

Listening carefully to what God tells us in the holy Qur'an, we can easily make the case that, fundamentally and clearly, Islam not only accepts the legitimacy of religious pluralism but considers it central to its system of beliefs. There are numerous Qur'anic statements that are unambiguous. Verse 5:48 is one of the most lucid:

> Unto every one of you We have appointed a (different) law and way of life. And if Allah had so willed, He could surely have made you all one single community: but (He willed it otherwise) in order to test you by means of what He has given you. Vie, then, with one another in doing good works! Unto Allah you all must return; and then He will make you truly understand all that on which you were wont to differ.

This seminal affirmation of the fact and value of religious and legal pluralism has not been recognized, or accepted, by many Muslims, especially Muslim rulers. Yet commentaries on this verse, by both classical and modern scholars, abound. In the context of this essay's theme, the most significant and operative words are: "Unto every one of you have We appointed a (different) law and way of life." The phrase "every one of you" obviously denotes different communities. Every community—that is, religious or religio-cultural community—has its own law *(shir'atan)* and its own way of life *(minhaj)*; thus, every community realizes its spiritual growth in keeping with its own law and way of life. The term *shir'ah* or *shari'ah* signifies, literally, "the way to a watering place" (from which humans and animals derive the element indispensable to their life); so in the Qur'an this word denotes a system of law necessary for a community's social and spiritual welfare. The term *minhaj*, on the other hand, denotes an "open road," that is, a way of life.[1]

So it is clear that Allah sent prophets to different communities *(ummah)*, and these prophets proposed laws and ways of life that corresponded to the people's genius and promoted their spiritual and material growth. This is further emphasized in the next part of the verse: "And if Allah had so willed, He could surely have made you all one single community." It was not difficult for Allah to fashion all of humankind into one single community. But

---

[1] Muhammad Asad, *The Message of the Qur'an* (Gibraltar, 1980), 153ff.

Allah graced us with pluralism in order to add richness and variety to life. Each community has its own unique way of life, its own customs and tradition, its own law. These laws or ways of life, in all their splendid diversity, are given to ensure the growth and enriching of life. Allah does not want to impose one law on all; Allah creates communities rather than community.

But there is a further purpose to the plurality of communities that Allah has brought forth. The diversity of scriptures and laws/ways of life is also meant to try and test human beings by calling them to use this diversity as building blocks for peace and harmony among all communities. Diversity, according to the will of Allah, is not meant to bring about the clash of civilizations but rather the cooperation and enrichment of civilizations. Allah creates diversity so that humans can live with and learn from their differences—and vie with one another in good deeds!

In the last part of the verse Allah says that unto Him all will return and it is He who "will make you truly understand all that on which you were wont to differ." So it is not for human beings to decide for themselves who is right and who is wrong. This will only lead to conflicts and the breaching of peace. Better, therefore, to leave it to Allah to make such final determinations when all humanity will "return unto Him." In promoting such an idea, the Qur'an is, I believe, a pioneer. Here we have a practical way to do away with interreligious and intercultural conflict and to promote the acceptance of the religious and cultural other with dignity and grace.

There is another pluralistic dimension to this verse—what Indian scholars such as Shah Waliyullah and Moulana Abul Kalam Azad have described as the concept of *wahdat-e-Din*, the unity of religion.[2] The earlier part of this verse (5:48) reads: "And We have revealed to thee the Book with the truth, verifying that which is before it of the Book and a guardian [*muhayman*] over it." Here the Qur'an is affirming the value of what has been earlier revealed to other communities through their prophets. Their *shari'ah*, their law and way of life, may be very different from that given in the Qur'an, but the essential origin of such other traditions—the *din* that constitutes all authentic religion—is the same. All religions are based on a revelation from Allah. Thus, the Qur'an affirms and protects earlier truth revealed through other scriptures.

This is a thoroughly pluralistic approach to the religious "other." Although the laws, the ways of life, may differ, still their *din*—their divine origin or essence or truth—can be affirmed. A divine revelatory presence can be expressed in multiple religions or spiritual traditions. Prophets, or vehicles of Allah's revelation, are multiple; they cannot be imprisoned in any one tradition. And when the Qur'an actually names other prophets besides Muhammad, we must remember that this list of prophets is illustrative, not exhaustive. Other faith traditions could be included in the list of those mentioned by the Qur'anic commentators. The Sufi saints from India were inclined to include Indian religions in the list of traditions containing authentic

---

[2] Moulana Abul Kalam Azad, *Tarjuman-al-Qur'an*, vol. 1 (Delhi, n.d.).

prophecy. We humans, therefore, have no right to reject on principal the "other" as false or illegitimate. If we do so, we are probably being motivated by our own egos and the desire for self-promotion rather than by an honest, divinely guided assessment of truth or falsehood.

This Qur'anic pluralism is contained in other forms throughout the sacred text. It affirms, for instance, that there is no one way in which humans can pray to Allah. "For each community there is direction in which it turns, so vie with one another in good works" (2:148). Commentators from the time of the Prophet's companions and throughout Islamic history interpret this verse as referring to other, different religious communities and their forms of "turning toward God" in worship. Ibn Kathir, in his commentary on this verse, emphasizes its resemblance to the same phrase found in 5:48 (discussed above): "Unto every one of you have We appointed a (different) law and way of life."[3] So the Qur'an tells us that no matter to which "direction" a community may turn in its prayer, the prayer can be a genuine submission to and worship of the one true God.

Furthermore, the Qur'an insists that all places of worship should be respected and protected: "And if Allah did not repeal some people by others, cloisters, and churches, and synagogues, and mosques in which Allah's name is much remembered, would have been pulled down" (22:40). So, according to the Qur'an, whether it is in church or synagogue or mosque, Allah's name is much remembered in these places. Though some religious sites will have prominence due to historical events, the plurality of sacred places is clearly affirmed. No single religious place is being privileged.

JUDGED BY WHAT ONE DOES, NOT BY WHAT ONE SAYS

But the Qur'an does not affirm diversity for the sake of diversity. It presupposes a fundamental criterion for determining the value and authenticity of religious prayer and belief. That criterion is primarily ethical, as the following text makes clear:

> It is not righteousness that you turn your faces toward the East and the West, but righteousness is the one who believes in Allah, and the Last Day, and the angels and the Book and the prophets, and gives away wealth out of love for Him to the near of kin and the orphans and the needy and the wayfarer and to these who ask and to set slaves free and keeps up prayer and pays the poor rate; and the performers of their promise when they make a promise, and the patient in distress and affliction and in the time of conflict; and these are they who keep their duty. (2:177)

[3] Ibn Kathir, *Tafsir Ibn Kathir*, vol. 1 (Deoband, n.d.), commenting on verse 2:148.

This verse makes it powerfully clear that the primary aim of the Qur'an is to form human beings who are virtuous, sensitive to the suffering of others, and who use their wealth to respond to the needs of the poor and orphans, who work to set slaves free, who are true to their word and patient in times of distress and conflict. Only such persons are truly *muttaqun,* that is, God-conscious and faithful to their duty to Allah. Needless to say, this verse also lends great support to the basic premise of the pluralistic model by de-emphasizing a particular way of prayer and extolling the importance of human conduct and sensitivity to the suffering of others as well as one's own steadfastness in the face of calamities and afflictions.

Unlike many present-day Muslim leaders and theologians, the Qur'an is not sectarian. Its general outlook is broadly humanitarian, and its emphasis is not on dogmas but on good deeds. It strongly condemns evil deeds that harm society and humanity. In this respect it makes no distinction between Muslims and non-Muslims. Thus the Qur'an says in 4:123: "It will not be in accordance with your vain desires nor the vain desires of the People of the Book. Whoever does evil, will be requited for it and will not find for himself besides Allah a friend or a helper." No one—Muslims or the People of the Book—can claim any exception to this iron-clad law of Allah; those who do good will be rewarded, and those who do evil will be punished. The Qur'an is graphically clear about this: "So he who does an atom's weight of good will see it and he who does an atom's weight of evil will see it" (99:7).

RELIGIOUS FREEDOM

The Qur'an is very clear about another essential piece of the pluralist platform: freedom of conscience. It states clearly and firmly that "there is no compulsion in religion" (2:256), and it affirms that all children of Adam are honorable (17:70). Further, the Qur'an endorses interreligious dialogue, but with decorum: "And argue not with the People of the Book except by what is best, save such of them, as act unjustly. And Say: We believe in that which has been revealed to us and revealed to you, and our God and your God is One, and to Him we submit" (29:46).

This affirmation of diversity and, further, of the ability of differing religions to live with and even learn from one another is based on the Qur'an's resolute recognition of the unity of humankind:

> Mankind is a single nation. So Allah raised prophets as bearers of good news and as warners, and He revealed with them the Book with truth, that it might judge between people concerning that in which they differed. And none but the very people who were given it differed about it after clear arguments had come to them, envying one another. So Allah has guided by His will those who believe to the truth about which they differed. (2:213)

In its affirmation of the freedom of belief and conscience, this verse is suffused with the spirit of pluralism. Although humanity is one, different prophets arise in different contexts, and through them Allah provides different revealed scriptures to guide people and to warn them. In this way, different ways of religious and cultural life take shape. But it happens that people begin to envy each other, and argue with each other, instead of respecting each other's particularity. So do divisions amid humankind arise and undermine the God-intended unity. But through the diversity of revelations, Allah guides those who believe to the truth about which they differed.

This theme of oneness of humankind is repeated in the Qur'an in a variety of forms. We are told that all human beings have been "created of a single soul" (4:1), that they are all descended from the same parents (49:13), and that they are as it were dwellers in one home, having the same earth as a resting place and the same heaven as a canopy.

But at the very same time that the Qur'an extols the unity of humankind, it continues with equal clarity to extol humanity's diversity. The various racial, linguistic, and national identities of people are not just creations of God; they are also signs: "And of His signs is the creation of the heavens and the earth and the diversity of your tongues and colors. Surely there are signs in this for the learned" (30:22). Differences, therefore, are not just to be accepted; they are to be engaged. They are necessary for establishing the unity of humanity. This seems to be the sense of verse 49:13: "O mankind, surely We have created you from a male and a female, and made you nations and tribes that you may know each other." In *knowing* one another's national or tribal or religious differences we are able not only to understand but also to learn from one another, and so to fashion a richer unity. For the Qur'an, unity and diversity are in dynamic relationship, each needing the other. Again, the Qur'an was pluralistic long before the so-called pluralist model for religious diversity was developed.

A PLURALISTIC CONSTITUTION

The Prophet of Islam, when he migrated from Mecca to Madina, found himself in a pluralist situation. There was religious as well as tribal diversity. Not only did he accept this diversity, he legitimized it by drawing up an agreement with different religious and tribal groups that accorded them a dignified existence and rights of their own. This agreement is known in Islamic history as *Misaq-i-Madina*. It begins:

In the name of God, the Merciful, the Compassionate!
This is writing of Muhammad the prophet between the believers and Muslims of Quraysh and Yathrib (Madina) and those who follow them and are attached to them and who crusade along with them. They are a single community distinct from other people.

This agreement can be called the Constitution of Madina. By establishing the foundation for a new political and religious culture, it certainly constitutes a milestone in the history of Islam, and perhaps of the Western world. Here was something new, something bold: groups from differing religious and politico-cultural traditions—Muslims of Quraysh from Mecca, Muslims of Madina belonging to the tribes of Aws and Khazraj, and Jews from different tribes—were called together to form a single community—an *ummah*. Differences did not have to divide or clash. They could be the materials for a new kind of community.

And it was a community that can be called an incipient democracy. The holy Prophet did not claim to be ruler of this community. While the emigrants *(muhajirs)* were a clan and the Prophet was their leader, there were also eight other clans with their leaders. According to the Constitution of Madina, the Prophet was distinguished from the other leaders on two counts: First, for the Muslims he was not only their political leader but their prophet; this meant that whatever was revealed to him was binding on their community. Second, the Constitution states that "whenever there is anything about which you differ, it is to be referred to God and to Muhammad." Thus, the Prophet was recognized as an arbiter between disagreeing factions whose function was to maintain the general peace in Madina. The Qur'an places high expectations on this role as arbiter: "And for every nation there is a messenger. So when their messenger comes, the matter is decided between them with justice, and they are not wronged" (10:48).

More recently and encouragingly, eminent Muslim theologians of India such as Jami'at ul-'Ulama-i-Hind have cited the Constitution of Madina as reason for Muslims to accept the composite national community that the Constitution of India has tried to inspire. They opposed, in other words, the separate nationalism based on religion that the Muslim League advocated. Indian Muslims, these theologians urged, should follow the example of the Constitution of Madina, in which the Prophet accepted differing religious and tribal groups into one single community—the *ummah wahidah*. Madinese society was a democratic, civil society that had tribal, religious, and racial diversity.[4]

The Prophet realized that no nation can become a strong, stable, prosperous, and violence-free society unless religious diversity or pluralism is accepted as a legitimate, indeed beneficial, ingredient in the organization and functioning of nation and state. So it is painfully unfortunate that most contemporary Muslim countries do not adhere to this spirit of pluralism and diversity in the Qur'an and sunnah. The extremists and fundamentalists among the Muslims in these countries attack the spirit of pluralism and want to create a monolithic society.

Many of the sociopolitical doctrines that are proposed and practiced today as "authentically Islamic" developed during the medieval period when

---

[4] Moulana Hussain Ahmed Madani, *Islam aur Mutatahad Qaumiyat* (Delhi, n.d.).

mulukiyat (personal and monarchical power structures) had become all pervasive, thus suppressing the Qur'anic values and the original spirit of Islam. During this time, of course, there could be no question of civil society, for the ruler was all powerful and could dictate whatever he wanted. The compulsion of power, rather than the spirit and requirements of the Qur'an, ruled. This arrogance of power and all-pervasive authoritarian atmosphere strongly influenced the formulation of Islamic political theory. Such medieval theories and doctrines should not be considered grounded in the Qur'an and valid for today.

Today, Islamic political theorists must develop new political theories that are both faithful to the spirit and demands of the Qur'an and sunnah, and at the same time responsive to the realities of the modern world. It must be made clear to the Islamic community and to the world that there need be no contradiction between the original vision of Islam and a pluralistic democracy. The ideal of a civil society that respects the autonomy of its citizens and their religious, cultural, and political rights is not in any way, as shown above, contradictory to the Qur'anic vision of Islam. An understanding of human rights that affirms and respects the dignity and freedom of conscience of every individual is integral to Islam. The Qur'an clearly states that all children of Adam have been honored (17:70). This, of course, includes the right to live with dignity and to promote one's own religious, cultural-linguistic, or ethnic interests.

Muslims, together with all peoples, can and must live in the twenty-first century not with a restrictive, imitative mentality *(taqlidi)* but with a creative and critical approach that adheres to Qur'anic values that call upon all Muslims to live free, full, and dignified lives and to assist and enable others to do the same. Fourteen hundred years ago the Qur'an affirmed the full dignity of Christian and Jewish "others" and demanded respect for their beliefs. Later, the Prophet recognized the Zoroastrians of Bahrain as People of the Book, and the fourth caliph, Uthman, extended such recognition even to Berbers. Many *'ulama* and Sufi saints have also embraced Hindus in this dignity of diversity.

We must bear in mind that the words *kafir* and *mushrik* have been defined and used in particular historical contexts and should therefore be used with great caution and restraint. Unfortunately, many Muslims take up these terms very easily and loosely and apply them to all religious others. Naturally, this stirs up resentment and animosity in others, for such terms are among the most depreciating a Muslim can use. But because they are so powerful, their use is clearly defined and therefore limited. Only those who refuse to accept truth in any form and who negate good *(ma'ruf)* completely and advocate *munkar* (evil) would qualify as *kafirs*. And only those who explicitly deny the fundamental oneness of God and associate partners with God qualify as *mushrik*. And still, we must note, even *kafirs* and *mushriks* have civil rights, as long as they do not disturb the peace of society. The Qur'an affirms that also the *kafirs* possess the right to worship in their own way and to maintain their own beliefs (109:1–6). For the Qur'an, freedom of conscience cannot be taken away from any human person, whatever his or her beliefs.

In no way, therefore, should Islam be an obstacle to the formation and maintenance of a genuinely pluralist civil society that assures and protects the dignity and freedom of conscience to all.

Admittedly, this is not the reality in many Muslim countries. But it *should* be, and it *can* be. This is the hope and the resolve that animates the belief and work of many Muslims throughout the world.

17

A Muslim Pluralist:
Jalaluddin Rûmi

MAHMUT AYDIN

The "problem" of religious diversity has been around for a long time. From the origins of the human species, as the spark of consciousness broadened and gave rise to the driving concern for the meaning of life, there have always been many religions, each with its own "ultimate" answers. Today the presence, power, and richness of other religious traditions have vigorously entered Muslim awareness. Our contemporary intercommunicating and interdependent planet has made us aware, more clearly but also more painfully than ever before, of the multiplicity of world religions and of the many different ultimate answers given by these religions. Because of this fact we, as Muslims, are facing questions and challenges we never had to confront before.

If these questions and challenges are used as positive impulses for reconsideration of our own past theologies, they can lead to new discoveries and insights about humanity, divinity, and Islam itself. The problem of the diversity of world faiths is not a new one. It is the will of our Creator. The Qur'an states clearly that even though humankind started its journey in unity as one community, the Creator soon brought forth an abundant diversity of peoples and religions. Why? In order to give humans, in their various cultures and faiths, the opportunity to compete with each other in good deeds (10:19; 49:13; 5:48). So, the diversity of humankind is not the result of the degeneration of human society or of a lack of divine guidance; it is, rather, the very will of God.

The challenges of this awareness of religious diversity have led some creative thinkers—Christians, Muslims, Jews, Buddhists, Hindus—to explore the following questions as part of an effort to develop a new theology of religions that would provide the foundation for better relations among all the religious traditions: Why are there so many different religions? Are all the religions valid in God's eye? Are the differences among the world religions more a matter of varied colors than of conflicting content? How should the followers of different world faiths relate to one another? Can religious believers learn from each other's religious traditions? If one religious community considers itself "the people of the right way," does this require it to view other ways as false or invalid? Is one's religious identity as a Muslim, Christian, Jew, Buddhist, or Hindu the result of one's free will or of the cultural identity given with birth? If being born a Muslim, Christian, Jew, Buddhist, or Hindu is regarded as a privilege for salvation, why has God given it only to a small minority and so deprived the majority?[1]

For many religious thinkers and practitioners, our present awareness of religious pluralism is such that it is simply not possible to claim that one's own religion is true while all others are false. As Edward Schillebeeckx states, "To say that one's Way is the only possibility for grasping religious truth is to live in a 'time warp.'"[2] And so in exploring the questions that the diversity of religions poses, many scholars in various religions have found themselves moving away from "exclusivist" and "inclusivist" understandings of other religions to a more "pluralist" model. In their view, according to Knitter, "the traditional theological telescopes that show other world faiths as ultimately having to be either replaced or fulfilled by one's own religion are not really showing what's there." The various moves toward a pluralistic view of other traditions have been described as different but complementary bridges, all making the same crossing: the philosophical-historical bridge, the religious-mystical bridge and the ethical-practical bridge.[3]

In this essay we make use of the religious-mystical bridge, and we do so specifically by examining the teaching of the great Muslim Sufi Jalaluddîn Rûmi. Clearly, especially in the West, Rûmi is one of the most popular of Muslim mystics. The works of Rûmi have become remarkably popular in the contemporary Western world to the extent that he is "reputedly the best-selling poet in America today."[4]

In this essay we examine Rûmi's views in relation to some of the central ingredients of the pluralist model: the ineffability of the Real, the diversity of faiths, the concern for salvation/liberation, and the necessity of a dialogical relationship with the other. Our main objective is to clarify how Muslim thinkers can respond to the challenges of today's religious pluralism by benefiting from Sufi thought. In dealing with the universal message of Rûmi, we offer it as a contribution to the development of a possible pluralistic Muslim theology of religions. Also, we respond to the criticism that the pluralist model is a product of the European Enlightenment and is therefore an imposition of one religious language on all the others. Rûmi is a clear indication

---

[1] For these questions see Paul F. Knitter, *Introducing Theologies of Religions* (Maryknoll, NY: Orbis Books, 2002), 1; Mahmut Aydin, "Religious Pluralism: A Challenge for Muslims—A Theological Evaluation," *Journal of Ecumanical Studies* 38, no. 2–3 (2001), 352.

[2] Quoted in Knitter, *Introducing Theologies of Religions*, 7.

[3] Ibid., 112–13.

[4] See Carl Ernst, *The Shambhala Guide to Sufism* (Boston: Shambhala, 1997), 170.

that the view of world faiths as different responses to the same Ultimate Reality was around centuries before any of the European Enlightenment thinkers were born.

THE MYSTICAL APPROACH TO RELIGIOUS DIVERSITY

The followers of this approach hold that within the many different world faiths the same Divine Being or Reality is experienced. By examining the lives of practitioners of different faiths, they claim, we can witness the same core mystical experience pulsating within each tradition; it is this core experience that has endured through the ages. So, if there is a core mystical experience in different faiths, there should be a core Mystical Reality within all of them. But this Divine Reality transcends anything that can be experienced in any one faith. According to this perspective, what is really important is not that the Divine Reality is infinite, but that the same Divine Reality is being experienced within the many world faiths. This means that each religious person or community hears and feels this Divine Reality through its own socially and culturally constructed antenna. As Knitter points out, by arguing in this way the defenders of this approach never "want to neglect the startling differences between faith communities."[5]

Yet despite these differences, despite the tensions between God as personal and God as supra-personal or even God as no-thing, those who take the mystical path to understand religious pluralism affirm that the differences do not dry up the deeper divine current that feeds all the different religious wells. Furthermore, proponents of this perspective claim that the more deeply followers of one faith enter into the religious experience of their own faith, the more they will be aware that what they are experiencing cannot be limited to their own religion. By making room for the possibility or probability of the presence of the same Divine Reality in other faiths, religious believers become more open and sensitive toward people of other faiths.

INEFFABILITY OF THE DIVINE REALITY

Like pluralists in general, those who take a mystical approach to religious diversity recognize and honor the fundamental ineffability of the Divine Reality. What John Hick calls "the Real" lies beyond the grasp of human images, ideas, and conceptual systems. Yes, we may encounter and feel the presence of the Real, but whatever we seek to think or say about it will be limited by our limited cultural and psychological categories. This means that as religious people we may know the Real's "phenomena," but we can never grasp the Real in itself, its noumenon.

Throughout his life and writings Rûmi affirmed and bowed to the ineffability of God. "Whatever you may think is liable to pass away; what does

---

[5] Knitter, *Introducing Theologies of Religions*, 125.

not come to thought is the Real/the Divine Being."[6] Therefore, for Rûmi, the Divine Being cannot be captured or contained in the finite categories of any one religion. "You are the One whom I worship both in Kaba and Synagogue; You are my only objective from both above and below."[7] "There is only one Divine Reality who abides no partner, agency or instrument."[8] For Rûmi, therefore, there is only one Divinity, who is the Lord of all humankind. Here Rûmi is in perfect resonance with the insistence of the Qur'an that Allah is not the Lord of one nation or one religious community but "the Lord of the whole universe" (1:1).

Rûmi tries to explain the ineffability of the Divine Being with the Indian parable about the blind men and the elephant. According to the story, a group of blind men were invited to touch an elephant and describe what they thought it was. The one who felt the trunk concluded that it was a hose; another, feeling the elephant's ear, thought it was a rudder plate; the third, who felt along its back, thought it was a throne; yet another, extending his arms around a leg, claimed it was a pillar. Thus all of them defined the elephant according to the limited part of its "reality" that they could perceive. After quoting the blind men's quaint descriptions, Rûmi underlines that "if there had been a candle in each one's hand; the differences would have gone out of their words."[9] Naturally, their views differed because of their differing and limited experiences. For Rûmi, this parable illustrates that in a sense we are all blind and can grasp the Divine only with our limited experience and categories. Therefore, each of the religions of the world will experience something authentic of the Divine, but that something will always be limited by its particular sociocultural context. No one religious tradition can claim to see all of the Divine Reality. No one religion can claim to be superior to all the others.[10]

Rûmi has a harsh admonition for anyone who tries to limit the Divine to only one religious faith:

> Since all forms were created
> Do not identify God with any form

---

[6] Jalaluddin Rûmi, *Mathnawi: Translations and Commentary,* ed. Abdülbaki Gölpinarli (Istanbul: Milli Eitim Basimevi, 1985), II, 3107. All subsequent references to *Mathnawi* are taken from the Turkish edition. I have consulted Reynold A. Nicholson's translation (see *The Mathnawi of Jajaluddin Rumi*, ed. Reynold A. Nicholson [Lahore: Islamic Book Service, 1989]).

[7] Jalaludin Rûmi, *Divan-e Kabir (Divan-e Shams-e Tabrizi)*, 2nd ed., ed. Abdülbaki Gölpinarli (Ankara: Kültür Bakanligi Yayinlari, 2000), VI, 2405. Translations from this book are mine.

[8] Rûmi, *Mathnawi*, VI, 486.

[9] Ibid., III, 1260–69.

[10] Cafer S. Yaran, "The Position of the Other according to Ibn Arabi, Mavlana, and Yunus Amra," in *Islam and the Other*, ed. Cafer S. Yaran (Istanbul: Kaknüs, 2001), 328.

Do not associate Him with any form
If that is so, who is worshiped by all people is the
   Same Divine Being.
But some have set their face towards the tail
   (phenomenal form) and have lost the Head,
   although the Head is the principal.[11]

So Rûmi affirms that all people worship the same God by defining God in the light of their own social, cultural, and historical circumstances; yet none of these definitions confines God. Different though they are, all the definitions point in the same direction—to the ineffable Infinite.

In the salutations and benedictions addressed to the
   righteous (saints) praise of all the prophets is
   blended;
The Praises are all commingled (and united):
the jugs are poured into one basin.
Inasmuch as the *object of praise Himself* is not more
   than One, from this point of view (all) religions
   are but one religion.
Know that every praise goes (belongs) to the Light
   of God and is (only) lent to (created) forms and
   persons.
How should folk praise (any one) except Him who
   (alone) has the right (to be praised)—but they go
   astray on (the ground of) a vain fancy.
The Light of God in relation to phenomena is as a
   light shining upon a wall—the wall is a link
   (focus) for these splendours:
Necessarily, when the reflexion moved towards its
   source, he who had gone astray lost the moon
   and ceased from praise.[12]

Furthermore, Rûmi holds that every human being has a natural desire or inclination to believe in God: "There is a taste of Divine Being in the heart/ soul of every religious community."[13]

THE DIVERSITY OF WORLD FAITHS

"The lamps are different, but the Light is the same." This is one of the most quoted of Rûmi's statements, especially by pluralists. Affirming diversity, Rûmi

---

[11] Rûmi, *Mathnawi*, VI, 3759.
[12] Ibid., III, 2122–28.
[13] Ibid., II, 3606.

also affirms unity. What makes them diverse is not the direction in which they are moving, but the vehicles in which they move. Every vehicle is different because it is conditioned by and adapted to the religion's particular cultural and historical context. The following verses indicate just how seriously Rûmi took the diversity of faiths:

> World faiths are not the same with regard to their
> character;
> But in the Hereafter they become one;
> The unity of faiths in the world is impossible.[14]

> There are invisible ladders in the Universe.
> All of them can reach the summit of heaven step by
> step.
> There is a different ladder for every nation;
> And there is a different heaven for every (traveller's)
> way.
> Every one is ignorant of another's condition (in) the
> kingdom (which is) wide and without end or
> beginning.[15]

From these verses of *Mathnawi*, we can clearly see that for Rûmi there were many different ways to God. But this diversity is one of appearances, not of inner essence, for in their goal he found all religions to be the same. This goal, or intent, is to bring their followers closer to the one Creator, or to make them acceptable to God. This is not far from the formulation of John Hick when he claims that all religious traditions seek to realize "the transformation of human existence from self-centredness to Reality-centredness."[16]

> Although there are many ways
> Their aim is the same
> Do you not see that?
> How many roads are there to reach Kaba?
> Some people's way passes through Greek lands;
> Others from Damascus;
> Others from the land of Persia;
> Others from China;
> And others from India by way of one sea.
> If you look at the ways
> The differences seem huge and limitless.

---

[14] Jalaluddin Rûmi, *Fihi mâ fîhî*, trans. M. Ülker Ambarcioglu (Istanbul: Milli Egitim Basimevi, 1990), 43. Translations in the text are mine.

[15] Rûmi, *Mathnawi*, V, 2556–58.

[16] John Hick, *The Rainbow of Faiths* (London: SCM Press, 1995), 18.

But when you look at their aim
You see that all of them are united in Kaba.[17]

The disagreement of mankind is caused by names
Peace ensues when they reach the reality (denoted by
the name).[18]

When you go to worship the external form
It seems like two to you.
But in reality it is only one.
. . . .
If ten lamps are in one place
Each differs from one another
Yet you cannot distinguish whose radiance is whose
When you focus on the light
In the field of the Spirit
There is no division, no individual exits.[19]

As you know, when the light of the sun enters the
inside of houses
It becomes like a thousand lights.
But when the walls of the houses are broken down
The light of all of them becomes one.
When the houses disappear
Believers turn to one person.[20]

In respect of the vessels there is number
But in respect of the flames of light
There is naught but unity
When the light of six lamps is mingled together
There is no number and plurality in their light.[21]

Do you not see that
When a person becomes hungry
The person declares:
"I want meat, yogurt
Or pastry or sweetmeat or beefsteak or fruit or
dates"?
In fact, all these things that the person desires derive
from the same essence:

---

[17] Rûmi, *Fîhî mâ fîhî*, 152.
[18] Rûmi, *Mathnawi*, II, 3680.
[19] Ibid., I, 680–84.
[20] Ibid., IV, 416–18.
[21] Ibid., V, 2882–84.

The person's hunger.
For hunger is only one thing.[22]

As is evident in all these verses, for Rûmi, despite their evident differences, all religions share one ultimate source in God, and their common aim is to enable their followers to lose their egos in order to relocate their identity in the Ultimate. It seems to me that all these verses of Rûmi imply that he believed in a type of universal faith belonging to all religions. Since, while Rûmi recognizes that the messengers and prophets who brought the Light of God to humankind differ greatly one from the other, yet the Light they bring is the same. He therefore declares those who set one prophet against the others or those who hold up one faith as superior to all others to be religiously myopic.

> There was an unjust ruler of the Jews.
> He was the enemy of Jesus
> And behaved unjustly to Christians.
> It was the age of Jesus and it was his turn.
> Moses was the spirit of Him.
> The Ruler became myopic in the ways of God.
> He saw Moses and Jesus as separated from each-
>   other.
>
> When a Master said to his squint-eyed assistant:
> "Immediately go to the room and bring me the
>   bottle."
> (There were two bottles in the room.) The assistant
>   told his Master:
> "Tell me more clearly which bottle I need to bring to
>   you from the two of them."
> The Master said "Do not be silly; there are not two,
>   but only one bottle.
> Look more carefully, and do not see the one as more
>   than one."
> The assistant said: "O my Master do not condemn
>   me!"
> The master said, "Okay, then break one of the
>   bottles."
> When the assistant broke it,
> Both of the bottles were no more.[23]

In contemporary terminology Rûmi argued strongly that the reality of religious pluralism was not just a "matter of fact" but "a matter of principle,"

---

[22] Rûmi, *Fîhî mâ fîhî*, 13.
[23] Rûmi, *Mathnawi*, I, 325–32.

that is, not just the way things are but the way things are supposed to be. For him, in other words, the reality of religious diversity was rooted in the reality of God, both in God's nature and in God's will. Regarding the divine nature, as we have already seen, Rûmi not only affirmed but happily embraced the ineffability of God. That means that the full reality and truth of the Divine will always be more than any one religious discovery or any one religious revelation. "More than" requires "many." The surplus missed by any one religion spills over, as it were, into another religion. Thank God that it does!

But for Rûmi, God also expressly wills the multiplicity of religions. The Qur'an told him that it is precisely by means of the differences among the religions that human beings have the occasion and the materials to deepen their quest for ever greater understanding of God's truth. In discussing differences, humans can, as it were, rank differences; they have the opportunity to figure out which human expressions of truth come closer to divine truth, or even, which claimed truth turns out to be error or ignorance. Using rather strong language, Rûmi implies that the predestination of God has led world faiths to fight each other. In the Hereafter, God makes manifest the real nature of each and displays the congenial by contrast with the uncongenial.[24] The engagement of open dialogue can bring about a fermentation that helps us distinguish the good from the bad, or the excellent from the mediocre.

---

[24] "The Suni is unaware of the Jabri's mode of glorification; the Suni has a particular (mode of) glorification; the Jabri has the opposite thereof in (taking) refuge (with God). This one (the Jabri) says, 'He (the Suni) is astray and lost,' (being) unaware of his (real) state and of the (Divine) command. And that one (the Suni) says, 'What awareness has this one (the Jabri)?' God, by fore-ordainment, hath cast them into strife. He makes manifest the real nature of each. He displays the congenial by contrast with the uncongenial. Every one knows (can distinguish) mercy from vengeance, or whether he be wise or ignorant or vile" (Rûmi, *Mathnawi*, III, 1501–6). When we look at the Qur'an, we see that God created human beings as different communities and gave them different ways of life for the following reasons: First, God wanted human beings to try to know each other. As is well known, human beings have never lived in isolation, and the history of humankind may be considered as an irreversible process of an unceasing, extending communication. Humanity's fulfillment is in community and relationship. This fact is underlined by the Qur'an as follows: "O Mankind, we have created you male and female and made you nations and tribes, so that you might come to know each other. Surely the noblest of you in Allah's sight is the most pious" (49:13). Second, God created human beings as different faith communities to compete with each other in good works in order to attain God's grace (5:48). When we look at world history, however, the followers of different religious traditions have wasted more time debating with one another about their own beliefs and ways of life than they have in trying to know and compete with one another both in good works and in the service of humanity. In short, God himself willed the creation of diversity. For that reason human beings should accept it in all humility because it is our test in this world. Also, as is well known, human ingenuity flowers in situations of diversity rather than in situations of monolithic sociocultural and religious structures.

For Rûmi, these two roots of religious diversity—God's nature and God's will—can yield the fruits of a peaceful society in which diversity is both affirmed and made productive. But Rûmi also recognized that diversity can be the cause of division and conflict; such negative effects stem not from God but from the way humans handle or understand their differences. This can happen, first of all, when humans become so focused on, or captured by, their differences that they lose touch with the fundamental similarities in the essence and aims of their religions. We have already pointed out how in one of his poems Rûmi warns against those who so stress the differences in the ways of the Prophet that they forget that all these ways share a common core. Elsewhere, Rûmi shows that this results from the way in which humans allow themselves to be caught up with externals so as to miss the internals:

> If you keep looking at glass [lantern] you would be
>   lost
> Because from the glass arise the numbers of the
>   plurality inherent in dualism.
> But if you keep your gaze upon the light
> You could be saved from dualism and numbers of
>   the finite body.
> From the place [object] of view,
> Oh, (that we might touch) the heart of Reality/
>   Existence.
> There arise the differences between believers
>   [Muslims] and those who worship fire
>   [Zorastrians] and Jews.[25]

With such beautiful poetry Rûmi urges us, as people of different faiths, to move from the forms of our religious thinking to the underlying religious reality.

Another reason, for Rûmi, why diversity can lead to division can be found in the lack of dialogical relationship between the religions. Sadly, the followers of different faiths do not try to know and understand and respect one another. Rather, all too often they are suspicious of one another and condemn one another, each claiming that only it is on the right path while all others go astray.

> Everything and everyone glorifies you in different
>   ways.
> Yet none of them is aware of the others.
> Man disbelieves in the glorification uttered by
>   inanimate things
> But those inanimate things are masters in
>   performing worship.

---

[25] Rûmi, *Mathnawi*, III, 1256–59.

> Nay, the two-and-seventy sects/nations, every one,
>   are unaware of the real state of each other and in
>   a great doubt.[26]

In all these verses Rûmi makes clear that "religiosity consists of something other than all those religions. Our prayers and other religious activities are the apparent side of religion. A real believer may only be recognized by his inner state, which is not observable to anyone else."[27] Making this even clearer, there is a beautiful story in *Mathnawi* about a shepherd and his foolish way of talking about God and Moses. According to the story, Moses listened to a shepherd, who addressed God as follows:

> O God! Where are You, that I may be your servant,
> I may repair your shoes, I may comb you hair
> I may wash you clothes, kill your lice, bring milk to
>   you;
> That I may kiss your little hand and rub your little
>   foot,
> And at bedtime I may sweep your little room.

When Moses heard such talk, he asked the shepherd: "O man! To Whom is this addressed?" The shepherd answered, "To that one who created us, who brought this earth and sky into sight." Upon this answer Moses became very angry and said to the shepherd that his words were blasphemous, that they made the whole world stink and that the utterer of such blasphemous words is an infidel. Despairing and confused, the shepherd turned his head toward the desert and went away. Upon this incident the following warning came to Moses from God: "You have parted my servant from me! You, Moses, as a prophet, did you come to unite me with my servants, or to sever me from them?" Then come the following powerful verses of *Mathnawi*: God says to Moses:

> I am independent of all purity and impurity;
> I take no benefit from my servants's worship.
> This is my kindness to them.
> In the Hindus the idiom of Hind, the Sindians the
>   idiom of Sind.
> Forms of speeches used by different peoples in their
>   worship,
> All are praiseworthy.[28]

---

[26] Ibid., III, 1497–99.

[27] Muhammad Este'lami, "Rumi and the Universality of His Message," *Islam and Christian-Muslim Relations* 14, no. 4 (2003), 433.

[28] See Rûmi, *Mathnawi*, II, 1718–58.

Rûmi makes clear, simply yet powerfully, how our failure to understand one another can lead to conflict. Starting with as basic a means of communication as language, he shows how when words fail us, we so easily resort to blows:

> A certain man gave a *dirhem* [a silver coin] to four
>   persons:
> One of them (a Persian) said: "With this money, I
>   will buy *angur* (grapes)."
> The second one was an Arap; he said: "No, I want
>   *ineb* (grapes) not *angur.*
> The third one was Turk; he said: "This money is
>   mine;
> I do not want *ineb*, I want *üzüm* (grapes)."
> The Fourth was Greek; he said: "Stop this talk. I
>   want *istafil.*
> These people began fighting in contention with one
>   another,
> Because they were unaware of the meaning of
>   names.
> In their folly they smote each other with their fists.
> They were full of ignorance and empty of
>   knowledge.
> If a master of the esoteric had been there, a revered
>   and many-languaged man,
> He would have pacified them.
> And then he would have said: "With this *dirhem* I
>   will give all of you what you wish."[29]

Rûmi's views on the diversity of religions are thoroughly compatible with Qur'anic teaching. According to the Qur'an, even though human beings started their journey in unity as one community, God willed that the unity should lead to diversity. And the reason for this was to provide humanity with the opportunity "to compete with each other in good deeds."[30] So according to God's revelation to Muhammad, humanity's religious journey is from unity to diversity. Muhammad Ayoub concludes that religious pluralism

[29] Ibid., II, 3681–88.

[30] "Mankind was one single community and Allah sent (unto them) prophets as bearers of glad tidings and as warners, and revealed therewith the Book with the truth that it might judge between mankind concerning it, after clear proofs had come unto them, through hatred one of another" (Qur'an 2:213). "Had Allah willed He could have made you one community. But that he may try you by that which He has given you (He has made you as you are). So vie with one another in good works. Unto Allah you will all return, and He will then inform you of that wherein you differ" (Qur'an 5:48).

is a divinely instituted phenomenon, and it will prevail up to the day of Judgement.[31] But we must remember that such diversity, affirmed by both the Qur'an and Rûmi, in no way is meant to lead to either relativism or chaos. It is, rather, a diversity grounded in, and productive of, unity.

RÛMI'S UNDERSTANDING OF RELIGION

As is clear throughout Rûmi's writings, religion for him is a message, not an established system. And as this message is heard and lived in individuals and in a community, it takes on both internal and external aspects. The inner quality is faith—the personal religious experience of individuals. Here one finds the transcendent ingredient of religion, where persons are touched by the Divine, where they feel and discover the meaning of their lives. But what is felt powerfully within must take on expression in external forms—words, deeds, ritual, morality, law, and the community itself. While the inner power of religion—faith—is what is common to all religious traditions, the external expressions of this faith will differ from religion to religion. It is such external differences that all too often become the combustible materials for discrimination and hatred between religious believers. So Rûmi admonishes followers of all traditions: "Shape is an obstacle and roadblock. Look beyond the shape of things and behold the meaning."[32]

For Rûmi, the external forms or shape of a religion are not static and homogenous; rather, they are the living, and that means the growing and developing and adapting, aspect of all religions. Therefore, external religious beliefs and practices not only differ from tradition to tradition, but they also

---

[31] Mahmoud M. Ayoub, "Islam and the Challenge of Religious Pluralism," *Global Dialogue* 2, no. 1 (2000), 56–57.

[32] Rûmi, *Mathnawi*, I, 2902. This distinction of Rûmi reminds us of W. Cantwell Smith's distinction between faith and cumulative tradition. As is well known, Smith in his modern classic *The Meaning and End of Religion* underlines that "religion" as a systematic entity, or "religions" as systems of beliefs or rituals, have been so understood in the Western world as a result of a complex process of "reification" that began in the seventh century and that has developed in a cultural context of polemics and apologetics. For that reason, he suggests that we drop these terms (*religion* or *religions*) and replace them with the terms *faith* and *cumulative tradition*. He describes *faith* as "an inner religious experience or involvement of a particular person; the impingement on him of the transcendent, putative or real." In this sense, according to Smith, faith refers to the transcendent aspect of religion. By the term *cumulative tradition*, too, he says, "I mean the entire mass of overt objective data that constitute the historical deposit, as it were, of the past religious life of the community in question: temples, scriptures, theological systems, dance patterns, legal and other social institutions, conventions, moral codes, myths, and so on; anything that can be transmitted from one person, one generation, to another, and that an historian can observe." See W. Cantwell Smith, *The Meaning and End of Religion* (Minneapolis: Fortress Press, 1991; originally published in 1962), 42–44, 156.

may differ in the very same tradition from century to century, or from culture to culture, or even from village to city. So, for Rûmi, the foundation of his pluralistic world view is based on his mystical epistemology.[33]

By separating the internal core or meaning of the religions from their external aspect or shape, Rûmi opens up the religious systems of the world, in all their splendid diversity, to historical investigation. But he also would warn investigators to proceed with caution. One's overall, or final, assessment of a religion should not hinge primarily on its external forms but on the quality or depth or ethical fruits of its inner, core experience. As a community seeks consciously or just naturally to give expression to the powerful, inner experiences that gave it birth and surge within it, distortions can easily take place. What was originally pure becomes contaminated in unclean or repressive containers; the subordinate services of external forms can be idolatrously elevated into roles more important than the transcendent experience or the Transcendent itself. So Rûmi reminds us:

> Is not the origin of the law or revelation the same?
> Yet when with the feelings, thoughts, and desires of
>   people,
> As well as their goodness and gentleness, have
>   disappeared,
> As is the case nowadays, what is left of that
>   goodness, grace, and revelation?
> Who can tell how clean and good this water
>   originally is as it flows down from Mount Sinai
>   to the city?
> For when it enters into the city
> And passes through gardens, vineyards, houses, and
>   toilets . . .
> And so many people wash their hands, faces, bodies
>   and clothes in that water . . .
> A man who is clean must try to understand the
>   water's original purity,
> And how many dirty things have been mixed into
>   it.[34]

As is clear from this poem, Rûmi maintains that all peoples, over the course of history, have interpreted, developed, and thus shaped the original or core revelation of God in light of their own social, political, and cultural circumstances. Here we have the reason for the great diversity of faiths. But here we also have the reason for the inadequacies and distortions of the many traditions. Rûmi uses another image to explain: "The water coming

---

[33] Lloyd Ridgeon, "Christianity as Portrayed by Jalal al-Dîn Rûmi," in *Islamic Interpretations of Christianity*, ed. Lloyd Ridgeon (Surrey: Curzon, 2001), 116.

[34] Rûmi, *Fîhî mâ fîhî*, 226–27.

from the heart to the breast is clean. But if the breast is not clean, everything is useless, for that water will become dirty."[35]

We can summarize at this point what Rûmi thinks of religious diversity: (1) We must recognize and affirm the multiplicity and variety of ways that lead people to Ultimate Reality. (2) Despite and amid this diversity, the primary intent of all religions is the same—to enable their followers to move beyond their own ego-identification and find their true identity in relationship to, or as part of, Ultimate Reality. (3) Given this common goal, we should evaluate religions according to their practical fruits—that is, how well they move their followers beyond self-centeredness. (4) The main cause of enmities, conflict, and hatred among the religions is to be found in the way believers so exaggerate their differences that they forget their common core. (5) Such enmities are augmented when religious people fail to speak with one another and so remain in ignorance of one another. (6) Given their common origins and their shared goal of promoting salvation/liberation, there is always the possibility of dialogue—and of peace—among the religions.

RÛMI AS A GUIDE
TOWARD A PLURALIST MUSLIM THEOLOGY OF RELIGIONS

This overview of Rûmi's understanding of religion and religions can serve as a guide toward a genuinely pluralistic Muslim theology of religions in our increasingly pluralistic world. Among the most helpful of the conclusions we can draw from his perspectives, I offer the following:

1. Muslims cannot claim, as many have in the past, that they are in possession of the fullness or the *totality* of divine revelation, as if what they know about God contains all that can be known. The Qur'an is truly God's revelation, but it is not the totality of God's revelation. The following verse from the Qur'an would seem to clearly state that what can be known about God cannot be limited to what the Qur'an knows about God: "Say if the ocean were ink (wherewith to write out) the words of my Lord, sooner would the ocean be exhausted than would the words of my Lord, even if we added another ocean like it, for its aid" (18:109).

2. Nor can Muslims make claims that their knowledge of God is *absolute and definitive*—as if whatever else others know of God would have to be already contained in what was given to Islam.

3. So neither can Muslims claim *unsurpassability* for their revelation, as if there could not be other religious paths by which people can experience their transformation from ego-centrism to Other or Reality-

---

[35] Rûmi, *Divan-e Kabir*, IV, 1200.

centrism; there are many ways by which people can be acceptable to
God.

Rûmi would heartily endorse all these statements. If Muslim theologians
could do likewise, they would be well on the way toward a new theological
model that would not allow them to absolutize the institutionalized teachings of the Prophet Muhammad as the only way or means of salvation; they
would be able, on the contrary, to acknowledge truly and even enthusiasti-
cally the possibility, if not probability, that other religions and their central
figures or prophets serve as vehicles for God's truth and love.

Rûmi offers this vision in the following beautiful words, which in a sense
summarize his "theology of religions":

> Come closer;
> If you are me and if I am you
> Why is there still yourselves and myself?
> We are God's lights.
> Why are we still fighting and being obstinate with
>   each other?
> Why does brightness escape from the light?
> All of us are only one mature person.
> But why are we squint-eyed?
> Why do the rich show contempt for the poor?
> Why does the right hand show contempt for the left
>   one?
> Both of them are your hands.
> Why is one of them regarded as lucky and the other
>   unlucky?
> All of us are from the same ferment.
> Our mind and our head are one
> But under this bent sky we are seeing everything as
>   double.
> . . . .
> Give up ego-centrism.
> Reconcile with everything and everyone.
> When you are alone
> You are only an atom,
> But when you unite and come together with the
>   others,
> You become like an ocean.
> Know that both the spirit and the flesh are one
> But they are millions in number.
> All of them are like almonds,
> There is the same oil in all of them.
> How many languages there are in the world?

But all of them are the same in terms of their
meaning.[36]

One final thought or question: Does the example of Rûmi suggest that the deeper the holiness of a Muslim, the greater the probability that that Muslim will be a pluralist?

---

[36] Rûmi, *Divan-e Kabir*, IV, 4088–94.

Index

Abe, Masao, 149
acceptance typology of religions, 76 n. 2
activists, religious, common concerns of, 40–42
Advaita Vedanta, 174
afterlife, Jewish doctrine of, 131
Albo in Ikkarim, Joseph, 128
al Haq, 9
All Kerala Inter-religious Students Fellowship, 164
Andrews, C. S., 47
apokatastasis theory, 15
Aquinas, Thomas, 9, 10, 35
Ariarajah, Wesley, 13–14
Arius, 154, 177
atheism/naturalism, 19, 21
Augustine, 142
Ayn Sof, 128
Ayoub, Muhammad, 231–32

Baar Statement (World Council of Churches), 7, 188–89
Baeck, Leo, 123
Bahya Ibn Pakudah, 127
Barth, Karl, 115, 137, 182–83
believers: as inclusivists, 31–32; lacking opportunity to learn about other religions, 47–48; regarding each others as neighbors, 45–46
Bernard, Reinhold, 15–16
Bhadrabahu, 168–69
Bhagavata Dharma, 166–67
Brinton, Howard, 89–90, 97–98
Brod, Max, 122–23
Buber, Martin, 123
Buddha Nature, 91, 93, 97, 99–100, 101
Buddhism: adjusting form of teaching, to aid in enlightenment, 98; approach to religious teachings, 81–87; double religious identity with Quakerism, 88; experiential truth in, 93–94; internal diversity of, 85; lacking imperative to become world's sole religion, 79; open to pluralism, 92; Spirit in, 146–50; as tool for understanding, 89

Calvin, John, 114
Cappadocians, 142
Chalcedon, doctrine of, 155
Chenchiah, P., 173
Christian, William, 18
Christianity: changes in approach to the Bible, 187; collision course with Islam, 78; history of awareness of God, 10–11; imperial legacy of, 177–78; negative attitude toward Jews and Muslims, 111; other religions from standpoint of, 155–58; pluralism of religions expected by Christian, 156, 157–58; pluralistic inclusivism in Indian theologies, 173–74; political influence on mission work, 180–81; presumed superiority of, 179–80; theological options in context of exclusivism-inclusivism-pluralism typology, 21; traditional faith claims, 7–8
Christian theology, reinterpreting and restating, 64
Christology: logic of, 153–55; orthodox, 151, 158–61; pluralist, 151, 158–61; plurality of, in New Testament, 154–55
Christ Within. *See* Light Within
Cobb, John B., Jr., 35, 36, 138
Cohen, Arthur A., 124
communalism, 53
comparative theology, 27
Constantine, 177–78
cultural pluralism, 56–61

Other Titles in the Faith Meets Faith Series